Praise for *The Black Girl's Guide to Building a Boutique Farm*

"*The Black Girl's Guide to Building a Boutique Farm* is a powerful and practical roadmap for the visionary building a farm brand with heart and purpose. Clarenda "Farmer Cee" Stanley blends deep agricultural wisdom with entrepreneurial insight, offering not only clear steps for profitability but also a philosophy rooted in community, resilience, and sustainability. This book will inspire and equip aspiring, new, and experienced farmers to cultivate business success and meaningful, long-lasting impact."

—Christa "FarmerJawn" Barfield

"*The Black Girl's Guide to Building a Boutique Farm* is a gift to the farming community! Rooted in years of experience and a family legacy of farming, Cee Stanely's writing is filled with essential wisdom from both the field and the marketplace. Farmer Cee is a masterful storyteller, sharing her journey of building a boutique farm that embodies her abundance mindset, business savvy, and dedication to the land. Farming can be an isolating and overwhelming endeavor, and that is why every farmer, from the newbie to the old salt, needs this book! Farmer Cee calls in the joy of claiming (or reclaiming) your space in the agricultural world. She also explores different models of boutique farms, illustrating the belief that 'if you can dream it, you can build it.' With every page, she reminds us, 'sis, don't play small,' and gives us the skills and encouragement to build a brighter future for farming. Big-time gratitude to Farmer Cee for her voice and her work!"

—Melanie and Jeff Carpenter, Zack Woods Herb Farm

"A huge part of decolonizing our relationship with agriculture, especially for Black girls, is drawing the parallels between nature, self-love, and adornment. We already know how to build and support boutique businesses that are stocked with fashion finds, accessories, fragrances, and homemade home essentials. We've built small businesses that are community sanctuaries of culture and beauty. Now Farmer Cee is expanding our boutique sensibility into farming so that we can remember how powerful our relationship with land, healing, and wellness is. Her ecosystem of wisdom in *The Black Girl's Guide* is the epitome of joy and abundance. She's helping us to continue to build life-affirming portals, and it's clear we can look and feel damn good doing it!"

—Dominique Drakeford, host and executive producer, Compost, Cotton & Cornrows podcast; cultural sustainability strategist

"Black women started the herbal industry in the United States. For hundreds of years, absent were hospitals and pharmacies where Black folk could seek medical help. Our doctors were Black women who caught babies, cured illnesses, and wrapped us in mantras of healing. Their care extended to white communities, too, and they collaborated with First Nations.

"What the annals left out is that Black women—both Indigenous and brought from Africa—kept America healthy. Through their medicinal flowers and plants grown in complex systems of gardens, plots, and farms, Black women's entrepreneurial savvy was unmatched. So much so that they are the root of American child birthing, floriculture, culinary arts, the herbal industry, and, of course, pharmaceutical professionalism, which started with plant medicine.

"Today, Farmer Cee exhumes the secrets of our mothers with incredible depth. Her book weaves together high-integrity herbal farming practices; a carefully cultivated business stratagem that includes social acuity; and the creation of a tightly knit global community. This book demonstrates her fearless acts of love to expand an agricultural ecosystem with care and her know-how to build a thriving enterprise. In short, you can farm and still be fly.

"What is entirely dope about Farmer Cee is her generosity with knowledge and time. I cannot count the many times she has directed people to Black Farmers Index and encouraged us to continue our work. All the while, she maintains a multigenerational family. Her dirt-divinity is most evident in what comes from her farm: the most brilliant harvests that produce superior herbs. That's more than magic; that is goddess-energy and ancestors returned."

—DR. KAIA SHIVERS, president, Black Farmers Index; founder and editor-in-chieftess, *Ark Republic*; clinical associate professor, New York University

THE BLACK GIRL'S GUIDE TO BUILDING A BOUTIQUE FARM

THE BLACK GIRL'S GUIDE TO BUILDING A BOUTIQUE FARM

Practical Advice to Keep Your Business Cute, Profitable, and Sustainable

CLARENDA "FARMER CEE" STANLEY

FOREWORD BY BONITA D. CLEMONS

Chelsea Green Publishing
White River Junction, Vermont
London, UK

First published in 2026 by Chelsea Green Publishing | PO Box 4529 | White River Junction, VT 05001 | West Wing, Somerset House, Strand | London, WC2R 1LA, UK | www.chelseagreen.com
A Division of Rizzoli International Publications, Inc. | 49 West 27th Street | New York, NY 10001 | www.rizzoliusa.com

Publisher: Charles Miers
Deputy Publisher: Matthew Derr
Project Manager: Natalie Wallace
Acquiring Editor: Fern Marshall Bradley
Developmental Editor: Amalia Herren-Lage
Copy Editor: Laura Jorstad
Proofreader: Rachel Markowitz
Indexer: Elise Hess
Designer: Melissa Jacobson

ISBN 978-1-64502-354-8 (paperback) | ISBN 978-1-64502-355-5 (ebook)
Library of Congress Control Number: 2026010385 (print)

Our Commitment to Green Publishing
Chelsea Green sees publishing as a tool for cultural change and ecological stewardship. We strive to align our book manufacturing practices with our editorial mission and to reduce the impact of our business enterprise in the environment. We print our books using vegetable-based inks whenever possible. This book may cost slightly more because it was printed on paper supplied by Versa from well-managed, FSC®-certifited forests and other controlled sources.

Authorized EU representative for product safety and compliance
Mondadori Libri S.p.A. | www.mondadori.it
via Gian Battista Vico 42 | Milan, Italy 20123

Printed in the United States of America.
10 9 8 7 6 5 4 3 2 1 26 27 28 29 30

First, to my TRINITEA, my children—Arionna, Amira, and Asher. You three are my grounding, my laughter, my why. Everything I build, every seed I plant, and every page I write carries a piece of you.

To my late grandmother Charity Mae (Rambo) Southall, who not only handed down her love of plants but also poured the deepest love into me during my childhood. Her hands taught me to tend, her heart taught me to hope. This book carries her fingerprints.

To all who support Green Heffa Farms, too many to name, but each one a felt source of support, wisdom, and accountability. You have poured into this vision in ways seen and unseen. Thank you for holding space for me and for this work.

To the plants for not only accepting me but embracing me.

And to Chelsea Green Publishing, thank you for trusting my voice, for giving it room to breathe on the page, and for believing that this story belongs in the world.

Contents

Foreword by Bonita D. Clemons *ix*

Introduction: Why This Book? Why Now? *xi*

1. What Exactly Is Boutique Farming? 1
2. Boutique Farming Starts Within 16
3. Cultivating an Abundance Mindset 29
4. Establishing the Vision for Your Boutique Farm 40
5. Build the Brand, Nurture the Land 61
6. Establishing Your Farm as a Legitimate Business 73
7. Visuals and Voice: Telling Your Boutique Farm's Story 89
8. Building Sustainable Relationships 107
9. Grow Slow So You Don't Owe 120
10. Planting Profitability 143
11. From Verified to Valued: Establishing Trust in Your Boutique Brand 167
12. The Land Chapter 183
13. Infrastructure and the Investment Behind It 198

Last Word: The Harvest Is Yours *233*

Resources *235*

Bibliography *238*

Index *239*

Foreword

The moment I started reading this book, my spirit said, "Well, look at God."

Ooooh yes, Sis, please pull up a chair, get cozy, and pour yourself a cup of RICH AUNTEA from Green Heffa Farms.

I grew up a little country girl in a tiny rural town. My whole world was playing in the fields where my grandfather farmed. He grew the food, and Grandma prepared the food. That land fed eighteen children, all the grands, those who claimed to be our cousins, and basically the whole community. From sunrise to sunset, I played in those fields, stopping only long enough to eat a tomato, cucumber, or watermelon.

Now, as a grown woman, healer, teacher, and farmer, I truly understand that the value of land is far deeper than childhood play and dirt. This book breaks down everything you need to know to build a boutique farm and a beautiful life simultaneously. It's not just another agriculture book. It is a blueprint for community, collaboration, coins, and connection. It's a guide for wellness, intention, joy, and gentle living while making money with a smile on your face.

Farmer Cee didn't just write a guide; she delivered what we've been waiting on for years. The wait is over. This book is all things because Cee left no stone unturned and no question unanswered. Everything you need to know about boutique farming and building a prosperous life is here. These principles go far beyond growing—they touch every corner of a woman's life. Everything from choosing seeds to choosing your systems. Cee went from the ground to grants, from the roots to AI, because she knows our brilliance.

This book is the answer to the prompt. It's both a permission slip for and a pathway to a life of abundance. This book honors our softness, our brilliance, and our hustle without asking us to choose between each of them. It speaks our language in ways we've longed to hear.

Farmer Cee rewrites what farming can look like when a Sista chooses economic independence, community impact, and personal fulfillment. Every chapter reminded me that farming is not just about planting seeds in soil, it's about becoming whole while you grow. It's about remembering that WE ARE THE MEDICINE.

Reading these pages will equip you with everything you need if you're willing to show up and do the work. These words encourage us to create farms that look and feel like us: beautiful, bold, soft, and fierce. Farms that heal us as we heal our communities. Farms that build wealth and legacy. Farms that look like our preferred future. That's the blueprint this beautiful work provides.

Farming isn't easy, and it's more than just planting seeds. It is a way of planting your true Self. Most importantly, this guide teaches us that we'll never need to break our backs or lose our peace to farm. The truth, presented in these pages, is the exact opposite. Continue to sip your tea and enjoy this journey that Farmer Cee has laid out for us.

We can farm with softness. With style. With intention. With boundaries. With joy. JOY is a ministry all by itself.

—Bonita D. Clemons, MPH,
creator and national leader, FarmaSIS Nation,
champion for Black women's health, wellness, and land sovereignty

INTRODUCTION

Why This Book? Why Now?

Why this book? Well, there are a few reasons. The main one is that the experience of farming as a Black woman is different and thus, we need different resources. Period. Most agricultural books out there are written from a perspective that doesn't reflect the Black woman's lived experience—whether a farmer or not. These books are often written from a white-dominant view, usually male. And I refuse to pretend that racism and sexism are not still very real and very present. They are.

Second, what's currently available in the agricultural space rarely speaks to those of us who want to create something different—something intentional, soulful, and boutique—especially not to Black women farmers. Yes, I came across a few books that skimmed the surface of these ideas, maybe with a chapter or two that mentioned niche markets or personal branding. But none of them went deep—certainly not into branding as an act of storytelling, as a form of resistance, as a tool for reclaiming space in a system that wasn't built for us.

Look Good, Feel Good, Do Good

When I first started farming, I found no shortage of information on soil science, crop rotations, and how to scale a traditional commodity farm. But I wasn't trying to do what had already been done. I was trying to build something rooted in purpose and pleasure. I wanted to grow plants, yes—but I also wanted to grow a business and a brand that felt good, looked good, and did good. I needed guidance on how to weave my culture, my values, my femininity, and my voice into every decision—from the logo to the labeling to the land stewardship practices I chose.

There were no resources that talked about the intersection of agriculture, identity, luxury, and liberation. Nothing that honored the reality of building a thriving, smaller-scale, boutique farm while also honoring myself—my joy, my wellness, my wholeness—as a Black woman in America.

So, I wrote the book I needed. The book I wish someone had handed me when I first felt the pull toward the land. This is for the women who want to grow beautifully, boldly, and sustainably. Who want to nurture not just crops but culture. Who want to cultivate not just food or flowers or herbs but a life.

I made it a point to document my journey and experience, and both helped to inform this book, which is about more than farming. It's about reclaiming space. It's about entrepreneurship and creativity. It's about cultivating a vision of success on our own terms. It's about recognizing that farming and building a boutique farming brand can be a vehicle for economic independence, community impact, and personal fulfillment. Most important, it is about building your very own customized joy factory.

That part.

This isn't a how-to-grow-lettuce or how-to-raise-goats book. This is a how to build a sustainable farming brand with purpose and power book, a How to Build a GOAT (Greatest of All Time) Boutique Farm. And it is written with Black women's success in mind. There are plenty of resources out there that will teach you the technical side of agriculture—what to plant, how to raise animals, how to get the most yield per acre. But this guide? This guide is about building the *soul* of your business. It's about strategy, identity, visibility, and sustainability—not just of the land but of your livelihood.

Customize Your Joy

I chose to focus on building a brand because scale isn't the only path to success, especially for Black women in agriculture. It is important for us to build a community-minded customer base. I didn't want to grow acres of low-margin crops to compete in a system that was never built for me. I wanted to grow high-value crops and create a wellness brand based on herbs truly grown with love and care. I wanted to create something that allowed me to give my best in a way that wasn't extractive or inauthentic and allowed me to sustain my desired livelihood without compromising what I stand for. I also wanted to meet a community need. That meant creating a brand with a story, a purpose, and products that people feel good about incorporating into their well-being program. It is not just about getting people to make a purchase.

When you build a strong brand, you're not just selling herbs or teas, eggs or designer chickens—you're selling an experience, a belief, a connection. That's what makes a boutique farm thrive. That's what creates longevity.

This book is your permission slip to dream differently. You don't have to grow more to grow your farm—you just have to grow smarter.

Another reason I chose to prioritize building a boutique farm brand is that agriculture is in urgent need of transformation, and I believe Black women have a critical role to play in leading that change. Agriculture, as it currently exists, is riddled with environmental harm, exploitation, and exclusion, especially of the very people who have historically contributed the most to its growth. Black women have long been stewards of the land, healers of the body, entrepreneurially minded, and innovators in the face of scarcity. We carry ancestral knowledge, cultural resilience, and a deep, spiritual relationship with Earth. That lived experience, coupled with a legacy of survival and transformation, positions us uniquely to reimagine what farming can be.

We're not just talking about diversifying the faces in the field—we're talking about redefining the field altogether. That means building systems rooted in sustainability, justice, wellness, and reciprocity, not just profit. It means creating an agricultural and entrepreneurial landscape that has an equitable representation of successful Black women. It means challenging who gets access to land, capital, and market share, and building models that prioritize community, health, and healing. I believe Black women can lead that revolution and will be a part of it, not because we have to but because we already are. And if both agriculture and entrepreneurship are to truly become

Photo courtesy of Maddy Gray.

forces for good, it will require a radical shift—one that centers those who've always known how to grow something from nothing.

Now, let me add this caveat. This book does not cover everything. I do not know everything. But it does cover a lot of what I have learned. I am but one person sharing her experience. I didn't grow up farming. While I spent a significant portion of my childhood on my maternal grandparents' farm, I wasn't encouraged to see it as a viable career. To them, farming was backbreaking work with little financial reward. While they always emphasized the value of land, farming was something they wanted me to escape, not embrace. My grandparents and parents pushed me toward higher education, believing a college degree was the key to a better life. And in many ways, I followed that path.

I explored a few career options. I knew I loved education, so I tried being a teacher. While I loved the children, I realized it was not my ministry to be responsible for them Monday through Friday. And the pay? Not nearly what such an important societal role deserves. I was so poor as a teacher. I called my paychecks "monthly reminders of insignificance." I then explored being a mental health clinician for a hot minute, but maintaining objectivity was a challenge when faced with other people's suffering. Eventually, I got on the path of marketing and fundraising, and here I found my lane. I hold both undergraduate and graduate degrees, and for a time I was a Certified Fund Raising Executive, or CFRE, the profession's leading certification. I climbed the ranks, won awards, and secured high-paying roles. I had a luxury car, established great credit scores, and had a home in a desirable neighborhood. On paper, I had made it. But behind the scenes, my world was unraveling. I was navigating relentless racial animus in my career, exhausted from the constant need to prove my worth in spaces that were never designed for me. At the same time, I was disentangling myself from a marriage that ended with me writing a check instead of receiving one. Ouch.

Reclaiming Agency over Your Life

At forty-two, I found myself at a crossroads. By this time, I had spent years excelling in high-level fundraising and marketing—work that paid well but drained me. I was tired. Tired of fighting for a seat at tables where I was only tolerated, not valued. Tired of code-switching, shrinking myself, and navigating microaggressions just to exist in predominantly white spaces. Tired of sacrificing my peace for a paycheck. And that tiredness affected my health; I was ultimately diagnosed with having anxiety. I knew I had to build something of my own that was rooted in my values, my identity, and my vision. That's how Green Heffa Farms was born. It wasn't just about farming; it was about reclaiming agency over my life and work. It was about creating a space where

I could be fully myself, where I didn't have to justify my presence or water down my truth. And it was about proving that Black women could—and should—thrive in agriculture and entrepreneurship on our own terms.

Many of you reading this are standing at a similar crossroads. You've built careers, maybe raised families, and have done your best to check all the boxes that were supposed to lead to stability. Or maybe you haven't quite found your space. The beautiful thing about building a boutique farming business and brand is that you are able to create your own path. But now you want something different. You want something that is aligned with your values, something that brings you joy without running you into the ground. Or maybe you have never really reached your pinnacle of success in the career path you have taken and you're wanting more than just to survive. You want to live. You want to grow. But you want to do it in a way that reflects who you are.

Maybe you want to grow herbs for wellness products, cultivate heirloom vegetables, or create a regenerative ranch that sustains both the land and your community. And you want to do it while living a life that sparks joy every day. Maybe you're not even sure where to start, but you know you want in. If that sounds like you, this book is for you.

Farmer or Founder?

Now, let's be clear: this is not a get-rich-quick guide. This is not one of those start-a-farm-with-zero-dollars books, either. This is a blueprint for building a boutique farm that is both profitable and sustainable. You have an advantage I didn't: this book. I'm giving you the game—the lessons I learned through trial, error, and perseverance—coupled with the knowledge I brought with me into agriculture so that you can start from a place of strength. And let me be real about something else: I am not about that struggle-farming life.

There is this narrative in agriculture that glorifies burnout and sacrifice, as if barely making ends meet is some kind of badge of honor. I reject that. I believe in farming and making money. I believe in farming and rest. I believe in farming and luxury. I like good food, comfortable-class flights, high-thread-count sheets, and regular massages. I absolutely love being a philanthropist and giving to the causes and people I care about and believe in. I refuse to buy into the idea that choosing boutique farming means choosing poverty. That's why when I stepped into this field—an industry where Black women are nearly invisible—I leveraged the lessons I had learned while working with some of the world's wealthiest. I knew that I wasn't just building a farm; I was building a brand. Even before my first harvest I was making money because I understood that the business side of farming is just as important as the production side.

Navigating this path as a Black woman comes with its own challenges. People hear "farmer" and may not picture someone like me or you. When I introduce myself as a farmer, I get a very different reaction than when I say I'm the founder of a trademarked wellness brand that vertically sources through its own organic and regenerative farm. The latter makes people pay attention because it challenges their preconceived notions. This book is about embracing that power—owning your narrative, building your brand, and showing up in ways that demand respect. If you're looking for a book that centers you—not just as a farmer or business owner but as a whole person—this is it. Throughout these pages, you'll find more than just technical knowledge; you'll find honesty in the "Real Talk" and "Groundwork" exercises to help you lay a solid foundation for your boutique farm.

And if you are not a Black woman and are wondering whether this book is for you, here's my answer: If you can see value in learning from someone who had to navigate countless barriers to create something meaningful, then yes—this book is for you. But understand this—I will not dilute my voice or my truth to make it more palatable. I'm writing unapologetically as I am, because my full journey holds the value. Take what resonates, let go of what doesn't, and trust that there is wisdom in perspectives outside the mainstream. This is more than a book; it's a movement. It's a declaration that we belong in this space and that we can build farming businesses that sustain us—financially, emotionally, and spiritually. This is about cultivating joy, reclaiming our power, and creating something that feeds both the land and our souls. If you're ready for that, let's get to work.

CHAPTER 1

What Exactly Is Boutique Farming?

I feel a sacred responsibility to the soil. It's not just farming, it's remembering.

—KAREN WASHINGTON, urban farmer and food justice advocate

When you think of farming, what comes to mind? Rows of corn and soybeans stretching to the horizon? Acres of farmland with combines and tractors that seem to work endlessly in the hot sun? Perhaps an older man, usually white, in denim overalls and a sun hat, casually spitting chewing tobacco for added razzle-dazzle? While these images may represent traditional agriculture, boutique farming is something entirely different. Boutique farming is small-scale, specialty agriculture that focuses on producing high-quality, often niche products for specific, targeted markets. It's about finding customers with aligning values. It's where luxury, nature, and profitability coexist in harmony. Boutique is for lovers of the unique: It is about truly creating your agricultural lane leading to your definition of quality living.

Unlike conventional farming, boutique farming is not about acquiring the most land or harvesting the highest volume of crops. Instead, it's about intention, value, quality, optimization, and storytelling. The power of boutique farming is that you get to define success on your own terms. Small is mighty: You get to cultivate your farm's unique identity, grow or raise products that align with your values, and serve your customers in ways that large-scale farms or brands can't. Every detail—from what you produce, to the packaging you choose, to the language you use in your marketing—flows from your values and vision. It doesn't chase trends. It doesn't try to replicate someone else's model but instead reflects your spirit, serves a specific purpose, and most important, feels authentically yours.

When I say I am a farmer and I live my version of a soft life, I often get the side eye—or at least some genuine curiosity. Farming is hard work, no doubt about it. So how can someone be a farmer and business owner, build a brand, and still claim to live a soft life? Easy. Because softness isn't about not working—it's about intention. For me, farming on my own terms means growing what I'm passionate about instead of chasing bigger and bigger production just because that is what's expected. Living a soft life as a boutique farmer looks like resting when my body needs it, saying no when something isn't right, and setting up systems that protect my well-being instead of draining it. In other words, I want to be both grounded and rested. As Tricia Hersey, founder of The Nap Ministry, reminds us: "Rest is a form of resistance because it disrupts and pushes back against capitalism and white supremacy." I believe that deeply.

This approach is also smart business. Many enterprises that borrow heavily to grow fast become fragile, especially when economic tides turn. In fact, a significant percentage of US businesses fail because of overexpansion, debt, and cash-flow problems, which are magnified during downturns. According to the U.S. Bureau of Labor Statistics, between 21 and 23 percent of US businesses fail in their first year, about 48 percent close within five years, roughly 65 percent close within ten years, and up to 82 percent of small-business failures are linked to poor or negative cash flow—often driven by overexpansion and excessive debt.

Photo courtesy of Maddy Gray.

Boutique farming is more than a farm and more than a business. It's what I call a customized joy factory. It's a deeply personal ecosystem you design to generate joy—for yourself, your customers, and your community. Joy, after all, isn't just about pleasure—it's about purpose, peace, and presence. In a world that often tells us to produce more, hustle harder, and shrink ourselves to fit systems that don't serve us, a customized joy factory says: *I'll build something that sustains me.* It's soft. It's strategic. It's sacred.

Why Choose Boutique Farming?

Boutique farming is especially ideal for Black women farmers. It is an opportunity to reclaim agricultural spaces, honor ancestral traditions, and cultivate economic independence without the heavy financial burdens of large-scale farming. It provides the flexibility to create niche markets that resonate with our personal values of sustainability and autonomy, our cultural heritage, and community wellness priorities. It enables high-value, specialized production on smaller plots of land. Boutique farming sparks innovation across diverse sectors, from heirloom vegetables and specialty fruits, to organic grains, to goat farming. With the opportunity to integrate direct-to-consumer models, agritourism, and online sales, boutique farming becomes a powerful pathway for building generational wealth and fortifying community food systems on our own terms.

Luxury has been defined through the lens of pop and celebrity culture—polished perfection, name-brand everything, and curated lifestyles meant to impress the masses. Luxury on social media looks like silk pillowcases and skincare fridges. Even farm-luxury is often presented online as something expensive, exclusive, and external, like influencer-filled farmscape photoshoots featuring cute alpacas and rustic aesthetics. But sis, here's the truth: Real luxury is personal, intentional, and sovereign. In boutique farming, especially as a Black woman, you have the power to redefine what luxury looks and feels like—on your land, in your business, and for your spirit. Redefining luxury through boutique farming is a practice of alignment that also allows us as Black women to showcase our unique flair as trendsetters and style icons.

The Healing Power of Horticulture

Here's a vital element of boutique farming that cannot be overlooked: the therapeutic nature of horticulture. I mentioned in the introduction that I was diagnosed with anxiety. And while I believe in holistic health that includes both Westernized and natural and ancestral health practices, I personally did not want to rely on prescription medication to manage my anxiety long-term. The first thing I needed to do was rid myself of toxic relationships. Around the same time I was getting legally "un-entangled" from my marriage, I was terminated from my high-paying job. While it was a wrongful termination, it was also a true blessing in disguise because it freed me from an oppressive work environment and allowed me to personally experience the therapeutic aspects of horticulture. This practice goes far beyond growing plants—it's about cultivating peace, grounding yourself in ritual, and creating space for emotional and spiritual healing. For Black women especially, the act of tending to the land can be a reclamation, a release, and a return. And what could be more luxurious than that? Not in the glossy, performative sense, but in the soul-nourishing way that makes you feel held. In boutique farming, luxury isn't just in the final product—it's in the process, the presence, and the power to make your land a sanctuary as much as it is a business.

No matter what challenges life threw at her, my maternal grandmother, Charity Mae, found solace in the soil. Most evenings she could retreat to her garden, a glass of sweet tea or water in hand, humming softly, pruning, and planting to process life's struggles and reconnect with herself. She taught me about the plants in her garden, and while I didn't always join her, the image of her nurturing the earth, tending it with intention and tenderness, left a lasting impression on me. She planted a seed within me—one that would take root years later and shape my own journey. It's a seed I now nurture in the hope that it will blossom in my children, too.

A little-known fact about me: Even though my undergraduate degree is in marketing, I originally majored in environmental science. Yep, I always wanted to play a role in saving the world. Organic chemistry, however, had other plans. It humbled me—deeply—and eventually pushed me toward a new academic path. But by then, I had already completed several college-level courses in plant and animal science and botany. Between that and the years I spent growing up on my grandparents' farm, I was no stranger to plants. Still, I hadn't yet understood their full power. Not even close. Back then, plants were either something you ate or something pretty to admire. I knew they were used in cosmetics, fashion, and beauty products, but it had never crossed my mind to think of them as tools for my own healing—to help me reclaim peace, balance, and well-being. Well, let me be real: I knew of *one* medicinal plant with mood-boosting effects. Ahem. But beyond that, I had no idea of the incredible variety of plants that could enhance our lives in so many ways. The more I learned, the more I was utterly captivated. Plants are absolutely amazing.

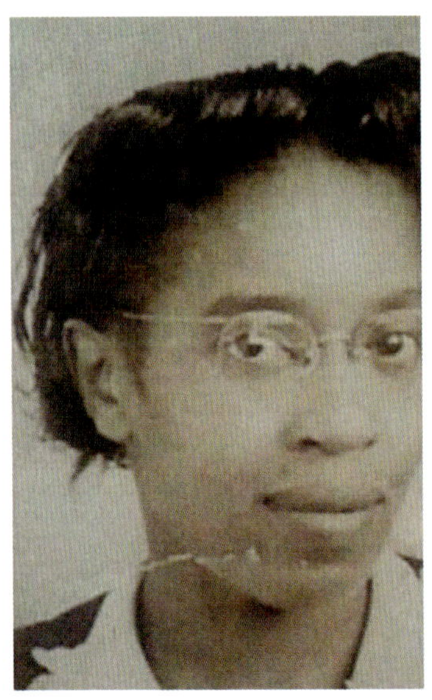

Cee's grandmother Charity Mae.

Evening primrose. *Photo courtesy of Maddy Gray.*

Throughout my career I've seen several examples of the healing power of horticulture. At one point I was leading the communications and fundraising teams at the Lucy Daniels Center, the region's largest children's emotional health center. I secured a corporate grant for a greenhouse designed as an educational and healing space, and I witnessed how tending to plants became a gentle refuge for children carrying deep emotional wounds. It offered them not just a safe space, but a space to express, release, and grow. Just a few years ago, I enjoyed the experience of teaching a workshop at the North Carolina Botanical Garden, home to a thriving therapeutic horticulture program. I focused on nervine herbs and how their cultivation can be a win-win both for growers and for those seeking plant-based support. Later, I brought members of my former subscriber community, the Sow Green Society, to the garden to learn more about the program firsthand. One of them was so inspired that she went on to teach her own workshop there.

When I started Green Heffa, I had this blank canvas of land—a sacred space to learn, experiment, and grow. I also had a healing heart—one opened up to discovery. I've continued to see that boutique farming can serve as a living extension of these therapeutic practices. It's about more than growing; it's about creating a farming ecosystem rooted in intention, emotional well-being, and authentic connection. In a world obsessed with hustle and scale, boutique farming gives us permission to slow down, prioritize quality,

Photo courtesy of Maddy Gray.

and cultivate a deeper sense of purpose. By incorporating therapeutic horticulture into our farm practices, we don't just grow plants—we grow healing, resilience, and joy. We nurture the land, and in return, it nurtures us. This is what true luxury looks like: a grounded, sustainable life that honors our wholeness and builds community from the soil up.

Boutique Prosperity Potential

One of the most exciting aspects of boutique farming is the limitless potential for revenue generation. I built Green Heffa Farms around the 4 E's: Economic Prosperity, Environment, Equity, and Education. There was never any question that one of the pillars of our sustainability framework would be Economic Prosperity. With a traditional farm, profitability is often tied to volume: You need to produce and sell as much as possible to turn a profit, and market prices can be restrictive. Boutique farms, however, operate on an entirely different model.

The global wellness industry is currently valued at over $4.5 trillion, showcasing a significant shift in consumer priorities toward health, wellness, and sustainability. As people become more conscious of their well-being, they seek high-quality, organic, and ethically sourced products—precisely what boutique farms provide. This growing demand creates opportunities for niche markets within the wellness sector, whether through herbal products, specialty foods, or wellness-focused experiences.

Unlike traditional farming, boutique farms can thrive by focusing on quality, uniqueness, and customer relationships. Consumers are willing to pay a premium for products that resonate with their values, such as sustainability, health benefits, and community engagement. By tapping into this expansive market, boutique farms can create diverse revenue streams, from specialty crops, to value-added products, to wellness experiences. The shift not only supports farmers' livelihoods but also nurtures a more holistic approach to agriculture—one that emphasizes innovation, passion, and the potential for transformative impact.

Boutique farm businesses carefully curate their customer experience. Years ago, I placed an order with a small boutique business. Funny enough, I can't even remember what I ordered, but I do remember the handwritten note I found in the package. That simple, personal touch left a lasting impression on me. I try to write as many personal thank-you notes as I can. It's a practice rooted in gratitude, and it helps me stay connected to the real people who support my work. It also lets me slow down, put a name to a customer, and practice my penmanship—something that's becoming a lost art! I am not able to write thank-yous for every order anymore, but I still pen as many as I can. And the impact? It's real. Customers often post pictures of their thank-you notes on social media or send a quick email just to say how much it meant to them. Is a handwritten thank-you note "boutique"? Without a doubt. It's thoughtful. It's personal. It's a small gesture that leaves a big impression—and to me, that's the true spirit of boutique.

Boutique farming isn't just about producing herbs, vegetables, flowers, or consciously raised meats; it's about cultivating an experience for your customers while also nurturing the land for future generations. The "boutique" aspect isn't defined by scale—it's defined by the narrative you craft around what you offer. While what you produce may be available elsewhere, when customers purchase from your boutique farm, they're investing in your story, your expertise, your dedication to sustainability, and your unique perspective. This is why boutique farms carry a built-in "cool factor," making them particularly

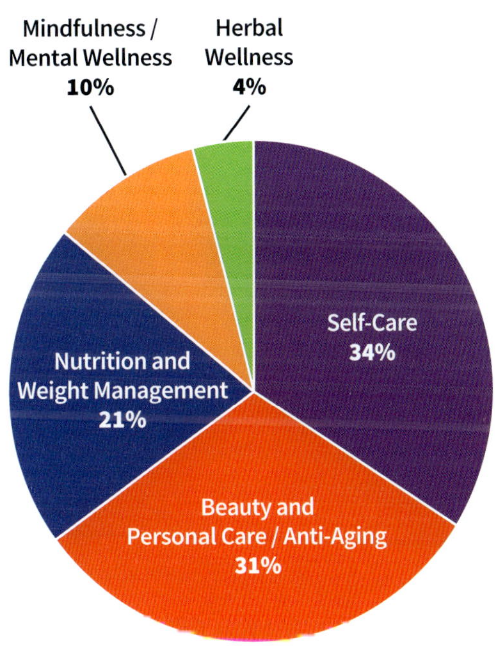

Percent of US wellness market by energy sector. *Source: Global Wellness Institute.*

Green Heffa Farms' 2025 holiday card.

attractive to today's discerning, environmentally conscious consumers.

Who Is a Real Farmer?

In the United States, the US Department of Agriculture (USDA) is the main federal agency that defines, supports, and regulates agricultural producers—including small, boutique farms like yours. While *farmer* may mean different things to different folks, the USDA has specific criteria for who qualifies as a farmer in the eyes of the government, particularly when it comes to federal funding. Whether you're growing on an acre or a backyard plot, if you plan to apply for grants, loans, or other support, it's important to understand the USDA

Photo courtesy of Maddy Gray.

definitions. The USDA supports over two million farms across the US. But here's the truth: Less than 2 percent of those farms are Black-owned, and even fewer are Black-woman-led. That's why it's so important that you know the rules of the game—and how to make them work for you. Let's walk through what the government's definition of a farmer is, and why one little number—the farm number—can open big doors.

The Thousand-Dollar Question

According to the USDA, to be officially recognized as a "farm" for program eligibility, you must have—or intend to have—at least $1,000 in agricultural sales annually. That means if your farm sells (or has the potential to sell) $1,000 or more of crops, livestock, or other agricultural products in a year, you qualify for most federal farm programs. That $1,000 can include fresh produce you sell at markets or to restaurants, herbal teas, flowers, livestock, or eggs. Farms also produce raw materials like hemp, timber, or plant starts.

Here's the part folks often miss: That $1,000 can be projected, especially if you're just starting out or if a natural disaster has impacted your sales. Let's face it: Life happens. Who knew that this would be the year that Japanese beetles declared war on your crop or your livestock animals weren't in the

Agritourism Income

Can agritourism income count toward the USDA's $1,000 threshold for defining a farm? Yes, but it depends on what you're charging for.

If your agritourism activity involves direct income from the sale or harvest of agricultural products, then that income can count toward the $1,000 in gross sales required for your farm to be recognized by the USDA. So, if you're charging admission for folks to enter your pick-your-own strawberry field, and they're paying for the experience of harvesting a crop—yes, that's agricultural income. It's tied to the production of a crop and is considered a farming activity.

On the other hand, if you're charging for access to your land for a non-agricultural event—say, a wedding or a yoga class in your field—that income likely wouldn't count toward the $1,000 threshold, even if it's earned on farmland.

Bottom line: The income needs to be directly connected to an agricultural product (growing, harvesting, or selling it) to meet the USDA's basic definition of a farm. And remember—the USDA may not check every dollar, but if you're applying for certain programs, you will need to show proof. So, keep those receipts organized and labeled clearly.

The interior of one of the agritourism tiny houses at Green Heffa Farms.

mood to procreate? The USDA recognizes that crop failures, weather events, and other obstacles can impact your bottom line. So even if you didn't make $1,000 in sales, you can still qualify for farm programs if you can show intent and evidence that your operation *would've* generated the sales under normal conditions. What matters is that you're operating with the intent to make that income by farming. Intent evidence could include: a record of your plantings, proof of weather events or natural disasters (like a drought or flood), pictures of pest damage, sales records from prior years, or invoices or receipts showing that you tried to sell your goods. This is where documentation is your best friend. Keep a folder—or digital file—with photos, notes, planting calendars, and all your receipts. It may feel extra, but it's the kind of "proof of work" that can unlock funding and support by demonstrating effort and sincerity.

The Farm Number

One of the first steps in establishing yourself as an official farmer is signing up for a farm tract number (often just called a farm number) through your local Farm Service Agency (FSA) office. A farm number is like a Social Security number—but for your farm's production. It's your farm's official footprint—and it shows the government (and grant funders) that you are in the game. It officially registers your land and operation in the USDA's system and tracks your farm's history over time. It builds a paper trail of what's been grown, how much land is in production, and what kinds of assistance or disaster support you've received. This record becomes powerful when you're applying for grants or loans, proving your operation was impacted by weather events, enrolling in conservation or crop insurance programs, or building a case for larger funding opportunities.

Getting a farm number is free, and you'll need it if you want to apply for USDA grants or loans, get disaster relief, qualify for conservation or technical assistance programs such as EQIP (see page 138), or receive federal insurance support. For those who are anti-government-support, I get it. Whether or not

Visiting the USDA in Person Versus Online

If you are unable to go to your local USDA's Farm Service Agency (FSA) office in person, you may be able to work with them remotely to some degree. But how much you can do from home varies quite a bit depending on your county, your state, and what specific service or program you need. Not all FSA offices are operated or staffed in the same ways. Here is what I know can be done virtually: You can do a lot through the farmers.gov portal, including submitting applications, researching program information, retrieving tract and farm maps, downloading certain documents, and even electronically signing some forms. And of course, if you owe the government some money, they are going to make sure you can pay it, so if you have any FSA loans, you can manage your payment via online systems. Ideally, you should be able to view your farm records, maps, and producer data reports online through USDA systems. However, information isn't always current or completely accurate. That's why I encourage you—if your farm is listed with the USDA—to review your records at least once a year. Catching discrepancies early can save you time and headaches later, especially when you're applying for programs, funding, or disaster assistance.

to get a farm number is a personal decision. As for me and my farm, I have no qualms with spending Uncle Sam's money, because he has never had an issue with spending mine. I remember getting an unexpected check for a few thousand because our state had received federal disaster funding for a hurricane.

There is no income minimum to get a farm number. You don't have to be making money yet to be recognized as a farmer by the USDA. However, some government assistance programs do consider your income, especially when determining eligibility for grants, cost-shares, or loans. For many of those programs, the USDA uses a $1,000 benchmark as a preferred threshold, but it's not always a hard requirement. It is also worth noting that there isn't a strict income maximum to receive all types of government farm funding, but many USDA programs have an adjusted gross income (AGI) limit of around $900,000 averaged over three years. However, if most of your income comes from farming, you may still qualify even if you exceed that limit. Specific programs may have their own rules, so it's best to check with your local USDA office for details.

For USDA program purposes, there is no real minimum size of land required to be considered a farm or to receive a farm number. Some data states that there is a minimum size of $\frac{1}{100}$th of an acre, which is equivalent to 435.6 square feet. However, the FSA has accepted acreage reports for plots as small as 0.000001 acre, which equates to approximately 6 square inches. Read that again. Six square inches. Perhaps someone was growing a Shenzhen Nongke orchid—often cited as the most expensive plant. I mean, these rare specimens can fetch up to $200,000 at auction! My point is not to let size be the determining factor as to whether or not you seek a farm number. Whether you are growing in a backyard garden, are on leased space at a community farm, run a container-based operation on a rooftop, or live somewhere urban, if you have the intent to produce and sell $1,000 worth of agricultural goods, you are eligible to apply for a farm number. You just have to navigate the local rules, document your setup, and be clear about your operation's scope and purpose. Even if you're leasing land, you can still get a farm number. You just need a copy of your lease and a map of the land you're farming.

It is important to know and remember that the farm number is tied to the land itself, not to you, the individual farmer. If you move farms, you'll need to register the new property and receive a new farm number. If someone else farmed the land before you, that history may already be attached to the number.

Farming in Suburbs or Cities

If you're in a neighborhood with a homeowners' association (HOA), your first step is to pull out those bylaws and read them like your next check depends on it—because it might. HOAs often have strict rules about land use, livestock, fencing, and even what kind of plants you can grow and how much of your yard you can use. Check for restrictions. Most HOAs draw a line between activities done for your own household (or for free educational/community purposes) and activities that generate income. For example, growing herbs in your backyard for your own kitchen, or hosting a free pollinator garden workshop for neighbors, is usually considered "personal use" or "educational." Those uses typically don't trigger HOA restrictions on commercial activity. Selling produce, cut flowers, eggs, or herbal products—even on a small scale—can fall into the category of "commercial" or "business" use. Many HOA bylaws restrict or outright prohibit commercial use of residential property, even if it's agricultural in nature. This doesn't mean it's impossible, but it does mean you must review your HOA's documents carefully and likely negotiate with the board.

Read the bylaws to see how *commercial*, *business*, or *agricultural use* is defined, and talk to the board about your plan. Some HOAs will grant a variance if you frame it as a community-benefit or low-impact activity. Document your activities and how they align with permitted uses—and be honest. If your end goal is a farm business, treat HOA bylaws as your first gatekeeper and, if necessary, plan to transition to land without such restrictions as your enterprise grows.

Apartment dwellers, balcony growers, and rooftop gardeners are farmers, too. But here's the honest part: Without direct access to land that you can designate for agricultural use, you're unlikely to be able to get a farm number in your name. Here's what you can do instead:

Partner Up: Team up with an entity that does have land, perhaps a community garden, a friend with a yard, or a local urban farm. Ask about forming a cooperative or sharing access in exchange for a formal lease or partnership agreement.

Lease a Plot: The USDA recognizes leased land if you can show a valid agreement and use the land for ag purposes. Even a small leased parcel can qualify.

Use a Land Host Model: More communities are embracing land hosting, where landowners offer unused yard space to growers in exchange for produce or a portion of profit. Secure a written agreement and apply from that location.

A great resource for those hoping to grow in urban spaces is Growing Urban Farmers (growingurbanfarmers.org). Though based in Arkansas, they have information that would be useful to farmers all over the country.

Real Talk

Don't let anyone tell you you're not a farmer because your farm is small, new, or different. If you're growing with intention, selling what you grow, and putting in that work—then you are a farmer. Period. Getting your paperwork in order and registering your farm is just another step toward making sure your operation gets the respect, recognition, and resources it deserves.

If I had listened to the doubt back in 2019—newly single, standing on raw land with no blueprint and no backup—Green Heffa Farms would still be just an idea. But I didn't. I showed up anyway. I worked the soil, I worked my vision, and I kept showing up until what I dreamed became what you're reading about today. And you can do it, too. Don't wait for perfect conditions or permission. Start with what you have, where you are, and let each small step add up. Your boutique farm may not bloom overnight, but it will grow over nights and days if you stay the course. You have what it takes. You dig?

GROUNDWORK

Claiming Your Growing Space

This exercise is designed to help you assess your current living situation and map out your path to securing a USDA-recognized farm location—even if your roots are currently planted in concrete.

Step 1: Define Your Current Growing Reality

What is your current living/growing situation? Do you live in an apartment or a condo? A single-family home with an HOA? Do you grow in containers or raised beds? Do you have access to a backyard or front yard? Are you currently growing herbs, vegetables, or flowers? Or do you have access to no land at all, but are ready to find some?

Write a few lines about your current growing setup and what your dream space looks like.

Step 2: Dig Into the Rules

If you rent your home or are part of an HOA, find your lease or bylaws and locate any clauses related to agricultural use, gardening or landscaping guidelines, restrictions on commercial activity, pets, or livestock, or any other restrictions that could limit farming. If you're not sure what's allowed, write down the exact wording from your lease or bylaws, then locate your nearby USDA FSA office or local ag extension office. Call to schedule an appointment, and bring any documents you've gathered—the lease or HOA bylaws, a land deed, or a farm sketch. Bring your list of questions, too. Showing up informed builds credibility and speeds up the process. FSA agents can help you interpret what you need for your farm number application.

Step 3: Get Real About Land Access

If you don't own land, where could you grow that would qualify for a USDA farm number? List a few potential spaces you could explore and reach out to. Options include a friend or family member's property; a community garden; a vacant lot; a school, church, or nonprofit space; or a local farm or land host open to partnership.

Step 4: Put It in Writing

To get a farm number, you need proof of land control. What documents do you currently have or could you work to secure? For example, a lease agreement, a memorandum of understanding, a land-sharing agreement, or a partnership contract. If you don't have one of these documents already, write down one action you'll take this month to secure a land access agreement.

Step 5: Build a Strategic Relationship with the USDA

Having a solid relationship with your local office can mean the difference between missing and seizing an opportunity. For example, my own FSA office has called me directly to alert me to important dates and program changes—a courtesy I know comes from developing genuine connections with the agents who work there. Every office is different, and not every agent will have a sunny personality. Some people may take issue with you simply because you're you. Still, cultivating relationships where possible increases your access to information, resources, and support.

We'll explore strategies for building and maintaining key relationships more deeply in chapter 8. The bottom line: Don't just complete the paperwork. Build the relationship. The USDA isn't perfect, but it holds tools and programs you deserve access to.

CHAPTER 2

Boutique Farming Starts Within

I come as one, but I stand as ten thousand.

—Maya Angelou

Green Heffa Farms would not exist today if I didn't first *believe* that it could exist. See, once you truly believe in something, your whole approach shifts. You move differently. You find energy where you thought there was none. You're willing to endure setbacks, to put in the work—even when no one else sees the vision. And some days you think the whole farm idea can kick rocks. But then you take a needed break and are ready to get back to building.

When I first shared my vision of Green Heffa Farms in 2018 with my fledging social media audience, I connected with so many others who told me that they had similar entrepreneurial goals, agricultural or otherwise. I'm still virtually connected with some of those people today, and while some have taken the leap and started their business, there are still several who profess a desire to start but have yet to move beyond that stage.

Don't Quit Your Day Job. Yet.

I started farming with a raw piece of land and almost no real growing knowledge. I mean, sure—I had a fledgling orchid collection, which was really just a collection of lonely stems adorned with a couple of oversized leaves (none of which ever rebloomed while in my care). And as I wrote in chapter 1, I spent a lot of my childhood years on a farm with my grandmother Charity Mae. But when it came to growing anything at scale? I knew absolutely nothing. I never asked my grandparents how the water actually made it from the well to the interior plumbing; I never even asked why we had a well. I just expected water when I turned on a faucet.

I wasn't technically broke, but I also didn't have the kind of money it takes to build a farm from scratch. When I bought my land and started farming, I was still employed, but the workplace was . . . tenuous. I was speaking up about inequities at the company and dealing with racial tension because of it. Then came the abdominal pain. Intense, erratic, and unnerving. I was sent to get a colonoscopy to rule out anything serious. What I learned was that I had developed anxiety. My body was screaming what I wasn't yet able to say: I was living in a state of dis-ease.

Of course, the solution offered was a prescription. Now, I am not one of those "Western medicine is the devil" folks. There is absolutely value in medication. But I also believe in holistic health: healing that honors ancestral wisdom, indigenous practices, spirituality, and, yes, science. That's when I began studying medicinal plants and herbs in earnest, starting with hemp flower (*Cannabis sativa*) and then expanding to other plant species. I was amazed at the variety and power of plants, their benefits, and the market potential. Despite all that I didn't know when I received my anxiety diagnosis, I did know three things: I couldn't put myself in another psychologically unsafe environment; I had to address the anxiety in a way that felt whole to me; and I was going to build an herb farm.

I can't tell you how many messages I receive that go something like this: "Hey, I bought some land and quit my job to start a farm. Where should I start?!" Every time, my heart skips a beat. I'm never quite sure what the person expects me to say. I absolutely understand the desire to leave a job that doesn't fulfill you, and truth be told, once you start farming, the idea of farming full-time will start to live rent-free in your mind all day long. But here's my advice: Stick with your day job for as long as you can. According to the 2022 USDA Census of Agriculture, nearly 60 percent of US farmers work an off-farm job to supplement their income. For many, farming alone does not provide enough financial stability—especially in the early years. Let your farm dreams grow steadily, without the heavy weight of financial desperation attached to them. Build the skills. Build the systems. Build the customer base. Give yourself time to reach a quality of life you're truly happy with *before* you bet it all. Because you are boutique, you will get there before you know it. Time really does fly when you are having fun, and there's no shame in easing into your dream. In fact, it's the smartest move you can make.

Finding Your Footing

For me to be truly successful, I couldn't afford not to believe in myself, especially at the beginning. I was in a financially vulnerable situation, and I didn't have time to dwell on what was missing, what I didn't know yet, or what still needed to be done. Instead, I decided to bet on myself and anchored myself in a new daily mantra: *Farming starts on the inside.* I stopped telling myself, "I don't have enough . . ." and started asking, "What can I do with what I have?"

I began honoring the invisible labor—the dreaming, the planning, the strategy sessions with myself. I focused on what I could control. That meant doing a lot of brainstorming and networking, but also self-care and taking steps to prepare myself for the farming lifestyle. The building blocks of a dream are often quiet and unseen—the slow, steady work that rarely gets celebrated but always matters. Do not discount the planning phase. It was in these early, invisible stages that I began making critical shifts to support the future I was determined to build.

We'll get into some of this work in the next few chapters. But the truth is, there were also changes I had to make in my daily life and routine long before the first seed went in the ground. Becoming more physically active became part of the job, whether or not anyone would call it exercise. Walking the fields, stretching before work, building strength—it all mattered. My body needed to be capable of the long days and heavy lifting that farm life demands. Learning business operations felt like stepping into a new world. I learned about bookkeeping, inventory, pricing, and permits. At first it was overwhelming, but understanding these systems gave me control and confidence to make smart decisions.

Harvesting butterfly pea flowers.

Researching herbs and their uses became a daily ritual. I read, experimented, and sometimes failed—but I fell in love with the deep knowledge each plant carries. Learning what an herb could do gave me the confidence to create products that really served people.

Thrifting cute overalls and vintage T-shirts was joy disguised as practicality. The clothes became my uniform but also a reflection of the farm's personality—fun, intentional, and real.

Engaging with and learning from other farmers and entrepreneurs became a lifeline. Their successes and mistakes became lessons I could borrow, adapt, and make my own. This wasn't networking—it was community and mentorship in one.

I downsized my living situation, choosing simplicity and financial flexibility over excess. I bought used vehicles instead of chasing something shiny and new, including my first tractor. I recommitted to sustainable shopping, which not only saved money but also rekindled my love for thrifting, antiquing, and upcycling—practices that felt aligned with the values I was nurturing for my farm and my life. This shift reawakened my creativity and inspired me to design small, meaningful spaces and displays around the farm; sweet little "moments" that tell a story, showcase the farm's history, educate about one of the crops, or simply add beauty and character to the land. See, I had made one non-negotiable promise to myself: My joy and psychological safety would not be compromised. And neither should yours. It's essential to be realistic about the changes you're willing to make, but they must come from a place of empowerment, not punishment. Any shift you make in service of your dreams should feel like you're investing in yourself—not punishing yourself for wanting more.

Take What Is Useful, Leave the Rest

At some point, I decided to enroll in a farm school program offered through a local university extension program. I had high hopes that it would deepen my knowledge and help me find community among other aspiring farmers. To be honest, it wasn't quite the transformative experience I had envisioned. The curriculum focused heavily on conventional agriculture—large-scale row crops, livestock operations, and commodity farming—models that had little to do with the boutique, regenerative farm I was working to build.

When I shared my plans to specialize in medicinal plants and herbs, I was met with a blunt dismissal: "That's not sustainable." The main instructor advised me to raise pork and create a pick-your-own-strawberries model. Imagine that. Still, I chose to stay the course. The program was affiliated with a respected agricultural university, and I knew that credibility mattered—especially as a Black woman stepping into a space where people already questioned my legitimacy. Even if the program didn't feed my spirit, it still offered valuable, practical lessons. I learned how to budget for essentials like compost and mulch, how to navigate the various types of insurance I would need, and how to factor in start-up costs I hadn't even considered.

Not every room you walk into will be designed for you. Not every program will see your vision. But even in spaces that weren't built with you in mind, you can still gather the tools you need to build a life that is. Funny thing? A few years later, a Black woman herb farmer in one of my learning communities told me that Green Heffa Farms was now part of the curriculum in her farm school course in another county. The same system that once said my dream wasn't viable was now using my farm as an example. You never know who's watching.

Here's something I want you to hear, loud and clear: Don't grow or produce something just because someone else tells you to. Their vision is not your vision. Yes, be open to advice and be willing to learn and discern what's useful. For example, someone once suggested I grow holy basil, and after doing my research, I learned that holy basil (tulsi) and cannabis have quite a few terpenes in common, which contribute to their healing properties. This partly explains why both are prized in herbal medicine—for relaxation, inflammation, and general wellness. So, the suggestion to grow holy basil was a smart one, and aligned with my mission. But I've also had folks encourage me to grow crops or raise livestock purely for profit, like pigs and strawberries. And you know what? I didn't do it. Remember: We are operating from an abundance mindset here. We attract money—we don't chase it. Always stay true to your vision. That's where the real harvest is.

Leverage Your Own Knowledge

It is important to remember that you are coming into this with some knowledge and skills, and that often those skills are transferable. Take stock of the skills and knowledge you already have and see if you can start generating revenue with that knowledge set alone. Early in Green Heffa Farms' journey, I launched a digital product called Big Hemping, which was a step-by-step digital course on how to get a hemp license and get started in the hemp farming business. I had navigated that process myself and I knew there was a demand for the knowledge because I was often asked for advice by other hemp-curious folks. And even though there were free resources available, I knew I could provide more detail for customers—even sharing some market entry tips for new hemp producers.

According to a 2021 report from Markets and Markets, businesses of all types from around the world are spending huge amounts of money on better ways to store, share, and use information. That spending is expected to grow from about $207 billion in 2021 to more than $300 billion by 2026, driven by

Photo courtesy of Donnie Rex.

companies moving their operations online and using cloud-based tools. As someone experienced in marketing and fundraising, I could see that this shift would create enormous opportunities to earn income from knowledge and expertise—and not just in tech. For example, as a boutique farmer, you can share what you know through online courses, virtual farm tours, digital guides, or subscription newsletters, turning your knowledge into a new source of revenue.

I didn't pull in six- or seven-figure numbers like some folks boasted about back then with their digital products, but I made enough to hit a few important milestones. I opened a business account. I got my first $1,000 deposit, then $5,000, and so on. And every time I hit a new milestone—no matter how small—I made it a point to celebrate that I had successfully leveraged my own knowledge to gain my footing in this business. Even if you're at the beginning of your farming journey, you might already have specialized knowledge that you could consider turning into a digital product.

Despite these accomplishments, I still had to deal with my number one hater: self-doubt. Impostor syndrome is real. It'll tell you that you're not doing enough. That you don't deserve the title of "farmer" because you haven't harvested your first crop, haven't secured your land yet, haven't made any revenue. Stop. That. Thinking. It is counterproductive. The fact that you're reading this book already says something: You're on the path. You're already a farmer. And once you truly believe that? Watch how everything starts to shift.

Finding the Silver Lining

Three years into my journey, life gave me a nudge I hadn't planned for: The job that had been draining me let me go. That place was never equipped to

There Are Bugs

Anyone who knows me knows I have had a lifelong fear of slugs. At one point it was really bad—I am talking full-body shivers, irrational panic, the whole thing. I used to tiptoe around the farm after a good rain, praying I wouldn't see a slug. Slugs don't care about your boundaries, though, and they sure don't care about your boutique dreams—and farming comes with slugs. One morning I was checking on my luxurious lemon balm when I spotted the sluggiest slug of all slugs just chilling on the underside of a leaf. And when I say chilling, I mean it was posted up like it paid property taxes. I could tell the slug had lived a very comfortable life and valued our efforts to ensure a boutique environment. I froze. This was my farm, my herbs, and I was scared to do what needed to be done. That was my wake-up call. You can't boutique-farm in theory. You've got to be about that soil life in real time.

Farming isn't always pretty. Yes, you can post gorgeous sunrise photos and tea-in-hand reels, but before that comes the not-so-cute part. If you're deathly afraid of bees, should you be planting lavender, echinacea, and other pollinator-attracting plants? Bees are vital, but they don't care about your boundaries, either. If you can't touch bugs, deal with soil, or get a little muddy, are you more in love with the idea of farming than the actual day-to-day? If you think rain is just romantic, wait until you're outside in it trying to fix a busted tarp or save seedlings from flooding. While aesthetics are important, boutique farming requires more. It demands emotional resilience, physical presence, and a willingness to confront your own discomforts. It's one thing to dream up a healing-centered farm surrounded by flowers and herb bundles. It's another thing entirely to actually weed those beds, manage pests, and keep that lavender thriving in 95°F (35°C) heat.

Take inventory of your real-life thresholds. What are your current no-go zones? Can you stretch them? Can you learn or hire your way around them? Don't design your farm around an Instagram dream—design it around what you can actually handle or are willing to grow into. Farming will stretch you—but it shouldn't break you.

create a healthy work environment for me as a Black woman. According to a 2023 report by the Green 2.0 initiative, Black women remain severely underrepresented in leadership positions across philanthropy and environmental conservation sectors, often facing hostile and isolating work environments. When I was offered a disrespectful severance, I refused to sign the NDA attached to it. Instead, I made sure their mistreatment was federally documented—for the record and for perpetuity. I wanted to ensure that a precedent was set, for the Black women and other marginalized folks who would come after me.

ACCOUNTABILITEA tea blend.

I had been farming for three years and was ready to commit to farming full-time. But without the extra income from my job, I had to be resourceful. When life handed me injustice, I made tea. During the early days of Green Heffa Farms, I found myself facing a legal battle against my most recent former employer that was draining emotionally, mentally, spiritually, and financially. But I want to share this part because it highlights something important: Life's challenges can inspire innovative solutions if we stay open. Instead of shrinking under the weight of the situation, I channeled my energy into creation. I formulated a detox tea blend using 100 percent plant material grown right here on Green Heffa Farms. I called it ACCOUNTABILITEA.

The symbolism was powerful: a detoxifying tea—cleansing the body—representing my own journey of purging toxic environments from my life and committing to full-time farming. The original packaging included a QR code that customers could scan to receive updates about my legal case. ACCOUNTABILITEA was more than a product. It was a movement. A reclamation. A way for customers to support me while also supporting their own health. And it resonated. The blend became one of our bestsellers and ultimately earned a permanent spot in our lineup of herbal teas. I was able to raise critical funds, awareness, and myself.

So, if you've already quit your job, been uninvited from attending work by your employer (ahem), or seen life throw an unexpected challenge at you, remember that you are resourceful and creative. Embrace the power of your own story, because it can be one of your most powerful tools. And it is a story that only you can tell.

But Sis, I Am Single

Look, this isn't a dip-your-toe-in kind of venture. If you want to build a successful and sustainable boutique farming business, you have to decide—with your whole chest—that you're in. And if you're in, then be all the way in.

FARMER HIGHLIGHT

Dr. Najmah Thomas, Earth People Farms, St. Helena Island, South Carolina

Tell us a little about your farm and your "why" for farming.

Earth People Farms is a micro boutique farm on St. Helena Island in the heart of the Gullah Geechee community. My siblings and I started the farm as a way to help support our parents and continue their legacy of being stewards of the Earth. We cultivate culturally relevant herbs, fruits, and veggies so our family and community members have a better chance at food sovereignty. We create value-added products and host on-farm agritourism and agri-education events so our farm enterprise can be "unbought, un-bossed, and un-bothered"!

What has been one of the biggest lessons you've learned through your farming journey?

Farming is messy, farming takes time, farming takes partners, and farming is freedom.

What is one piece of advice you would offer to other Black women interested in starting a boutique farm?

Do it, QueenSis! But do it with your eyes and ears wide open. Don't let the "after" pictures you see on social media be your measuring stick—make your own definition and description of what boutique

Photo courtesy of Najmah Thomas.

farming success will look like for you. Then build a plan based on your vision. Identify the resources you will need to implement that plan. Link up with sisters and groups dedicated to ecowomanism; curate your contacts and your content. Take it step by step, bit by bit, and give yourself plenty of grace along the way. Also, go 'head and treat yourself to a dope straw hat, some cute boots, fancy gloves, specialty overalls, and snap-front long-sleeved shirts—'cause we boutique with this, okay? Ain't no need in looking bedraggled just 'cause you working hard!

How do you care for yourself while doing this work?

I am so serious about taking loving care of my body, mind, and spirit in this work. I meditate and write in my journal (shameless plug for the Dayclean Devotion Queen journal!) each day without fail. This practice has positively transformed the last five years of my life. I drink and eat with intention on longevity and pleasure. I time myself in the field, especially during the hottest months—early morning or late evenings only. I protect my schedule from excessive meetings and others' expectations. Time is not money, time is life, and I take care to spend my blessed minutes wisely. I have an amazing partner (truly the best of good men), and we grow love together. My ancestors ground me; I hear them reminding me that they sacrificed so I don't have to sacrifice as much. I rest, play, and love in tribute to them.

As a single woman, I'll be real with you—it's hard sometimes. There are days I wish I could hop into one of the six gassed-up, well-maintained vehicles I'm responsible for, without a single concern, because my partner had it handled. I'd love to be a passenger princess with nothing but my ID and lip gloss. My man, my man, my man . . . But that's not my current reality. Regardless of your identity, I know this for a fact: Being single is far better than being with someone who doesn't support your vision. It doesn't matter whether it's family, a business partner, or romantic relationships and marriages. Had I stayed in past relationships, Green Heffa Farms wouldn't exist as it does today—and I wouldn't be the woman, or the business owner, I've become. I seriously doubt I'd be writing this book.

So, if you're single? Start single. You'll be building something that will attract people who see you and value your mission. Don't let your relationship status stop you from stepping into your purpose. If being single is the thing holding you back, I'll be honest—you may not be cut out for this. If you're going to do this, do it fully. Now, if you're in a relationship or partnership, I truly hope it's one where you feel supported as you go after your dreams. I have a good farmer friend who's married. She's the farmer. He's not. He helps

Single and botanically unbothered. *Photo courtesy of Visual Chronicles.*

occasionally, does some things because he enjoys them or because he loves her, but the farm is her dream, and they both respect that. She doesn't expect him to follow her lead just because they share a life. I've seen beautiful joint ventures where both partners are all-in, building a shared vision. But I've also seen the other side—unsupportive partners, power struggles, or outright tension. Whether it's a spouse, domestic partner, or family member, I will tell you this: A farm will not fix your relationship. In fact, the stress and responsibility of running a farming business will amplify what's already there. One of the defining features of a boutique farm is that your well-being is a priority. If the foundation of your personal life is shaky, don't expect farming to stabilize it.

Let's address a few things I hear often: "I'm not physically capable." "I don't have enough money." "I don't have the time." "I am a caretaker/have small children." "I don't know anything."

And my response is: Okay. If that's your truth right now, I respect that. I'm not here to convince anyone to start a boutique farm. That would be irresponsible. This book is not about hype—it's about helping women build something real. But I will say this: The agriculture industry needs new voices. According to the USDA's 2022 Census of Agriculture, the average age of all US farm producers is 58.1 years, a number that's been steadily increasing to reflect an aging farmer population. But as the old guard ages out, the industry is slowly becoming more diverse. Here's more of what the latest census data shows:

- Beginning farmers (ten years or less experience) are an average age of 47.1 years old.
- Producers under thirty-five make up 9 percent of all producers.
- Women account for 36 percent of all producers, and 58 percent of farms have at least one female decision maker.

If you really want to farm, there is room for you, even if you're also dealing with variables like raising children or being a newcomer to agriculture. Boutique farming is customizable, meaning you can set up your business to fit with your needs and lifestyle and then adjust as needed. For example, it would be remiss of me to not mention that one of the farmers who inspires me the most is of a "seasoned" age. Cheryl Alston, lovingly known as Mama Cheryl, started farming later in life after an awarded career as a scientist and educator. Now she's in her eighties. Believe me when I tell you, I can't keep up with her! It is never too late to build your dream.

Farming can be physical, and if that's a concern, make body movement part of your preparation phase. That might mean stretching more, walking regularly, or doing the kind of work your future self will thank you for. Personally, once I started Green Heffa Farms, I found myself waking up earlier or staying up later—not because I always had to but because I wanted to. The joy outweighed the fatigue. But I still had a kid at home and had a full-time job. This doesn't include my board commitments, showing up for adult children (and grandchildren), being a friend, and all of the other hats I wore. I had bills, and there I was, starting a new business. And not just any business but a farming business as a *Black woman*.

Another important thing I did? I documented my journey. Every decision. Every mistake. Every step. Experts are built through experience, not perfection. And the notes I took back then? You're reading them now. Let that sink in. Even if you don't plan to write a book, documenting your process positions you for so much more—speaking gigs, workshops, curriculum development, creating a private learning community, or just being able to look back and see how far you've come. You have skills that matter. Your story matters. Your voice matters. And yes—you're already enough.

So, as we go through this journey together, I hope you'll learn not only how to build a boutique farm from the ground up but also how to cultivate the mindset and resilience it takes to thrive—whether you're planting herbs, raising animals, or sowing the seeds of your dreams.

Cee's mentor, Mama Cheryl. *Photo courtesy of Little Washington Growing Group.*

GROUNDWORK

Accessing Your Own Wisdom

A core component of building a boutique farm is ensuring that you're supporting a strong foundation within yourself. This exercise is about recognizing the wisdom you've already earned. While you may be considered a beginning farmer, that doesn't mean you are inexperienced. You are building from your lived experiences—not just from information. This is your opportunity to reflect on the strength, insight, and resilience you already carry, and how it can ground the path ahead.

Step 1: Describe Your Starting Point

Begin by detailing what your initial "raw piece of land" looked like—whether it was a literal space, a career path, or a personal goal. What were the obstacles you encountered that made you feel unprepared or overwhelmed?

Step 2: Identify Your Turning Point

What moment or realization helped you take ownership of your situation? Did you have a side-eye moment like mine, when you recognized a lack of support or resources? How did that moment shift your perspective?

Step 3: Embrace the Journey of Learning

Consider how your mindset evolved as you faced challenges. Write about the lessons you learned and how remaining teachable has influenced your growth. What new skills or insights did you gain along the way?

Step 4: Cultivate Resilience

Reflect on how you nurtured resilience during this journey. What practices or affirmations helped you stay grounded and focused on your goals? How did you celebrate your progress, no matter how small?

Step 5: Connect to Your Dreams

Finally, envision the future you're cultivating. What dreams are you planting today, and what actions are you taking to ensure they thrive? Write in your journal about how this journey, much like building a boutique farm, involves continuous growth and adaptation. Dig deep.

In boutique farming, your farm can be anything you dream it to be. It's where purpose meets profitability. And when you embrace the unique power of boutique farming, the sky isn't even the limit—it's just the beginning.

CHAPTER 3

Cultivating an Abundance Mindset

To free ourselves, we must feed ourselves.

—Fannie Lou Hamer, civil rights leader and founder of the Freedom Farm Cooperative

I lived with my maternal grandparents in rural Alabama during the 1980s and '90s—a time when the scent of fresh-plowed earth mingled with the tension of uncertainty. The land was both sanctuary and battleground. My grandparents raised livestock, tended rows of field peas and collards, and lived with the quiet dignity of folks who knew how to coax life from stubborn soil. But behind every harvest loomed the shadow of discrimination. This was the Pigford era, when Black farmers like my grandparents were fighting for justice—battling USDA loan denials and systemic neglect that threatened to erase generations of Black landownership. As a child, I didn't fully understand the weight they carried, but I knew that farming, for us, was more than work—it was resistance, legacy, and love.

I always associated farming with the land itself. I rarely heard my grandparents talk about the business of farming, except when there were complaints about how little compensation was being offered for the cattle taken to market. This gave me the impression that farming was not a profitable endeavor and that farmers had little to no control over how much their hard work could yield. This impression was reinforced by my grandparents, who strongly encouraged us to go to college, get a degree, and get a good pension-paying job. As a child, I absorbed the following beliefs and carried them into adulthood: (1) There was no money in farming; (2) Farmers were at the mercy of external forces when it came to making a living; and (3) Farming was a joyless occupation.

But when I began my own farming journey, I realized very early that understanding the distinction between viewing a farm merely as a piece of

Photo courtesy of Maddy Gray.

land and recognizing it as a thriving business was essential. Whenever someone says to me, "I can't wait to start a farm," I ask them why they are waiting. The response is inevitably, "I'm waiting to get access to land." This is a common misconception. A farm is often viewed as just a plot of soil where crops are grown and livestock is raised, but when we shift our perspective to see it as a business, we unlock its full potential. This shift involves embracing the entrepreneurial mindset, where every decision is driven by strategic planning, financial management, and sustainable practices. Instead of just cultivating herbs or vegetables, you're cultivating a brand, a community, and a legacy that reflects your values and vision.

When I talk to aspiring or beginning farmers, the topic of money—and often, not having enough of it—almost always comes up. And honestly, it's no surprise. Many of us are navigating systemic barriers that make accessing resources a constant challenge. The scarcity mindset—believing there's never enough, that opportunities are scarce, or that financial success is out of reach—is deeply ingrained, especially for those of us who have had to fight for progress.

But here's the truth: Minding your money isn't just about what's in your bank account. It's about setting yourself up for success by aligning your financial management with the vibrant, sustainable vision you have for your boutique farm. Let's break down what that really means and how you can cultivate a financial mindset that supports your long-term success.

It's easy to get caught up in the logistics of funding your farm—budgeting, applying for grants, securing loans, and generating revenue. But one of the most overlooked factors in your farm's financial future is your own personal relationship with money. As a farmer—especially as a Black woman entrepreneur—your financial mindset isn't just about dollars and cents; it's about how you perceive wealth, opportunity, and sustainability. You're not just running a farm; you're running a business, and that means your personal money habits, financial literacy, and confidence with numbers directly impact the growth of your farm. If you don't have a healthy relationship with money in your personal life, it will inevitably show up in your business.

Just like your crops need healthy soil to thrive, your farm business needs a solid financial foundation—starting with you. Farming is not just about growing crops; it's about growing wealth, sustainability, and independence. By shifting your money mindset, getting clear on your financial health, and making strategic financial decisions, you position your boutique farm for longevity and success.

This mindset shift begins with getting your personal financial house in order. Just like a house built on a weak foundation won't stand, your farm needs a stable financial base to thrive. Take time to review your finances, create a budget, and set up separate accounts for your farm, no matter how small it currently is. Every decision you make from a place of financial clarity sets the tone for how you will run your farm. It's an act of care and respect—not just for your money but for your dreams.

When you take control of your personal finances, it does more than set your farm up for success. It allows you to operate with confidence, authenticity, and integrity. You'll feel empowered to say no to opportunities that don't align with your vision and say yes to investments that push your farm forward. And when you bring that energy into your business, you're planting the seeds for a harvest that goes far beyond dollars and cents.

Farmer Coo's maternal grandparents, Johnny and Charity Mae (Rambo) Southall.

Let's get into the steps toward strengthening your financial health from the inside out.

Adopt Abundance Thinking: First, shift your perspective away from a scarcity mindset and toward abundance. Instead of focusing on what you don't have, start recognizing and leveraging what you do have. Maybe you don't have $50,000 in start-up capital right now, but you have community support, unique skills, a developing plan, and the ability to generate revenue creatively. Adopt the mindset that money is a tool, not a limitation. As your business and brand(s) grow, so will the money. You have to become comfortable with prosperity.

Get Intimate with Your Numbers: If you don't know exactly how much money is coming in and going out—both personally and in your farm business—it's time to change that. Get familiar with your credit report. Track every dollar. Create a budget that accounts for your farm's needs while also making sure your personal financial health isn't neglected. Separate your personal finances from your business finances. This might seem basic, but it's crucial. Keeping your personal and farm finances separate not only makes accounting easier but also helps you treat your farm like the business it is. Open a dedicated business bank account, track farm expenses meticulously, and pay yourself—even if it's a small amount at first.

Invest in Your Financial Education: No one expects you to be a financial expert overnight, but the more you understand about managing cash flow, pricing your products, and funding your business, the more empowered you become. Take the time to read books (like you're doing now!), take online courses, or connect with financial experts who understand money, entrepreneurship, and farming. (For a list of other financial education options, see "Resources" at the end of this book.)

Diversify Your Revenue Streams: We'll cover this in upcoming chapters. Farming can be unpredictable, so multiple streams of income can create stability. Maybe your boutique farm sells premium herbs, but you also offer farm tours, workshops, or value-added products. Finding creative ways to generate income will help you stay financially resilient.

Abundance Mindset: Think Like the Boss You Are

Shifting your mindset is just as important as shifting your money habits. From the moment you decide to start your farm, whether it's a few herbs on your windowsill or a plot in your backyard, you have to embrace the role of a business owner. Why? Because that mental shift is the foundation for everything that comes next. Think of yourself as the CEO from day one. This isn't about waiting until you have acres of land, a large budget, or a thriving customer base to start treating your farm like a business. It's about adopting a mindset that allows you to be proactive about your finances, make decisions with confidence, and cultivate a vision of abundance even when resources are scarce. When you approach your farm with a business mindset, you're not just reacting to what's in front of you. You're strategizing, planning, and taking intentional actions that shape the future of your farm.

You do not have to own land to start your farm. It is important for you to know that you can begin establishing your farm as a legal business right now while you move through the planning stages. Many aspiring farmers skip over the business planning and establishment phase because they believe that without a physical location, their farm doesn't really exist. I encourage you to challenge that mindset. Every business, every idea, exists twice—first in your mind and then in reality. So, it's crucial to invest the time needed to plan, research, and strategize your farming business even before you put a single plant in the ground.

Starting a boutique farm costs money. There's no sugarcoating it. And if you're like me and want to grow slow so you don't owe as much as possible, you'll need to be strategic, creative, and intentional about securing funding. But before we get into all the possible funding sources in chapter 9, let's make sure your mindset is in the right place. Lack and scarcity thinking can destroy your confidence before you plant your first seed. If you start with the thought that you'll never have enough money to make it work, you'll find yourself acting out of fear, making poor financial choices, or hesitating to invest in opportunities that could benefit your farm in the long run. Instead, focus on developing a mindset of financial empowerment. Even if your bank account doesn't yet reflect abundance, your attitude should. Why? Because you need to be ready to put your business out there and show potential funders that you're serious, prepared, and trustworthy. When you approach funding from a place of abundance, you're not just chasing money—you're creating opportunities for mutually beneficial partnerships and long-term stability.

Real Talk

Remember, you are the foundation of your farm's financial future. And just like any good farmer, you'll need to cultivate your resources with care, intention, and a mindset rooted in abundance.

The Truth About Credit

Even though I ascribe to the *grow slow so you don't owe* mantra, I do still maintain a strong personal and business credit score. I make sure to stay on top of my credit rating, and I check credit reports regularly. I have talked to many aspiring boutique farmers who have shared that they do not check their credit reports annually. Pulling your credit report might sound intimidating, especially if you've had a less-than-perfect relationship with money in the past. I get it; I've been there. I've had bad credit more than once. I'll never forget the shock of checking my credit one time and seeing a score in the low 400s. I was so embarrassed and overwhelmed. I felt like I was on the financial equivalent of a desert island with no lifeboat in sight. I couldn't even get approved for financing at the "no-credit, bad-credit, buy-here-pay-here" car dealerships that claim to approve anyone. It was a wake-up call.

Why Your Personal Credit Matters

You might be wondering, "Why does my credit score even matter if I'm planning to establish business credit?" Here's the thing: Your personal credit isn't just a reflection of your past—it's a mirror of your money mindset. And it has everything to do with how you'll manage your farm's finances. If you have challenges managing your own money, chances are you won't manage your farm's budget any differently. Plus, when you're first starting out, your business credit and personal credit are deeply intertwined. Lenders often look at your personal credit history to gauge whether you're a risk. A solid personal credit score can fast-track your access to business credit, loans, and investment opportunities. It's a stamp of approval that tells the financial world you can handle responsibility. Raggedy credit is not in alignment with CEO or boutique energy—I say this with love. Raggedy credit and financial disorganization do not match the energy you need to operate as the CEO of your farm. Your credit score isn't just a number; it's a reflection of your financial intentions. But it goes even deeper than that. Repairing my credit taught me discipline, focus, and a growth mindset. It wasn't just about getting a better score; it was about transforming how I viewed money, wealth, and abundance. It was about reclaiming my power and stepping into my role as the CEO of my life and my business. So, yes, this journey started with pulling my credit report, but it ended with me redefining what was possible for myself financially.

My Credit Story

For years, I avoided checking my credit because I didn't want to face the reality of it. Whenever I thought about it, my credit seemed like a list of my financial failures, an indictment of all the mistakes I'd made. The report was filled with painful reminders of the tough times I had been through. Some items were there because I had been irresponsible—but more often, they were there because I had been broke. Really broke. Eventually, I got tired of feeling tired, and that exhaustion extended far beyond my bank account. My financial stress was draining my mental, physical, and emotional energy. I hit a point where I decided enough is enough. I got serious, and I put in the work to turn things around. It took two years of focused, consistent effort to clean up my credit and rebuild my financial health, but the results were worth every hard-fought step.

Now I've maintained a credit score in the high 700s to low 800s for over a decade. My highest score has been 817, and even with all the ups and downs over the past decade, the lowest it has dropped is 747. But this wasn't always the case. Some years ago, my credit took a major hit after getting financially liberated from my ex-husband during our divorce, and it dropped again when my student loans were forgiven through the Public Service Loan Forgiveness Program—just before I transitioned to farming full-time. These dips, while frustrating, didn't stop me. I had been there before, and I had acquired the tools to bounce back.

But I didn't grow up with a solid understanding of financial literacy, and it showed. Both of my parents were college graduates, but they divorced when I was still a little girl. While I won't go into details here, I was the victim of and witnessed a lot of abuse and violence. Money was always a point of contention growing up, and I ended up with a lot of emotions wrapped up in it but no practical knowledge of how to handle it myself. When I finally left to live with my grandparents in middle school, things did stabilize. The schools I attended taught the basics of balancing a checkbook, but nothing about how to build wealth, avoid debt traps, or leverage credit. My grandmother, on the other hand, tried to impart what she knew. She had excellent credit, and she guarded it fiercely. Still, she never had "McDonald's money." She wasn't frivolous. Every dollar had a purpose, and she'd look at me over her glasses and remind me, "You can't eat credit, baby."

The concept of good credit with no cash flow was foreign to me and, frankly, confusing. I didn't get it. I just knew that money was scarce, and being financially irresponsible seemed to run in the family. All of this set the stage for my own chaotic relationship with money. And when I became a mother at just fifteen years old, everything went from bad to worse. Money became synonymous with survival. I was terrified of my daughter experiencing hunger. With inconsistent support from my daughter's father and the challenge of navigating a life in a community with almost no economic resources, I was thrust into a cycle of financial trauma. This trauma would manifest itself repeatedly throughout my teens, twenties, and even into my thirties.

I spent a good part of my life viewing credit as an indictment. Every time I'd muster the courage to check my score, it felt like a list of financial failures.

And there was no escaping the racial bias baked into the entire system. Studies show that Black individuals are often penalized more harshly for the same financial mistakes as their white counterparts, and this reality only added to my feelings of inadequacy and frustration. I wasn't just broke; I was being judged for it. My score didn't just reflect a lack of money—it reflected a lack of grace from the institutions that were supposedly there to help me. And every new ding on my report was like an echo of that trauma.

When I finally decided to get serious about rebuilding my credit, I gave myself a clear time frame—twenty-four months—to increase my score by a hundred points. I wasn't trying to erase my entire financial past. I just needed the good to outweigh the bad. This was back in the early 2000s. I was in my *first* unhappy marriage, with the father of my youngest child. I knew I would have to leave with nothing more than I came with unless I was willing to drag the dissolution out. I only needed a 620 credit score to qualify for an FHA (Federal Housing Administration) loan to purchase a little house. My budget was $90,000, which seemed such a large goal. I reached my credit goal in a year, though, and that allowed me to leave even sooner. I started small, pulling my credit report from all three bureaus to get a clear picture of where I stood. Then I made a plan to tackle the issues one by one, prioritizing the quick wins (like paying down small balances) and slowly chipping away at the bigger problems. I ultimately purchased a small house in a cul-de-sac for a whopping $93,000.

This experience taught me a few lessons. One, credit plays a major role in your ability to make financial moves. I learned about debt/income ratio and the importance of staying on top of my credit utilization rate. I learned to negotiate with creditors and to strategically pay off debts in a way that would have the most impact. I learned that I operate better when I utilize automatic payments for recurring bills to avoid late fees. I remember how it felt when I finally saw my score climbing. I felt capable—like I was regaining control of my narrative. And let me tell you, that is one of the best feelings in the world.

Later, when I secured a farm loan to build Green Heffa Farms, I was in a completely different financial situation. I had the down payment and a high credit score. Granted, they still tried to deny me a loan, but that was more based on my melanin and estrogen than my financial standing. ALLEGEDLY. It would be remiss for me to not acknowledge that. But the way credit scores are calculated often reflects systemic inequities, making it harder for Black women and other marginalized entrepreneurs to get the same opportunities.

Small Steps That Made a Big Impact

So, what's the ideal credit score for someone running a boutique farm? Ideally, you want your credit score in the low 700s or higher. But let's be real: If you're currently sitting at a 580, don't let that discourage you. This isn't about

Annual Preseason Besties' Trip

One of my biggest cheerleaders—and my best friend—is Candice. A few years ago, she surprised me with birthday tickets to see Usher in Las Vegas. Candice is the consummate experience curator. I'm talking full-on vibes. She even had a custom logo designed for us.

That trip was in March, right before the farming season started rolling—and it was such a reset. It turned into a tradition: a little preseason Bestie Trip to ground, laugh, and exhale before the work kicks in. Since then, we've hit up NYC for Broadway (my first time seeing a Broadway show—we saw three!), and most recently we took over LA.

We keep it short—usually three to four days. She has a demanding career as a communications executive for an affluent municipality, and I've got Green Heffa Farms. But during that window, we eat well, shop a little, rest hard, and have a good time. No financial stress, no hustle—just joy. This is what boutique means to me: designing a life that includes joy and connection, not just productivity. Think about what kind of experiences you want to build into your life. Instead of an Usher concert, maybe you'd rather rent a house somewhere peaceful and have your family join you. Maybe you dream of hiring a chef for a week and just being. Whatever your version is—claim it. Make space for it. Build it into your model of success. Joy is not a reward; it's a right.

beating yourself up; it's about progress. Start by understanding where you are and then develop a plan to get where you want to be. Focus on discipline, not the dollar amount. Expect abundance, not struggle. When your mindset is directed toward growth, your actions will follow.

Back when I was doing the work of shifting my financial mindset, I had to get my financial house in order. I knew I had to get creative about finding ways to make and save money. I tried a few things. I began to use coupons to save money, took on seasonal jobs during the holidays, and became an expert at finding discounts and deals at the grocery store. Any little bit of extra cash I could save, I funneled straight toward paying down debts. When tax refund season rolled around, instead of splurging on a "treat yourself" purchase, I used the bulk of the funds to chip away at outstanding balances. I was tired of being caught in the vicious cycle of overdraft fees and late payments, so I made a personal vow: no more NSFs (non-sufficient funds). I set up reminders, made minimum payments if that's all I could afford, called to make arrangements if I was unable to make the minimum payment, and eliminated the small leaks that were silently draining my finances.

I've always loved shopping—probably too much, if I'm honest—so I also had to set firm boundaries for myself. I channeled my inner bargain hunter by thrifting. Not only was it kinder to my wallet, but it also felt more aligned with my commitment to sustainability. At one point, I even turned this side passion into a small business, running an online vintage clothing store. That little venture not only gave me some extra cash but also taught me valuable lessons in inventory management, marketing, and pricing—skills I didn't realize would later serve me when I launched my boutique farm. All these experiences—cutting costs, budgeting, side hustles, and learning to live within my means—shaped me into a more resourceful and resilient entrepreneur.

Building a boutique farm as a Black woman requires that same resourcefulness and relentless creativity. In full transparency, when I first began building the farm, I was still making multiple six figures as a professional fundraiser, and that continued for my three years building both Farmer Cee and Green Heffa Farms as revenue-generating brands. This may not be your reality. Many of you may be working with more limited resources. As a former teen and single mother, I can relate to making a dollar stretch in ways that most people can't even imagine. And let's not forget that we are also

GROUNDWORK

Credit Check, Reality Check

Step 1: Face the Facts

If you haven't already, pull your annual credit report from all three reporting agencies (Experian, Equifax, and TransUnion). Yes, this might be uncomfortable, but you need to face the facts before you can make meaningful changes. Remember, you are focused on abundance. There is nothing in any of those reports that is insurmountable.

Step 2: Feel the Feels, Then Analyze

Sometimes the first step toward getting better is just being real about how you feel. After you've pulled your credit reports, take a minute to sit with them. Were you surprised? Relieved? Discouraged? Motivated? Was it better or worse than you expected? No need to sugarcoat it—just be honest with yourself. This isn't about judgment. It's about understanding where you are so you can figure out where you're going. Now look at the reports a little more closely. Do you notice any patterns? Are there areas where you've consistently struggled—or places where you've made progress? Write down whatever stands out. These insights are your starting seeds for change.

navigating systemic barriers. When I no longer had that six-figure income, I did not panic. I knew that I had the needed skills to connect with resources. Not only because I'd done that professionally but also because I have experienced poverty. Anyone who has been in a situation that only their creativity got them out of knows exactly what I am saying. I approached every expense and investment with the same strategic thinking I had used to rebuild my credit and get my personal finances in shape. I also changed my life. I went from living in a four-bedroom house in the suburbs to a tiny house on my farm. I did keep my fancy cars (they were paid off), but I downsized my wardrobe and reduced my retail shopping, which I found out was an emotional outlet. Farming filled that void. I learned to be receptive to opportunities to grow in profitability and impact, which allowed me to begin generating revenues as a speaker, teacher, and now author. I now expect good news to come my way. This would not have been possible had I not transformed my financial habits. Once you do that, it's not just about getting your numbers right—it's about preparing yourself to build a business that can thrive, even in tough times. Most important, it helps you in creating your desired quality of life. So, don't skip the personal work. Your financial resilience is a cornerstone in the foundation for the entire operation you're about to build.

Real Talk

If there's one takeaway I want you to hold on to, it's this: Your credit score is not a life sentence. It's a starting point. Whether you're at 480 or 780, you have the power to improve your financial health—starting today.

CHAPTER 4

Establishing the Vision for Your Boutique Farm

We all have the power to make our dreams a reality, but you must believe in your own magic first.

—FAWN WEAVER, CEO of Uncle Nearest Whiskey

When creating a boutique farm, I believe firmly that defining and clarifying your values should come first. Why? Because your values are the core beliefs and principles that guide how you make decisions, interact with the land, and shape your brand's identity. They are your "why"—why you farm, why you choose specific practices, and why customers and communities should care. So, the first step is to think about the values that will guide your farm's development; then you can narrow down your vision and farm model. Your values are the roots of your operation—they will naturally inform your vision by defining the purpose and impact you want your farm to have. Once your values are in place, your vision for what your farm will become and achieve can be articulated in a way that aligns with these guiding principles.

A vision rooted in solid values is more than just a business strategy. It becomes a meaningful expression of your farm's commitment to sustainability, community, or any other priorities that matter most to you. Starting with values ensures that as the business evolves, it remains authentic and purpose-driven. This is literally peace protection for future you.

Your Farm's Values

So, how do you determine and clarify your values? Start by reflecting on what matters most to you—both personally and in the context of the legacy you want your farm to build. Consider the impact you want to have on your community, the type of relationships you want with your customers, and the kind of environmental stewardship that aligns with your ethics. For Green Heffa Farms, these reflections took shape in the 4 E's framework, which guides every aspect of the business:

Graphics like this can be a way to market your boutique business's values to customers. *Illustration by Visual Chronicles.*

Economic Prosperity: Ensuring that the farm is financially sustainable and that its economic growth supports not only the business but also the broader community. This value extends to creating opportunities for others and empowering more marginalized farmers to thrive.

Environment: Prioritizing regenerative farming practices that honor the land and preserve its health for future generations. Green Heffa Farms is committed to cultivating herbs in a way that respects the soil, water, and biodiversity, striving to be a model for responsible land stewardship.

Equity: Recognizing the historical and present-day disparities in agriculture, this value is a commitment to creating a more inclusive and accessible space for Black women farmers and others historically excluded from agricultural entrepreneurship.

Farmer Cee visiting Gaia Herbs in western North Carolina. *Photo courtesy of Nate Burrows*

GROUNDWORK

Clarifying Guiding Principles

This exercise will help you clarify the guiding principles that will shape your farm's identity and impact. Take some uninterrupted time to answer the following prompts.

Step 1: Reflect on What Matters Most

Write down your responses to each of the following questions:

- What led you to want to start a farm? Perhaps it was a passion for sustainable agriculture, a desire to reclaim ancestral land practices, or a commitment to providing healthier options for your community. Define the deeper "why" behind your motivation.
- Who or what are you most committed to supporting? It might be a specific community, like underrepresented farmers or local families. Perhaps it's the natural environment itself. Consider who or what you want your farm to ultimately benefit.
- What do you want to stand for in the agricultural space?

Step 2: Figure Out What You Aspire To

Think of three to five words or phrases that capture the essence of your desired reputation. This could be "innovation in herbal wellness," "regenerative land care," "economic empowerment," or "healing through food."

Step 3: Set Your Boundaries

What are three non-negotiables for your farm? These are actions or behaviors that you will not compromise on. For example, if sustainable practices are a core value, using chemical fertilizers might be a non-negotiable. Or if community impact is crucial, neglecting fair wages for staff could be a deal breaker. Write these down.

Step 4: Make a Mind Map

Review your responses. Circle any recurring themes, and then group similar ideas together. Label each group with a word or short phrase that best captures the concept. For example: If you frequently mentioned "stewardship," "soil health," and "protecting water," a value might be "Environmental Responsibility." If "uplifting marginalized voices" and "creating economic opportunities" appeared often, you might use "Equity" as a core value.

Step 5: Define Your Core Values

Using the themes you identified, define three to five core values with a few words or a brief statement. For example: Sustainability: prioritizing regenerative and eco-friendly practices that nurture the land; or, Community: building a farm that serves and uplifts the local community.

Step 6: Make Your Values Actionable

For each value, list two practical ways

you can bring it to life in your farm's daily operations. Ask yourself what decisions or actions will reflect this value. How will you communicate this value to customers and partners? For example, if one of your core values is "community," you could source materials locally to support other small businesses and offer educational workshops for aspiring farmers.

Step 7: Revisit and Refine

As your farm grows, revisit these values periodically to ensure they still resonate and guide your vision. Adjust as needed, but let them remain the foundation of your decisions and direction. By grounding your farm in these values, you create a business that is not only profitable but also purposeful and aligned with the impact you want to make.

Once you're clear on your values, don't just let them live in a notebook or your head. Create a visual representation—an infographic, a poster, or even a cute card—that breaks down what you stand for in a way that others can quickly understand and connect with. This isn't just for aesthetics (though visuals do hit differently)—it's a tool for alignment. Whether you're pitching to a retailer, onboarding a team member, or just reminding yourself why you started, having your values visually represented keeps you rooted. Remember, in this business, your "why" is part of your brand. Storytelling is essential. So make it visible. Make it shareable. Make it you.

Education: Using farming as a platform for sharing knowledge. This means not only educating customers on the benefits of herbs but also offering insights and resources to help new and aspiring farmers navigate the complexities of building a farm-based business.

These values define Green Heffa Farms' approach and ensure that every decision, from the crops grown to the collaborations pursued, stays aligned with a deeper purpose beyond profitability.

The Mission and Vision for Your Boutique Farm

While *vision* and *mission* are often used interchangeably in casual conversation, they play two distinct roles in shaping your farm's identity and strategy. Your vision statement is your big-picture dream. It answers the question: "What impact do I want my farm to have on the world?" It's a future-oriented statement that paints a picture of the world you want to help create through your work. Your vision statement is meant to be inspirational and aspirational—a

FARMER HIGHLIGHT

Rachel Herrick, Slow Farm, Cameron, North Carolina

Tell us a little about your farm and your "why" for farming.

My reason for farming really comes down to three things: people, the land, and the animals. All of it boils down to wanting to live honestly and do my part in the world. I grew up on a farm, and I saw firsthand how incredibly hardworking and skillful the old farmers were. It always bothered me that these talented people, doing such important work, were paid so little and respected so little that their kids didn't want to take over. Farming started becoming more industrial, and with that, centuries of valuable skills began to disappear. I saw it in how people stopped understanding the soil, how they forgot the careful way to raise animals, and the old wisdom about working with nature. This loss, this forgetting of what we once knew, made me sad and worried.

Photo courtesy of Rachel Herrick.

When I realized I still had a lot of that basic farming knowledge, I left my arts career of ten years. I came back to this life, but I wanted to do it my way. I wasn't going to repeat the old mistakes that left my ancestors exhausted and broke. Instead, I wanted to do better, to honor them by learning from their errors—especially the big ones they made with the environment and animal welfare. So, my goal is to help fix what's been broken, to restore what's been lost, and to play my part in making things right.

What has been one of the biggest lessons or truths you've learned through your farming journey?

A long, happy career in this demanding work hinges entirely on finding balance. The farmers who truly thrive are the ones who manage to connect their own values and personal strengths with the unique features and abilities of their specific land. From this alignment, they then build a diverse array of products and experiences for customers to invest in. This isn't just about selling one thing; it's about offering several types or tiers of products (which could be anything from fresh produce, shelf-stable goods, and value-added products, to classes, workshops, and apparel). The key is that all these offerings build on each other, telling one cohesive story about the farm that directly reflects your core strengths and values.

The final piece of this balance puzzle is rethinking what "payment" means. Yes, financial savvy is crucial—you need to invest wisely, grow slow, and know your worth. But equally vital is valuing the intangible forms of riches this life brings: the independence of being your own boss, the outlet for creativity, the health gained from physical work, and the profound connection with nature. It's about being smart with money, yes, but doing so while always noticing the abundance all around us, in all its forms.

What is one piece of advice you would offer to other women interested in starting a boutique farm?

Build your business around things you genuinely love and use yourself every day. This strong personal connection, this real affection for what you do, will keep you going when the newness wears off and the work gets tough. Starting with what you love means you'll always be interested, turning hard work into something you're passionate about. It pushes you to learn more, because you become your own toughest critic, always trying to improve. And from this real, lived experience, your business gets a voice that isn't just convincing but true. It's a voice that talks about an honest life, not just clever marketing, and that's the kind of voice that truly resonates with people looking for real connections in a world that often feels fake.

How do you care for yourself while doing this work? What grounds you?

The biggest way I stay grounded in this demanding life is by really noticing and appreciating the small, good things that happen daily: a new plant I've never seen on my farm before, learning something cool about an insect, or just a really nice snuggle with my pigs. These are moments where I deliberately pause and let the sound of the bees or the warmth of an animal in my hands reset my mind. This collection of small victories, this quiet gathering of good feelings, is a crucial source of strength. Farmers know that bad times will pile up and try to knock you down. So, having these small triumphs in your memory, being able to pull them out when you feel low, is a necessary practice.

And then there's Sunday, a necessary break from the farm's constant demands. Besides taking care of the animals, my Sundays are sacred—a time to walk in the woods without a plan, read a book, or just sit on the porch and watch the light change, letting my mind wander from the endless to-do list. And during this time of rest, I find comfort in the very products of the farm's labor, like using an herbal mud mask that makes my skin feel alive again, or a rich hair butter that brings back softness. It's a way of participating in the farm's own generous cycle, a give-and-take that takes care of both the land and the person who works it.

reminder of why you're doing this in the first place. It's your farm's "why." Your mission is about the journey. It answers: "What will my farm do, day in and day out, to make that vision a reality?" It's more concrete and action-oriented, describing the core purpose of your farm and what makes it unique. It's your farm's "what" and "how."

The path you take to build your farm might not be straightforward—and that's okay. Defining your farm's identity is an iterative process that evolves as you gain more clarity, resources, and experience. What matters most is starting with intention. Take the time to map out what success means to you, not what it looks like to others. A well-defined vision will help attract the right people, align your efforts, and build a business that's deeply rooted in your values. In essence, your vision and mission are more than words on paper; they are the heart and soul of your farm, influencing everything from what you plant to how you engage with customers.

Because boutique farming is inherently smaller in scale, every decision you make carries weight. With less margin for error or waste, having a clear vision and mission helps keep your farm aligned with your overall goals and identity. Think of them as your North Star—your guiding light when challenges arise and when it's tempting to chase trends that don't serve your long-term purpose.

Vision Statement

A strong vision also reflects what your farm stands for. Whether you aim to contribute to food sovereignty in marginalized communities or promote environmental healing, your vision is your compass. Now, I am not one of those "manifest and it shall be" folks. No. While mindset is critical, so is doing the work. But you will find that your mindset will be your greatest motivator.

EXAMPLE VISION STATEMENTS

- "To be a model of sustainable farming that empowers Black women to reclaim our agricultural heritage and build economically viable businesses."
- "To cultivate a thriving gourmet spice brand rooted in reverence for the land and the legacy of ancestral foodways that celebrates the power of flavor as nourishment and serves as a hub for culinary wellness and community healing."
- "To nurture a space where nutrient-dense and culturally significant vegetables are grown with love and intention, fostering environmental stewardship and holistic health for generations to come."

So, dream big. Be bold. Even if your goals feel a little out of reach now, remember: Every step you take is a seed planted for future harvests—whether

GROUNDWORK

Creating Your Vision Statement

These steps will help you create a statement—and a visual representation—that reflects your deepest intentions and aspirations. Keep it inspiring. Let it energize you every time you read it. In a quiet space, take time to answer the following prompts.

Step 1: Think Beyond the Farm

What impact do you want your farm or business to have on others? How do you want to feel when working toward this goal? Who do you want to serve, and how will they benefit from your work? What long-term change do you hope to create? Revisit the core values that you defined in the Groundwork exercise "Clarifying Guiding Principles" on page 42. As you reflect on these questions, jot down key words, images, symbols, or phrases.

Step 2: Create Your Vision Board

Now bring your vision to life visually. Gather images, quotes, textures, or anything else that represents the future you're building. You can use a physical board or go digital using tools like Canva or Pinterest. Include elements that reflect your farm's purpose, the environment you want to create, the customers you want to serve, and how you want to feel in your role as CEO. Place your vision board somewhere you'll see it often—it's not just pretty decoration; it's a visual affirmation of your intentions.

Step 3: Draft Your Vision Statement

Using the words and themes that emerged from your reflection and vision board, craft a clear, powerful sentence or two that captures your farm's purpose. Your statement should be clear; avoid vague or overly complex language. It should be inspiring and reflective of your passion and commitment. And while visionary, it should also be grounded and actionable.

Step 4: Refine and Commit

Read your vision statement out loud. How does it feel? Does it feel honest and energizing? Adjust the wording until it aligns fully with your values. Then post it near your vision board, in your planner, or wherever you'll revisit it regularly. If you have trusted supporters, share it with them and invite feedback. Just remember: Their input should affirm and enhance your vision—not reshape it beyond your truth.

it's investing in education, building community, or purchasing your first greenhouse. Your vision is the heartbeat of your farm. It should reflect your values, your long-term goals, and the impact you want to make. When you have tough days (and you will), this vision is what will keep you rooted and

Real Talk

Remember that your farm isn't just where you grow crops or raise livestock—it's where you grow a life. Don't be afraid to dream in full color. Your vision board isn't fluff—it's a strategic farming tool that reminds you why you're doing this work on the days when it feels hard. Make sure you put it somewhere you'll see it at least once daily.

Green Heffa Farms' vision board.

resilient. Whatever it is, your vision should feel authentic and inspiring. You'll likely revise it as you grow, and that's part of the process. Your farm should evolve just like you do.

Mission Statement

For large-scale farms or industrial agricultural enterprises, a mission statement might focus solely on profitability, production goals, or supply chain

GROUNDWORK

Crafting Your Mission Statement

Find a quiet place, bring a journal or open a fresh document, and reflect honestly on the following prompts. These are not business questions first—they're soul questions, rooted in your personal goals, your purpose within your community, and the legacy you hope to create. Answer them from your gut, not just your goals.

Step 1: Spend Time with Soul Questions

Personal: What are three things I deeply care about in the world? What traditions, ancestral knowledge, or healing practices do I feel called to carry forward? What would success look like beyond money or productivity?

Community: What need or void do I see in my community that my farm could speak to and that I desire to help meet? Who am I growing for? Who do I want to reach, teach, feed, or inspire?

Legacy: If my farm could be known for one thing ten years from now, what would I want that to be and why? When someone says my farm's name, what do I want them to think or feel? What do I want to leave behind—not just on the land, but in the lives of others?

Step 2: Write Your Mission Statement

Now that you've journaled, write a rough draft of a mission statement. Your mission is your daily why—what drives your farm forward every day. This doesn't need to be perfect. It just needs to be honest.

Focus on What Sets You Apart: Think about your niche in the market and what makes your farm different from others.

Keep It Short and Powerful: Aim for a concise statement that captures the essence of what you do and how you do it.

Emphasize Action: Use strong verbs that reflect the daily work and commitments of your farm.

efficiency. But as a boutique farmer, your goals are likely much more nuanced. You're not just growing crops—you're cultivating an experience, a brand, and a set of values that are reflected in every aspect of your business.

For example, if sustainability is one of your core values, it will show up in the practices you adopt, such as composting, using organic inputs, eco-conscious packaging, and prioritizing water conservation. If social equity is a value, maybe your farm will have a pay-it-forward model that helps low-income families access fresh produce or a mentorship program for young Black women interested in agriculture once your farm has the capacity to offer programs such as these. Social equity will also show up in how you expand your team and use your brand's platforms to amplify. Values are not just buzzwords—they are the framework that will support your farm's growth and longevity. Your values are what will ensure you continue to do good business as you experience increased success.

EXAMPLE MISSION STATEMENTS

- "To grow high-quality medicinal herbs using regenerative practices, while providing educational resources to empower women farmers."
- "To cultivate specialty crops with a focus on environmental stewardship and supporting local economies, delivering fresh and ethically grown produce."
- "To create a farm that serves as a center of wellness, using sustainable practices and heritage herbs to promote holistic health and build community."

Remember, your vision is what keeps you going on tough days, while your mission is the reason you get up every morning and put your boots on. Your vision and mission are the DNA of your boutique farm. They should be reflected in every decision you make, from the crops you choose to plant to the way you market your products. Keep them visible and revisit them regularly, especially as your farm grows and evolves. When you lead with a clear vision and a strong mission, your farm will resonate with the right customers, partners, and community members—those who not only appreciate what you grow but also believe in why you grow it.

Knowing What to Grow or Raise

It's crucial to remember that boutique farming isn't just about making money—it's about aligning your passion with your profitability. There's a reason this book is called *The Black Girl's Guide to Building a Boutique Farm*. This is about more than just growing a business; it's about growing a legacy. It's about cultivating a life that reflects your values, your culture, and your purpose. When you connect with your customers on this deeper level, there's no limit to the ways your farm can generate income. So, whether you're growing medicinal herbs for women's wellness, producing small-batch teas with your signature blends, or handcrafting herbal beauty products, you have the power to design a boutique farm that's truly one of a kind. Your farm is an extension of who you are, and there's no cap on the creativity you can bring to it.

Boutique farming isn't about doing everything. It's about doing something special—intentionally. It's the art of growing with purpose, centering your values, and offering something that feels both authentic to you and valuable to others. Unlike large-scale industrial agriculture, boutique farms focus on high-value, small-batch production and creative business models that align with personal passion and purpose. Your niche is more than just your product. It's the unique intersection of your mission, your skills, your story, and your customers' needs. The clearer you are about that sweet spot, the stronger your business will grow. Once you've grounded yourself in your real capacity and values, it's time to explore models that can align with both your vision and your bandwidth. Boutique farming is not a one-size-fits-all approach—it's about curating a life and a business that works for you.

When you're getting started in boutique farming, it's tempting to want to grow or raise everything under the sun. But let me tell you from experience: Finding your niche is one of the smartest moves you can make. Your crops or animals should not only match your skills and interests but also align with what your market is looking for. I can't emphasize enough how vital market research is in choosing what to grow or raise. Before planting my first herb, I researched industry trends, product demands, and pricing strategies. And what I found is that the herbal market is booming. The global herbal supplements and remedies market alone is projected to reach over $130 billion by 2027. The herbal tea industry, specifically, has seen substantial growth, driven by rising interest in natural wellness. This trend made herbs a strong fit for Green Heffa Farms, particularly since herbs allow for niche, premium products that customers are willing to pay more for, especially when marketed with wellness and sustainability values.

My decision to grow herbs was also about lifestyle. Herbs have a relatively gentle growing cycle that doesn't demand the same all-day physical labor as some other crops. It's work, but it's work that matches my energy. Herbs also provide a creative outlet—there are countless ways to blend, market, and brand them. I saw herbs as a way to combine my interests in health, wellness, creative branding, and education while giving me the freedom to set my own product offerings. Beyond the practicalities, herbs allow for specialty crop pricing—when you're offering a product that's perceived as unique or therapeutic, customers are willing to pay more. Boutique farming isn't about selling by the ton but focusing on the value and quality of each ounce, and herbs have been ideal for that approach.

According to the USDA Agricultural Marketing Service, specialty crops are defined as "fruits and vegetables, tree nuts, dried fruits, horticulture,

Considerations for Farms with Animals

I am often asked why I do not have animals outside of my pets. My number one reason is that I do not want the responsibility that comes with it. I want to be able to travel, and finding pet sitters is hard enough. As an empty-nester and former teenage mom, I like the flexibility plants give. Don't get me wrong—there are months when we have daily harvests and getting away is more of a challenge, but even then, it's still possible. Adding animals to a boutique farm can bring many benefits, including fertility for the soil, diversified revenue streams, and a deeper ecosystem balance, but animals also require careful planning and can be very expensive to maintain. Here are key factors to consider before integrating livestock into your farm.

Part of Your Business Model: Will the animals contribute to your farm's financial sustainability by providing products to sell, such as sheep for high-end specialty yarns? Or are they associated with meeting your own needs, like having chickens for eggs? Are they part of a regenerative farming approach (rotational grazing for soil health)? Do they support any of your certifications? Are you prepared for the long-term commitment, even if their output fluctuates seasonally?

Availability of Veterinary Care: Do you have access to a veterinarian who specializes in the type of animals you plan to raise? Large-animal and poultry vets can be scarce in some rural areas. Can you learn basic animal husbandry skills to handle minor issues yourself? What are the costs of routine vaccinations, deworming, hoof trimming, or emergency care?

Quality of Life: Are you able to handle the odors and sounds? How squeamish are you? How will you cover animal care while you're traveling?

Space Requirements: Different animals have vastly different land needs. Cows require about 1 to 2 acres each for grazing, depending on soil fertility and climate. Goats and sheep can thrive on ¼ to ½ acre per animal but need secure fencing. A small flock of chickens can live on a few square feet per bird in a coop plus 10 to 15 square feet per bird in a run. If rotational grazing is part of your plan, consider fencing needs, pasture rotation schedules, and land regeneration periods.

Predators: Common threats include coyotes, foxes, hawks, raccoons, and stray dogs. Do you need livestock guardian animals (dogs, donkeys, llamas)? Is your fencing predator-proof? Consider electric fencing, secure enclosures, and proper nighttime shelter.

Water: How will you provide fresh, clean water year-round? Is there an on-site well or a nearby stream, or do you need to install troughs or rainwater catchment systems? Consider seasonal concerns—freezing water in winter or droughts in summer.

Feed and Nutrition: Will you grow your own feed, or will you need to purchase it? Can your land naturally sustain grazing animals, or will you need to supplement with hay and grain? Are you using organic, non-GMO, or conventional feed, and what are the cost implications?

Manure Management and Composting: How will you handle waste? Composting can be a great way to cycle nutrients back into the soil, but proper management is necessary to avoid contamination or odors. Are there local regulations about manure disposal?

and nursery crops (including floriculture). Eligible plants must be cultivated or managed and used by people for food, medicinal purposes, and/or aesthetic gratification to be considered specialty crops. Processed products shall consist of greater than 50% of the specialty crop by weight, exclusive of added water."

One of the biggest benefits of choosing a specialty crop like herbs is the potential for premium pricing. Specialty crops often have higher retail value per acre compared with commodity crops. Many are sold fresh, processed, or as value-added products, which can significantly increase revenue potential for small-scale producers. Markets for organic, local, and culturally relevant crops continue to grow. Think about your niche—can your crop offer something unique to your target market? Specialty crops give you the freedom to work with fewer plants or animals but still make the profit needed to sustain and grow your business. Many specialty crops—especially herbs, legumes, and certain vegetables—are excellent for diversifying crop rotations, improving soil structure, and increasing biodiversity on the farm. Some also act as natural pest repellents or pollinator attractors, which contributes to an overall healthier growing environment.

While specialty crops themselves are not classified as animal products, they can support animal health. Herbs like nettles, calendula, and mint can be used in herbal formulations for livestock wellness or included in foraged diets. Crop residues and trimmings from specialty crops (like greens, fruit rinds, or stems) can sometimes be safely composted or used as supplemental feed, depending on the species. Specialty crops can improve pasture systems—for instance, when using cover crops or intercropping with forages that benefit both soil and grazing animals.

Farmers growing specialty crops are eligible for specific federal funding and support programs, such as the Specialty Crop Block Grant Program

(SCBGP) and various USDA Value-Added Producer Grants. These resources can help cover marketing, infrastructure, or research costs—opportunities that may not be available for producers of commodity crops alone.

Boutique Farm Models and Revenue Streams

To help you explore what's possible, here are some boutique farming models—each with revenue opportunities and ways to adapt them to your unique mission. You might feel drawn to one or see a way to combine elements of a few to create your own niche. Keep in mind that each of these models will require different kinds of permits and licenses. If you're selling skincare products, you'll need different certifications than if you're selling products that are meant to be ingested, or if you're hosting people on your farm. More on that in the chapters ahead.

The Healing-Centered Farm

For many Black women, farming is more than cultivation—it's reclamation. It's resistance. It's ritual. A healing-centered farm honors that legacy by prioritizing wellness, rest, and connection to the land as core values. As highlighted in a September 2025 article in *Civil Eats* titled "Farmers of Color Offer Community Wellness at 'Healing Farms,'" this approach to farming emphasizes trauma recovery and improved health, connecting neighbors to ancestral practices. A farm that exemplifies this model is Hawk's Nest Healing Gardens in Durham, North Carolina. Stewarded by BIPOC farmers Phoebe Gooding and Hector Lopez, the farm integrates permaculture, community gardens, and traditional ceremonies like temazcal sweat lodges to nurture both land and spirit. Their mission is to heal bodies, the land, and communities through practices of reciprocity and cultural legacy.

Real Talk

Black women have always been close to the land—as herbalists, midwives, growers, and caretakers. But accessing that land in today's system isn't always fair or easy. That's why these models matter. They don't just offer space to farm—they create space to thrive, to dream, and to build something lasting.

REVENUE STREAMS

- Guided farm meditation and yoga sessions
- Herbal CSA subscriptions or wellness kits
- Apothecary workshops and seasonal retreats

- Partnerships with wellness professionals for farm-based therapy

EP Farmacy's Skin Soothing Balm is an example of a high-quality, value-added boutique product. *Photo courtesy of Najmah Thomas.*

The Specialty Fruit and Vegetable Farm

This model centers on cultivating rare or heirloom produce using organic or regenerative methods. You're not just selling vegetables—you're offering taste, texture, and tradition. FarmerJawn, in Elkins Park, Pennsylvania, exemplifies this model. Founded by Christa Barfield, FarmerJawn is the largest Black-woman-owned regenerative organic produce farm in America. The farm operates on 128 acres, offering a range of specialty fruits and vegetables grown using sustainable practices. In addition to providing fresh produce, FarmerJawn is dedicated to reintroducing farming into urban lifestyles through educational programs and community engagement, aiming to cultivate physical, social, and environmental health.

REVENUE STREAMS

- Sales to restaurants, food co-ops, and boutique grocers
- U-pick experiences featuring unique seasonal offerings
- Artisan products like jams, pickles, and fruit vinegars
- Curated CSA boxes and farmers market sales

The Luxury U-Pick Experience

Think of this as elevated agritourism—where guests don't just pick produce, they make memories. Earthseed Farm in Sonoma County, California, is an Afro-Indigenous woman-owned, solar-powered farm that provides a U-pick experience from May to November. Visitors can harvest fruits and berries while learning about permaculture design.

REVENUE STREAMS

- Reservation-only harvest days (lavender, champagne grapes)
- Private farm picnics, proposal settings, and photo sessions

- DIY bouquet- or jam-making workshops
- "Harvest & Create" events with take-home products

The Grass-Fed and Ethical Livestock Farm

For those called to raise animals with dignity, boutique livestock farming offers sustainable, humane alternatives to conventional systems. Swanson Family Farm in Georgia is a Black-owned farm delivering grass-fed beef, lamb, poultry, and pork nationwide, emphasizing sustainable farming practices. They also work with other farms and ranches to source pasture-raised meats. Each farm has been personally vetted to ensure it meets the highest standards of sustainability and regenerative farming practices.

REVENUE STREAMS

- Direct-to-consumer sales of grass-fed meat and artisanal dairy
- Fiber products from alpacas, sheep, and rabbits
- Farm education tours and ethical butchery workshops
- Goat yoga or livestock sponsorship programs

The Culinary and Agritourism Farm

This model blends farming and flavor, inviting others to experience meals rooted in the land. Bloom Ranch is Los Angeles County's largest Black-owned ranch. It combines agriculture with tourism, offering seasonal festivals and fresh produce picking, making it a perfect weekend getaway. It offers

Rachel Herrick's pigs on her farm. *Photo courtesy of Rachel Herrick.*

high-nutrient produce boxes for sale, along with farm-fresh eggs, natural olive oil, specialty wines, and other wholesome culinary finds.

REVENUE STREAMS

- Seasonal tasting dinners and farm-to-table events
- Cooking classes using farm-fresh ingredients
- Collaborations with local chefs for pop-up experiences
- Sales of spice blends, infused oils, and artisanal condiments

The Floral and Apothecary Farm

Perfect for those who find magic in petals and plant medicine, this model turns beauty and wellness into business. Nappily Naturals & Apothecary in Los Angeles's Leimert Park neighborhood is a Black-owned herbal apothecary that curates plant-based wellness products. While it is not a farm in the traditional sense, it embodies the principles of a floral and apothecary farm by sourcing herbs and botanicals to create holistic products, offering education, and emphasizing the healing potential of plants.

REVENUE STREAMS

- Flower CSA subscriptions and custom bouquets
- Dried floral arrangements, bath blends, and herbal skincare
- DIY floral or apothecary workshops
- Wedding packages and seasonal pop-ups

The Sustainable Mushroom and Exotic Crop Farm

Growing niche crops like gourmet mushrooms or spices allows you to serve specialty markets with big flavor and high margins. Sierra Saffron (a former member of Sow Green Society, a membership group I founded to help support other farming brands) specializes in producing its namesake herb, saffron. A Black-woman-owned operation located in California's mountains, the farm grows organically and regeneratively.

REVENUE STREAMS

- Culinary mushrooms for chefs and foodies
- Rare crops like saffron, turmeric, and ginseng
- DIY mushroom grow kits
- Crop-specific virtual and on-farm classes

The Regenerative, Carbon-Sequestering Farm

This model puts ecological stewardship front and center—great for climate-conscious farmers with a passion for systems thinking. New

Communities in Albany, Georgia, is a Black-led organization that operates a 200-acre pecan orchard as part of its 6,000-acre land trust. Founded by Shirley Sherrod, an agricultural icon, the orchard employs sustainable farming practices that not only produce high-quality pecans but also contribute to carbon sequestration through the trees' biomass and soil organic matter. Research indicates that pecan orchards can serve as significant carbon sinks, with a substantial portion of fixed carbon remaining stored in the trees and soil, thereby mitigating greenhouse gas emissions.

REVENUE STREAMS

- Organic grains, nuts, and produce
- Carbon offset programs for soil conservation
- Native plant nursery sales
- Regenerative agriculture education and consulting

The Rare and Indigenous Crop Farm

This niche honors and preserves ancestral knowledge through cultivation of traditional and heirloom crops. Sistah Seeds in Philadelphia is a Black-woman-owned farm founded by Amirah Mitchell. Sistah Seeds focuses on seed keeping—preserving and cultivating culturally significant vegetable seeds for the African diaspora. The farm emphasizes the stories and memories associated with these seeds, aiming to pass them down to future generations.

REVENUE STREAMS

- Sales to chefs seeking unique or heritage ingredients
- Seed saving and heirloom seed kits
- Storytelling and sovereignty workshops
- Value-added goods like ancient grain flours or heritage teas

The Micro-Dairy and Artisanal Cheese Farm

With the right infrastructure, a micro-dairy can offer a boutique twist on milk, yogurt, and cheese production. An example of this model is Tieton Farm & Creamery in Tieton, Washington. The creamery was started in 2010 by Lori and Ruth Babcock after they left careers in software. Ruth is the herdswoman and Lori is the cheesemaker. Their solar-powered creamery specializes in artisan cheeses from sheep's and goat's milk with a zero carbon footprint. They also raise grass-fed and grass-finished cattle, whey-fed pigs, and pastured free-range chickens, ducks, turkeys, and geese.

REVENUE STREAMS

- Raw milk shares and cheese subscriptions

- Cheesemaking classes and tastings
- "Adopt-a-Cow" programs
- Specialty farm-branded dairy products

The Bee and Pollinator Conservation Farm

This niche merges ecological impact with beauty and business. These farms are dedicated to supporting pollinator populations through habitat preservation, education, and sustainable farming practices. Mother's Finest Urban Farm in Charlotte, North Carolina, is a Black-woman-owned farm that focuses on pollinator conservation and community education. Farmer Samantha Foxx Winship offers urban apiary programs, habitat planting, and hands-on experiences to protect bees and other pollinators. She also produces delicious honey and honey-based products.

Photo courtesy of Candice Brown-Murray.

REVENUE STREAMS

- Infused honeys and beeswax products
- Beekeeping workshops and bee sanctuary tours
- Pollinator garden kits and educational content
- Conservation partnerships for habitat protection

Many boutique farms incorporate multiple models to diversify income and create resilience. For example, a farm could combine specialty produce with agritourism, or a healing-centered farm could also offer culinary retreats. The key is finding what aligns with your vision, mission, audience, and available resources. Boutique farming isn't just about growing food—it's about curating an experience, crafting a brand, and building a business that nourishes both land and people.

GROUNDWORK

Customizing Your Boutique Farm's Model

Before you move on to developing your business strategy, reflect on which of these models sparked your curiosity or aligned with your mission. You don't have to know exactly how you'll get there, but you do need to know what direction you're heading.

Step 1: Do the Research

This is the moment to begin shaping your farming model—a practical expression of your mission, aligned with your values, strengths, and lifestyle. Explore different farming models through research, conversations, or observation. Reach out to farmers you know or follow, and ask them about their business.

Step 2: Explore a Couple of Ideas in Depth

Pick one or two of the models you researched that resonate most with you. For each, write a few sentences exploring how it aligns with your mission and values, the kind of life you want to live, your natural strengths or lived experiences, and the audience you most want to serve. What crops or animals will you grow or raise and what products or services will you offer that directly support your mission? What scale feels manageable and sustainable for you—financially, emotionally, and physically? How do you want to interact with your customers or community? Will you host events, offer subscriptions, or provide educational experiences? You are allowed to dream boldly and specifically. Your niche isn't a limitation—it's the fertile ground where your vision starts to grow roots.

Step 3: Describe Your Farm

Based on these reflections, write a short description of what your ideal farm might look like. There's no need to have everything figured out—but putting a vision of your mission in motion will help reveal your niche in the next section.

CHAPTER 5

Build the Brand, Nurture the Land

You don't have to know the how—you just need to be clear on the what.

—Bea Dixon, founder of The Honey Pot Company

This quote from Bea Dixon resonates deeply with me because in my journey, the what has always been clear. I knew I wanted to create something that honored the Earth, served my community, and reflected my values. I also am a part of the land, so I include myself in that nurturing. It doesn't take long to realize that a vision alone doesn't cover the cost of soil tests, fencing, irrigation systems, or conservation work. Let alone the cost of a vacation, organic foods, and foot massages. It takes green—financial green—to stay green. If you want to farm sustainably, you need an income that sustains you, too. That's why building a brand isn't optional—it's a strategic necessity. A well-built brand attracts opportunities, reinforces your values, and allows you to nurture the land. And it can provide you with the quality of life you desire. That's what I mean when I talk about boutique farming with purpose.

A brand is more than a logo or packaging—it's an asset. A well-established brand builds recognition, trust, and emotional connection. And those elements are what allow you to command premium pricing. When you are building a boutique farming business, you are building a brand. You have the freedom to create a brand identity that reflects your mission, your values, and your unique offerings. Boutique farming has such high revenue potential because customers aren't just buying a product—they're buying into your brand story. And that story has as much power as any crop you grow.

When done right, your brand becomes a revenue engine. That revenue doesn't just cover costs—it can underwrite your sustainability goals. Whether that means implementing regenerative practices, investing in renewable energy,

Photo courtesy of Visual Chronicles.

or starting a community garden program, your brand's profitability makes those initiatives possible. This is especially important in boutique farming, where margins can be thin and every dollar counts. If you want to grow without compromising your values or burning out, your brand needs to carry its weight. It needs to generate income that allows you to reinvest in the land, in your systems, and in your community.

Boutique farms thrive on building relationships. When you're producing at a smaller scale, you can offer personalized customer service, customized products, and even direct-to-consumer experiences that larger farms can't provide. This level of care and attention creates loyalty and a deep sense of trust, making your farm a go-to for clients who value that one-on-one connection. A strong farm brand can significantly enhance opportunities for securing funding partners, co-marketing opportunities, brand deals, and collaboration in grants, leading to fruitful partnerships that can drive your business forward. Funders are often looking for projects that align with their missions and values. Furthermore, a recognizable brand can facilitate connections within the agricultural, entrepreneurial, and nonprofit sectors. As your brand gains visibility, you may receive invitations to participate in industry events, conferences, and panels, where you can network with potential funders and collaborators. These relationships can lead to opportunities for subgrants or partnerships that might not have been accessible otherwise.

A Brand with Roots

People are hungry for authenticity. They want to know where their food, herbs, and wellness products come from. They want to support people and practices that align with their values. Your brand is the bridge between your mission and your market. When it is rooted in your story, your land, and your values, it doesn't just sell—it connects. And connection is the foundation of long-term success.

Think of it this way: A tomato from a traditional farm might sell for $2 a pound at a farmers market. But a boutique farm specializing in heirloom tomatoes, grown using organic practices and harvested at peak ripeness, can easily command $5 a pound or more. Why? Because customers aren't just buying a tomato—they're investing in an experience. They're purchasing produce that's been meticulously cultivated, handpicked with care, and presented by a farmer whose values resonate with their own.

Now take it a step further: When you transform those heirloom tomatoes into a signature spaghetti sauce, the value multiplies. Suddenly, it's not just about the tomato or the sauce—it's about the story behind it. Customers pay a premium because your brand represents quality, authenticity, and transparency. They're buying into your commitment to sustainable farming, your unique heritage varieties, and the artistry that goes into every jar.

Ultimately, it's the established brand, not just the product, that creates the perceived value. It's why people don't just see a tomato on their plate—they see a symbol of mindful agriculture, community support, and a culinary experience they're willing to pay more for. This can apply to any model of boutique farming. Customization, personalization, and specialized value-added products and services mean you can target a niche audience, command a higher price point, and also have access to diverse income streams because you aren't relying solely on a large quantity of raw product. Whether you're growing heirloom vegetables, cultivating rare medicinal herbs, or producing small-batch herbal teas, you can set your prices based on the uniqueness and perceived value of your offerings. And unlike large-scale farms that focus primarily on raw produce, boutique farms can easily pivot into value-added products. These products allow you to carve out a space that few others can occupy, making your farm's offerings highly sought after and nimble.

On top of that, with a boutique farm, you're not limited to just selling products. Your farm can be a space for agritourism, workshops, farm-to-table dinners, and even wellness retreats. If you develop your own personal brand in addition to your farm's brand, you can also establish an online presence that generates income through e-commerce, subscriptions, and digital content. The options are endless because you are in control of the narrative and the experience. It's about crafting multiple ways for your farm to be profitable—each rooted in your specific talents, capacity, and interests.

Your Personal Brand as a Boutique Farmer

When I embarked on my journey with Green Heffa Farms, I quickly realized that my personal brand as a boutique farmer could grow alongside the farm's brand. While Green Heffa Farms represents the mission, products, and values of the farm, Farmer Cee became my voice—an extension of my experiences, knowledge, and advocacy for Black women in agriculture and entrepreneurship. This dual-branding approach has allowed me to establish a revenue-generating personal brand that not only complements my farm but also expands my influence far beyond traditional farming.

My personal brand has opened doors I never imagined when I first started farming. By showing up authentically—as a Black woman, a farmer, and an entrepreneur—I've been able to attract opportunities that not only align with my values but also expand awareness of my work and my businesses. One of the most rewarding partnerships I've had was with Dovetail Workwear, the largest women-owned workwear brand in the Northern Hemisphere. They named me a "Maven," featured me in their catalog and on their website, and flew out a team for an amazing photo shoot right on my farm. It wasn't just about the clothes—though I did get some fantastic workwear—it was about being seen and celebrated for who I am and what I do. And yes, I was compensated for the partnership, which is important. Exposure is great, but equitable collaborations are even better.

Building a personal brand isn't just about visibility; it's about authenticity, connection, and purpose. I started by sharing my journey—offering insights into my farming practices, the challenges I faced, and the lessons I learned. I did not romanticize my journey. Through transparency and storytelling, I cultivated trust and built a community of individuals who resonate with my experiences and values. Farmer Cee the brand became more than a

Photo courtesy of Cliford Mervil.

personal brand; it is a platform for education, empowerment, and advocacy. Best part: Farmer Cee is truly me.

To tie it all together, I eventually launched a dedicated Farmer Cee website that serves as a hub for my personal brand, showcasing my journey, resources, and offerings.

While not required, you can also develop your personal brand alongside your farm brand. A strong personal brand isn't strictly essential for a farm brand to succeed, but it can be a powerful tool for building trust and creating connections with your audience. If you already have a personal brand—perhaps on social media, through public speaking, or in another professional field—you can leverage it to amplify your farm's values, share your story, and introduce your products in an authentic way. Your audience already knows you; connecting your personal brand with your farm brand helps them understand why your products matter, who is behind them, and what you stand for.

For those who haven't developed a personal brand yet, start small: Share your journey, your philosophy, and the lessons you've learned. Be intentional about your messaging and consistent in how you present yourself. This could be as simple as posting behind-the-scenes photos of your farm, writing short reflections about your practices, or hosting educational content that aligns with your farm's mission. Over time, this transparency builds credibility, fosters loyalty, and positions you as both a thought leader and a trusted source in your niche. Ultimately, a personal brand can serve as a bridge between your values and your farm's story, helping your audience connect with both in meaningful ways.

More than Just a Name

The next critical step in shaping your farm's brand is choosing a name and determining how it will be recognized—by your customers, your community, and yourself. Your farm's name is more than a label. It's the beginning of your story, the first impression you make, and a reflection of the values you carry into your work. And trust me, choosing the right name can feel just as weighty as writing your business plan, because it holds energy, legacy, and intention. Some of you may eventually change your farm's name. It happens. As you evolve, so does your vision, and refining your brand identity is a natural part of growth. But that doesn't mean you shouldn't put deep thought into your farm's name from the very start.

There is profound meaning behind the name Green Heffa Farms—just as there is intentionality behind the name Farmer Cee (a little play on "pharmacy" because I grow herbs—though very few people actually get it. I just knew that one was going to be a winner. Ha!). But this isn't just about picking something that sounds good. You're not merely naming a piece of land—you are defining your boutique brand. A farm isn't just soil and crops; it's a narrative, a value system, and a promise to your customers. As with any strong brand, the name becomes a powerful asset, encapsulating everything you stand for. Choose wisely and own it.

Green Heffa Farms' logo.

Your business name is often the very first thing potential customers, investors, or collaborators will learn about you. It sets the tone for your entire business. Whether your focus is boutique herbal products, farming workshops, or premium hemp, your name should instantly convey what your brand stands for. A well-chosen name can communicate your values, evoke emotions, and attract your ideal audience. It influences everything from your logo and website design to your social media handles and marketing materials. Deciding on a name early helps set a clear direction for your brand's identity, voice, and messaging. This consistency is key for building a cohesive and recognizable brand.

A well-thought-out business name should be easy to remember, pronounce, and spell. This is essential for word-of-mouth marketing, especially in industries where customers often refer others to trusted brands. Whether someone sees your name on a product label, hears about it in conversation, or stumbles upon it online, a memorable name makes it easy for them to find you again. Conversely, a complicated or generic name might lead to lack of interest or lead to confusion with other businesses, making it harder for customers to return.

One of the most practical reasons to decide on a name before registering your business is to ensure it is legally available. Imagine spending months building your brand, designing labels, and establishing your online presence, only to find out someone else already owns the rights to the name. Conducting a thorough name search, including domain availability, trademark databases, and local business registries, helps you avoid this pitfall. Be sure to search your proposed name on your state's business entity database to make sure it's not already taken.

In today's digital age, having a strong online presence is essential. Registering a name early gives you the opportunity to secure the corresponding website domain, social media handles, and other digital assets. If you wait too long, you may find that your ideal web address or social profile names are already taken, forcing you to settle for less optimal alternatives or creating inconsistencies across your platforms. Your business name should be easy to search and find across all channels, which helps build a strong, unified presence. Marketing becomes much easier when you have a clear business name. It acts as a hook for storytelling and can be the basis of a compelling brand narrative. From catchy taglines to memorable hashtags, your name will be central to all your promotional efforts. If you've ever seen a brand's marketing and thought, "Wow, that's clever," it's likely because the name itself played a role in shaping the brand's campaigns. Choosing a name that aligns with your mission, products, and target audience ensures that your marketing strategies are rooted in a strong foundation.

Registering your business under a name that you haven't fully vetted or aren't entirely committed to can lead to headaches later on. Rebranding is not only expensive but can also confuse your existing customer base. It's not just about changing a logo or updating a website; it can mean re-educating your audience, overhauling marketing materials, and sometimes even losing brand equity that you've worked hard to build. Getting the name right the first time saves you from these complications, allowing you to focus on growing your business.

A Name That Grows with You

A good name should be able to grow with your business. When you decide on a name early, it allows you to think strategically about the future. Will this name work if you expand into new products, open a second location, or pivot slightly in your business model? Can it appeal to a broader audience, or is it niche enough to resonate deeply with a specific customer base? Choosing a name that aligns with your vision for growth ensures that your business won't outgrow its own identity.

So, as you brainstorm names, think beyond what's trendy or catchy in the moment. You want something timeless—something that reflects your values, your story, and your vision for the farm. Your name should evoke a feeling, paint a picture, and hint at the experience you want people to have when they encounter your farm. It should be a beacon that draws the right people to you—those who connect with the soul of your brand and who become lifelong customers, ambassadors, and advocates. Choose a name that speaks to what you want your farm to represent today, but also what it could become in the future. While you may decide to sell a product line or even partner with a larger company down the line, owning your brand name and its associated intellectual property ensures that you hold on to the legacy you've built. Names matter because they carry your values and vision forward—even if you're not the one at the helm forever.

GROUNDWORK

Nailing Your Name

By naming your farm, you are laying down the foundation for your business's identity. You're telling the world: This is who my brand is and this is what my brand stands for.

Step 1: Revisit Your Why

Go back and find your vision and mission statements and the journal reflections you wrote in the Groundwork exercises "Creating Your Vision Statement" (page 48) and "Crafting Your Mission Statement" (page 49). Circle words or phrases that jump out to you as potential name inspiration.

Step 2: Create a Farm Mood Board

Visuals can often trigger ideas in a way that words alone cannot. Here, I am sharing my farm's branding mood board. You can also create one for naming. Spend some time gathering images, colors, and textures that reflect your farm's aesthetic and values. Pinterest or a simple vision board on your wall can help. Include pictures of the crops or animals you might raise, flowers, landscapes, vintage farm signs, or anything else that resonates with the vibe you want your farm to embody. After your board is complete, describe the images aloud as if explaining your farm to someone new. Listen to yourself—often, descriptive terms that flow naturally can become inspiration for a name.

Step 3: Do Word Association and Mind Mapping

Write your core values from the Groundwork exercise "Clarifying Guiding Principles" (page 42) in the middle

Green Heffa Farms' mood board.

of a sheet of paper and build a mind map by branching off related words. Allow your thoughts to wander. One branch may lead you to a powerful keyword that perfectly captures the spirit of your farm. If one of your core values is "Environmental Stewardship," for instance, you might end up with connections like "roots," "nourish," or "bloom." You may even discover unexpected words that trigger the perfect farm name.

Step 4: Dive into Local or Cultural Inspiration

Think about the location of your farm and any local history, dialect, or stories that could serve as a name. Maybe there's an old folk saying, a name for a natural feature nearby, or even a family tradition that could be meaningful. Sometimes, honoring regional history or culture can lend depth and distinction to your farm's identity. Research the etymology of place-names around you or interview a family member about local stories and traditions that have been passed down. Let these serve as seeds for ideas.

Step 5: Use Acronyms or Word Combinations

Sometimes combining words or creating acronyms can help craft a unique farm name. Think about your core principles, your initials, or the key products you want to highlight. Combining meaningful words or phrases can result in a fresh and unexpected name. Take two of your top values, like "Nurture" and "Nourish," and blend them into something new. This might spark ideas like "NurtureBloom" or "The Nourish Nest."

Step 6: Play with Sound and Symbolism

Say potential names out loud and listen to how they sound. Does it feel inviting and easy to pronounce? Consider the emotional tone you want your name to convey. Pay attention to how different combinations of words feel when spoken, and don't be afraid to let symbolism or whimsy lead the way. Try on different names as if introducing your farm at a networking event: "Welcome to [your farm name], where we . . ." This helps you identify which names roll off the tongue and which have the right energy.

Step 7: Look to Nature and Literature for Inspiration

Nature can be a beautiful and bountiful source of name ideas. Consider the plants, herbs, or flowers you'll grow and see if any of their Latin names, symbolic meanings, or even folklore resonate. Look into literary or historical figures related to agriculture, healing, or resilience. Make a list of your farm's main crops, herbs, or flowers, then research their symbolic meanings. You might find inspiration in names like "Elderflower Farm" and "Hibiscus Haven."

Step 8: Use a Name Generator to Get Unstuck

Sometimes when you're brainstorming, it's easy to hit a wall and feel like nothing fits. If that happens, don't panic!

One easy way to break through a creative block is to use an online name generator to spark fresh ideas. Using a name generator doesn't mean you'll settle for one of the exact suggestions it spits out. Rather, it's a tool to expand your thinking and explore new possibilities you may not have considered. Sometimes seeing unexpected word combinations can trigger a lightbulb moment and help you discover what resonates. And even if the results are a bit offbeat, they might help you get clearer on what doesn't work, which can be just as valuable as knowing what does.

Step 9: Test Your Top Choices

Take some time to test your top choices. Say them out loud, imagine them on labels, and see if they still resonate after a few days. Sometimes a name that looks great on paper doesn't roll off the tongue as easily, or it doesn't capture the essence of your brand when you really sit with it. Don't rush the process! Naming is part art, part strategy. Using these tools can make the creative process fun and less overwhelming, helping you find a name that truly fits your vision. Remember: A name is the first step in telling your story—make it one worth remembering.

The Origin of the Name Green Heffa Farms

A huge part of Green Heffa Farms is rooted in storytelling. When I chose the name for my farm, it reflected both my personal story and my aspirations for the business. At the time, I was going through what I'll generously call a "legal entanglement." I knew deep down that the relationship wouldn't last and I wanted a name that would carry positive meaning for me and wouldn't hold any negative emotional baggage.

My maternal grandmother, Charity Mae, loved her name. She insisted that I pronounce it correctly and taught me to expect the same about my name. Her name suited her well, as she was one of the kindest, most generous souls I've ever known. She rarely used harsh language, and when she was angry with another woman, her sharpest insult would be to call her a "mean heffa." Now, if you're unfamiliar, *heffa* is Southern vernacular for "heifer," which is a young female cow. In this context, it wasn't meant to be complimentary. But that phrase stuck with me because it carried a sort of tongue-in-cheek humor and truth. So, when it came time to name my farm, I knew I didn't want to be a "mean heffa." I wanted to flip that phrase into something positive, powerful, and distinctly me. That's how "Green Heffa Farms" came to be. The "green" represents our commitment not only to environmental sustainability but also to economic prosperity. The "heffa" is a nod to the strength and resilience of women in agriculture—our fight to take up space and reclaim what has historically been denied to us. In that one name, I could capture our commitment to cultivating land, values, and a business that honors the legacy of strong women like my grandmother, while also planting the seeds for the future of what farming could look like for women of color.

The Basics of Boutique Farm Branding

Once you've decided on a farm name (and hopefully checked that the domain and social handles are available!), it's time to think about your logo, wordmark, color palette, and fonts.

These elements form your brand book—a living document that keeps your visual identity consistent across platforms and over time. A logo is the visual symbol or icon associated with your farm. A wordmark is a stylized version of your farm name in a specific font and layout. You can use them separately or together, but they should be consistent and easy to recognize. Keep in mind that your logo will need to work across multiple sizes and backgrounds—from websites to T-shirts to product labels to signage.

No matter what you grow or raise, your boutique farm has a unique fingerprint. The visuals and voice of your brand are how people get to know you, believe in you, and support you.

So, don't play small. Show up. Be seen. Let your colors speak, let your story be told, and let the beauty of your farm reflect the beauty of your purpose.

You don't have to be a graphic designer to create polished, on-brand visuals for your boutique farm. One of the best things I did was work with my graphic designers to set up my Canva Brand Kit and reusable templates. This gives you the best of both worlds: pro-level design and DIY flexibility. Look for a designer with experience in brand development. They'll help you define your logo, color palette, fonts, and visual style. These are the building blocks of a strong and memorable farm brand. For my own branding, I partnered with an international graphic design firm based in Colombia. They were not only far more affordable than many US-based options but also incredibly talented. The principal designer, Saida, is an

Green Heffa Farms' logo icon.

Family

African art

Strong patterns and colors

Jazz posters

Diaspora

Your brand is more than a logo. It's a feeling, a rhythm, and a visual language.

extraordinary artist who created original pieces for us. Once that foundational work was complete, I brought in my own graphic designer to build on what the international team delivered. This ensured we had a complete, cohesive visual identity and the flexibility to create additional materials as needed.

Have your designer upload your brand assets (logos in full color and black and white, fonts, color hex codes, and any design elements like illustrations, textures, and patterns) into the Canva Brand Kit. You'll need a Canva Pro account for this, which is $120 per year (at the time of writing). Ask your designer to build a few core Canva templates for content you'll use often: social media posts and reels, labels, flyers, newsletters, and so on. Having these templates keeps your visuals consistent and makes content creation way faster and fully editable by you.

Once your system is in place, you or your team can create new content on the fly without sacrificing style or cohesion. Whether it's a farm announcement or a new product label, your visuals stay professional and on-brand. Hiring a designer to create a full set of graphics every time you need something can get expensive—especially for social media or seasonal content. But by paying them once to build your Canva Brand Kit and templates, you invest in a repeatable system. You'll be empowered to make your own graphics without starting from scratch or going off-brand. Even factoring in the Canva Pro subscription, this approach can be far more affordable over time—and far less stressful.

Remember, as a Black woman entering a space that has historically excluded us, defining your farm with intention is a radical act. It's about claiming your place and building something that honors your identity, your heritage, and your vision for the future. Your farm can be anything you want it to be—whether it's a space for healing, a source of nourishment, a means of economic empowerment, or all of the above.

CHAPTER 6

Establishing Your Farm as a Legitimate Business

You can't plant a seed and expect to eat the fruit the same day.

—YVONNE VERA, Zimbabwean author

So, we got a lot done in the previous chapter. You are putting in the work! You have defined your values, vision, and mission. You are clear on what you want to create and, hopefully, you have a name for your boutique farming business. Now it is time to get into laying the administrative foundation of your operation. This ensures that your boutique farm has a solid base to grow on and that you're protected legally and financially as you build your brand.

But first a disclaimer: Yes, Green Heffa Farms is a whole corporation out here in these agri-streets. I've been through the paperwork, the tax filings, the meetings, the registrations—the whole shebang. But let me be clear: I am not your attorney, accountant, insurance agent, or corporate compliance officer. I'm a Black woman who has learned through experience, grit, a lot of googling, and asking the right people the right questions. This chapter shares what I've done and what I've learned, not what you're legally required to do. So, while I can tell you what worked for me (and what didn't), please talk to a qualified professional before you make any major money moves, legal decisions, or IRS declarations.

Translation: Don't be out here telling folks, "Farmer Cee said I could deduct my designer chicken's birthday party." That's between you, your accountant, and your chickens.

Do send me an invite to the party, tho!

Now, I did file a lot of my own forms to establish my business. I have a do-it-yourself attitude when it comes to filing paperwork. I also will hire a professional if I feel something is out of my scope of knowledge or comfort. North Carolina's process is pretty straightforward—some states' are. Some are more complicated. Before you make big decisions like forming your own corporation, filing tax elections, or drafting up contracts, really think about whether you will DIY or work with a professional. If the latter, find someone who respects your vision. My rule of thumb: If you do not respect my Black, I am not trying to give you my green.

Use this chapter as a road map, but understand that you still need your own navigation tools. This isn't legal advice—it's boutique business game from someone who's living it.

Common Types of Business Structures

Before selecting a business structure for your boutique farming enterprise, it's essential to understand the implications each option carries. Your choice will affect everything from how you're taxed, to your personal liability, to how you can raise money and grow. Some structures, like a sole proprietorship or LLC, offer flexibility and can be adjusted later—such as converting an LLC to a C corporation if your business scales and seeks investors. However, other decisions are more permanent. For instance, if you choose a nonprofit model and gain 501(c)(3) status, transitioning to a for-profit structure later can be extremely difficult, if not legally impossible, due to restrictions around how assets and revenues are managed. Taking time to understand both the current and future implications of your business structure will help you build with intention and avoid costly missteps down the line. Some points to consider include:

Liability: How much personal risk are you willing to take on? If protecting your personal assets is important, structures like LLCs or corporations offer more safeguards.

Taxes: Different structures are taxed in different ways. Consult a tax professional to understand which structure offers the best benefits based on your income and business model.

Flexibility: Do you expect your farm to grow or change significantly over the next few years? Choose a structure that can accommodate these shifts without too much hassle.

Future Plans: Do you want to attract investors? Do you see the possibility of selling your farm down the line? If so, becoming a corporation might offer more flexibility.

Paperwork and Compliance: Some structures are easier to set up and maintain than others. Make sure you have the time and resources to keep up with the compliance requirements for more complex structures like corporations.

Your farm is more than a business—it's a representation of your vision and a vehicle for achieving your personal and financial goals. Choosing the right structure from the start will save you time, money, and potential headaches down the road, allowing you to focus on what really matters: building a farm that's aligned with your values and dreams. Take the time to map out your vision and goals so you can choose the business structure that best supports your path forward.

Sole Proprietorship

A sole proprietorship is the simplest structure to establish. It's inexpensive to set up and requires minimal paperwork. However, it comes with a major downside: There is no legal separation between you and your business. This means that if your farm faces financial or legal trouble, your personal assets—like your home or savings—are at risk. While this structure can work for farms that are just getting started or as a temporary arrangement, it's not ideal if you plan to grow your business beyond a certain scale. It's best for micro-scale operations or test phases where you're dipping your toe into farming and haven't yet committed to long-term growth.

LLC (Limited Liability Company)

An LLC is one of the most popular choices for boutique farms because it offers the best of both worlds—liability protection and operational flexibility. With an LLC, your personal assets are shielded from business liabilities, giving you peace of mind. This structure also provides the flexibility to choose how you want your business to be taxed (as a sole proprietorship, partnership, or corporation), which can be beneficial as your farm evolves. You can have a single-member LLC or add partners as needed without drastically changing your structure.

This option is probably best for boutique farms focused on scaling up or introducing value-added products, where liability protection is important but you still want a straightforward structure.

Partnership

If you're going into business with someone else, a partnership might be a viable option. There are two main types: general partnerships (where all partners share equal responsibility and liability) and limited partnerships (where liability and management responsibilities are divided based on the partnership agreement). Partnerships are relatively easy to form and offer shared management responsibilities, which can be helpful when different partners bring unique skills or resources to the table. However, partnerships can be risky if not managed properly. Make sure you have detailed agreements in place that define roles, responsibilities, and profit-sharing arrangements to avoid misunderstandings down the road. This is best for farms started by multiple people who want to share ownership and decision making but who also have strong, clear agreements about how the business will operate.

Corporation

While less common among small farms, establishing a corporation can be a smart move if you have big plans for your farm's future. This structure offers the highest level of liability protection and allows you to issue stock, which can make it easier to attract investors. A corporation can be taxed as a C corp (subject to corporate taxes) or an S corp (where profits and losses pass through to your personal taxes). Forming a corporation involves more paperwork, higher costs, and stricter regulations, but it's a strong option if you plan to grow significantly or want to keep your options open for selling your business in the future. This is a good option for farms that have high growth potential, plan to seek investors, or want to build a brand that can eventually be sold.

When I established Green Heffa Farms, I chose to set it up as a corporation rather than as an LLC or sole proprietorship. Why? Because I see this farm as more than just a day-to-day operation—I see it as a brand. One that, with time and strategic growth, could become valuable enough to sell if I ever decide that's the best move. My motto is: "We can sell the brand. We can keep the land." Establishing Green Heffa Farms as a corporate entity gives me flexibility and options. I want the ability to scale, attract investors if needed, and create a legacy that could outlast my direct involvement.

Real Talk

Remember, your business structure should align with your ultimate goals, so don't be afraid to think big. You are not "playing business"—you're building one. And that means having your house in order. You deserve to operate with the same clarity, professionalism, and security that legacy farmers and brands do. Starting a boutique farm as a Black woman is revolutionary in itself. Doing it right—with legal, financial, and operational structure—is your armor. It's how you protect yourself, your vision, and your legacy. So, let's root deep, sis.

Making It Official

With your business name chosen and your legal structure selected, it's time to complete a few essential steps to make your farm business legal, legitimate, and ready to grow. This is the moment where your vision begins to take form on paper—and in policy.

Registering Your Business

You are going to start by registering your business. Depending on your state, you may need to register your farm's name—especially if you're using a name that differs from your own legal name. This is often done by filing a DBA (Doing Business As) or trade name with the appropriate state or county agency. In my state, that's the department of commerce, but in others, it may fall under the secretary of state, department of revenue, or even your local clerk of courts. Registering your business name makes your farm business official in the eyes of the law. It's also required for opening a business bank account under your farm name. In some states, it's a prerequisite for receiving farm-specific tax benefits or exemptions (such as on equipment, seeds, or supplies), so be sure to check with your department of agriculture or state revenue office. After registering your business name, apply for an EIN (Employer Identification Number). Even if you're a sole proprietor with no employees, you should still apply for an EIN. Think of it as your farm's Social Security number. You'll need it to:

- Open a business bank account
- Apply for business licenses or permits
- File state or federal taxes
- Apply for grants or loans
- Establish credibility and separation between personal and business finances

You can apply for an EIN for free through the IRS by visiting irs.gov and searching for "Apply for an EIN." The online application is available Monday through Friday, 7 A.M. to 10 P.M. (EST). Once you complete the application, you'll receive your EIN immediately. This is the fastest method. You can also do it via mail or fax by completing form SS-4 and submitting it via mail or fax to the IRS. This method takes longer—usually four weeks for mail and about four business days for fax. If your business is based outside the US, you can call the IRS at 267-941-1099 (not toll-free) to obtain an EIN. Important tips: Never pay a third-party site for an EIN; EINs are free directly from the IRS. And keep your EIN in a secure place. You'll need it for tax filings, banking, and other official documentation.

Snagging Your Digital "Land"

Secure your website domain and social media handles. Think of your URL as your digital acreage—you want to own that land before someone else does. In today's world, your digital presence matters just as much as your physical one. Before you launch your products or tell folks where to find you, lock down your domain name (URL). Use platforms like Namecheap, Google Domains, or GoDaddy to find and register your website. I recommend getting the .com if it's available, even if you plan to use .farm or something more creative. Once you've got your domain, claim your social media handles—even if you're not ready to post yet. You're protecting your brand. Imagine someone else posting under your farm's name. You might not be ready to launch your brand fully online, but get your digital "land" while it's still available. Also, snag your personal brand name if you haven't done so already.

Business Accounts

Once your business is legally established, it's essential to set up a robust accounting system to track your income and expenses accurately. This can be done using accounting software or by hiring a professional accountant familiar with agricultural businesses. Understanding your financials will enable you to make informed decisions and help you navigate the complexities of running a farm as a business. Open a business checking account and, if needed, a savings account for taxes or reinvestment. Use a bookkeeping system like QuickBooks, Wave, or FreshBooks. There are also some systems more tailored to some farming models, so do your research. While these systems only include home and general business income and expense categories, farm income and expense categories are easily added. And of course, a solid spreadsheet system is fine if you're just getting started. Just make sure you are keeping track of your farm's financial activity, which is much easier if you have separate business and personal accounts and credit cards (as we discussed in chapter 3). Your financial records will also come in handy for filing taxes, applying for grants and loans, tracking profitability, and knowing your numbers for informed conversations with potential collaborators.

Permits

Register for state and local licenses and permits. Requirements vary by state and county, so don't skip this. The last thing you want is to complicate your business due to not having necessary licenses and permits. You may need:

Sales tax license or seller's permit: Required in many states if you're selling products.

Agricultural or nursery license: May be required if you sell plants or produce.

Food handling permits: May be required if you're producing teas, tinctures, or any ingestible items.

Home occupation permits: May be required if you're operating out of your home or farm.

Tip: Call your county's small business or agricultural extension office. They'll help you cut through the noise.

Getting Insured

Now that you've got land or equipment—or are working toward securing it—it's time to talk protection. Insurance isn't just for big operations. Whether you're growing chamomile in a side yard or running farm tours with your goats, coverage gives you a safety net. I did extensive research into insurance and made a few insurance mistakes, so I cannot impress upon you enough—insure your assets.

Let me tell you about The Fire of 2023. I had just driven to the post office to drop off some orders and decided to take advantage of the trip by swinging by the local Goodwill. I had some things in the truck I'd been meaning to donate, and I also wanted to take a quick look around. I do love a good thrifting break. My phone was dead, but I didn't think much of it. Honestly, it was nice to be disconnected for a little while. On my way back to the farm, I noticed plumes of smoke rising in the distance. I thought maybe it was just a burn pile—common enough in rural areas. But as I got closer, I heard sirens. I sped up, just a bit. It was the middle of summer—July 10, 2023, to be exact. We weren't running heaters or using anything flammable. There was no reason to think there'd be a fire at the farm. Until I turned the corner and saw it—those sirens were at my farm. My heart sank.

My son had called 911 the moment he saw flames shooting out of our beloved herb cabin. He'd tried calling me, but my phone was dead. Yeah . . . the mom guilt hit hard. While the truly irreplaceable things—my loved ones—were safe, the damage was almost total. The herb cabin, our production and storage hub, was nearly destroyed on the inside. I had insurance, but not nearly enough. That $20,000 machine we bought to start making plant-based tea bags? Gone. Along with all our packaging, supplies, computers, furniture—almost everything. And of course, we lost our entire herb inventory. One of the firefighters remarked that it was the best-smelling fire he'd ever experienced.

That day, I learned I was seriously underinsured. I also learned that insurance companies aren't too enthusiastic when it comes time to actually use the policies you've been faithfully paying for. I didn't have adequate insurance coverage for the building, the contents, or the lost business income. It

Images of the damage from The Fire of 2023. The farm lost $40,000 worth of equipment (pictured) that was not properly insured.

was a costly lesson, and one I hope you won't have to experience yourself.

As I demonstrated with ACCOUNTABILITEA, there are creative ways that your community can help support you during challenging times. If you find yourself in a bad spot with inadequate insurance, I hope this story inspires you. After the fire, I developed RESILIENCEE: A Blend Rooted in Recovery and Resistance. It's made with passionflower, lemon balm, butterfly pea, and red clover. These herbs were chosen for their traditional use in healing from physical and emotional fatigue, making them ideal allies in times of rebuilding. And rebuild we did. Proceeds from RESILIENCEE directly supported our ongoing rebuilding efforts,

RESILIENCEE Herbal Tea Blend helped raise support after the fire.

De-stemming herbs by hand.

helping us restore infrastructure, replenish stock, and continue crafting small-batch herbal offerings with integrity. Like ACCOUNTABILITEA, RESILIENCEE is more than a blend—it's a brand ethos. A statement. A remedy. A resistance. It reminds us that healing—both personal and collective—isn't a luxury. It's a necessity. When we show up for one another, we all grow stronger.

All that said, do make sure that you have adequate insurance protection and complete an annual review of coverage. Build your coverage like you build your farm. You're not buying insurance for a big commercial operation when your farm is just sprouting—and that's exactly how it should be. You can layer your coverage over time, based on your current needs—not where you hope to be five years from now. Let's break down the key insurance types you should know and consider having.

GENERAL LIABILITY INSURANCE

Think of general liability as your first line of defense when it comes to insurance. General liability insurance covers legal fees and medical costs if someone is injured on your farm or as a result of your farm activities. If you plan to host events, from workshops and farm tours to U-pick days, pop-ups, weddings, corporate volunteer days, or even family gatherings, then you absolutely need it. Even if it's just your grandmother and her friends stopping by, accidents can happen, and this insurance ensures you aren't financially liable. For Black women farmers, this coverage isn't just about paperwork. It is also about protecting our hard work. Too often, we face heightened scrutiny in agricultural spaces. Showing up prepared and insured signals that you're serious, professional, and here to build a lasting farm business.

PRODUCT LIABILITY INSURANCE

Listen, if you're making anything people put in or on their bodies—tea blends, tinctures, salves, herbal smoke mixes, infused oils—product liability insurance is critical. I would even consider it a non-negotiable. Skipping it can cost your business and even more. Life happens, and even the best intentions can't prevent allergic reactions, accidental misuse, or claims that your product was contaminated. And while building an authentic relationship with your customer base is key to resolving issues, having insurance adds peace of mind. Product liability insurance protects you if someone decides to sue you over your goods. Most wholesalers and retail stores require it before they'll touch your products. Many farmers markets also require that you have coverage. After the fire on my farm, I had to show proof of product liability insurance before I was able to rent the temporary kitchen space used during the transitional period while repairs were made to my farm's kitchen. Think of it as a safety net for your farm hustle: You do the work, craft the magic, and this insurance has your back if something goes sideways.

FARM PROPERTY INSURANCE

Farm property insurance protects the physical assets of your farm, including greenhouses, high tunnels, sheds, tools, equipment, irrigation systems, and, in some cases, livestock and crops. This coverage is crucial for safeguarding your investments and ensuring that your farm can continue operating smoothly in the event of unforeseen circumstances. One of the biggest mistakes new farmers make is underestimating how insurance actually works. It's not enough to jot down a list of tools, equipment, or crops. You need a full inventory, and you need to insure everything based on replacement value, not what you paid at a discount or a sale.

Replacement value matters because the price you originally paid often doesn't reflect the true cost of getting back to business after a loss. That $50 garden hoe from a big-box store might be enough to dig a small garden, but if it breaks in the middle of a season, replacing it with a heavy-duty, professional-grade hoe—the kind you rely on day in and day out—could cost twice as much. The same goes for your dehydrator, greenhouse heater, tractor and other farm equipment, or even a batch of harvested crops or processed livestock. Market prices change, equipment upgrades are often needed, and quality replacements aren't always cheap. If your coverage is based on what you paid, you could find yourself underinsured at the moment you need the money most.

For farmers, underinsurance can be devastating. Trust me, I experienced it firsthand. A fire, storm, or theft can wipe out not just property but months of labor and planning. Insurance that reflects true replacement value ensures that you can restore your farm to the condition it was before disaster struck, without cutting corners or delaying operations. It's about more than money; it's about continuity, reliability, and preserving the life and livelihood you've built.

Being meticulous about inventory and realistic about replacement costs also signals professionalism to your insurer, which can make claims smoother and strengthen your relationship with the agent. In short, it's not just paperwork. Proper insurance is a proactive strategy that protects your farm, your income, and your peace of mind.

FARM VEHICLE INSURANCE

If you're driving a vehicle for farm business, you need to make sure that vehicle is properly insured for farm use. The type of coverage depends on who owns the vehicle and how it's used. If the vehicle is owned by your farm

Photo courtesy of LMO Productions.

business, the best option is a commercial farm vehicle policy. This is a full business vehicle insurance plan that protects both the vehicle and its use for farm operations. It provides higher coverage limits and typically includes liability protection if the vehicle is involved in an accident while performing farm tasks. If the vehicle is a personal one that you occasionally use for farmwork, you don't need a full commercial policy. Instead, you can add a farm use endorsement to your personal auto insurance. A farm use endorsement is essentially an add-on that extends coverage for farm-related activities. It protects your vehicle and provides liability coverage when you're using it for tasks like transporting produce, visiting markets, or moving supplies around your property. Farm use endorsements are particularly useful for boutique farms, where personal vehicles are often pulled into farmwork. However, it's important to read the fine print: Endorsements may include limits on coverage amounts, who can drive the vehicle, or what types of farm-related tasks are included. The key takeaway is that insurance should match how you use the vehicle. Using a pickup to haul CSA boxes or a utility ATV to run across your property may seem simple, but without the proper coverage, one accident could cost far more than the vehicle itself. By choosing the right policy, you ensure that you're protected, whether on the farm or on the road

CROP INSURANCE (EVEN FOR SMALL PLOTS!)

Small farms need crop coverage, too. The USDA actually offers Micro Farm insurance through the Whole-Farm Revenue Protection program for farms making under $350,000 per year. This program simplifies record keeping and

Tractors: Property or Vehicle?

Should a tractor be insured as a farm vehicle or under farm property insurance? The answer depends on how you use it, but in many cases, it can be covered under both, depending on your policy structure.

If the tractor is primarily used on your farm property for planting, cultivating, or hauling materials around your fields, it often falls under farm property insurance. In this case, it's treated like a piece of equipment; if it's damaged by fire, theft, or natural disasters, your property policy may pay to repair or replace it. However, if you're using the tractor on public roads to haul goods to market, drive to a neighboring field, or transport equipment, then it may need farm vehicle coverage. Farm vehicle policies or farm use endorsements extend coverage to vehicles in motion and can protect you in the event of collisions or liability claims while driving.

For many farmers, the safest approach is a combination: Insure the tractor under farm property for on-farm risks, and make sure your farm vehicle policy or endorsement covers any off-farm use. This dual coverage ensures that no matter where your tractor is or what it's doing, you're protected. The key takeaway: A tractor isn't just a tool—it's a critical part of your farm business. Proper coverage means you can use it confidently without risking the farm's financial security.

provides coverage for all commodities on the farm under one policy, including specialty and organic crops, livestock, and value-added products.

While the USDA administers and subsidizes the Micro Farm program, the policies are sold and serviced through private crop insurance agents. These agents are approved by the USDA's Risk Management Agency (RMA) and operate in partnership with the federal government to deliver crop insurance products. Therefore, even if the USDA were to discontinue the Micro Farm program, private insurance companies might still offer similar coverage options, though the specifics would depend on the insurance providers and available programs at that time. For Black women farmers, it is important to know that your creativity and labor are backed by real protection. Programs like USDA's Micro Farm insurance options help mitigate the risk of a single bad season wiping out your farming business.

LIVESTOCK INSURANCE: PROTECTING YOUR HERD, FLOCK, OR BEES

If you're raising animals, even bees, you need to think carefully about livestock-specific insurance. Standard farm property or crop insurance usually doesn't cover animals, or if it does, the coverage is limited. That's why there are policies designed specifically for livestock, giving you financial protection if your animals are lost or stolen, or their market value drops.

The USDA offers several programs through the RMA, including multi-peril livestock insurance, which can cover death due to disease, accidents, or extreme weather. Programs like Livestock Risk Protection (LRP) and Livestock Gross Margin (LGM) insurance help protect against market price declines as well as the difference between feed costs and commodity prices, respectively. In order to purchase these policies, you will have to work with a private insurance agent approved by the RMA. You can find a list of agents using the RMA agent locator found at https://www.rma.usda.gov/tools-reports/agent-locator.

When considering livestock insurance, think about both replacement costs and revenue and income protection. Replacement coverage helps you pay to replace animals lost to theft, fire, or accidents. Revenue protection safeguards the income you would have earned from selling your animals, protecting your cash flow and your ability to keep your farm operating. For small-scale and specialty farms, it's critical to work with an insurance agent familiar with boutique operations. They can help you determine which type of coverage matches your animals, herd size, and revenue goals. Without livestock insurance, a single outbreak of disease or an extreme weather event could devastate your farm financially. But with the right coverage, you can recover, rebuild, and keep your animals thriving.

INSURANCE RIDERS

A rider is essentially an add-on to an insurance policy. It is how you can customize your coverage to fit the exact needs of your farm. No two farms are exactly alike, so your insurance needs to fit your operation. Your base policy covers the basics. For example, your farm property insurance may cover buildings, some equipment, and general inventory. But what if you have harvested crops stored in your greenhouse, or agricultural goods waiting to be packaged and sold? What if your income stops because of a fire or storm? That's where riders come in.

Riders allow you to expand your coverage. You can add protection for harvested products, specialized equipment, livestock, or business interruption. You can get a rider to cover the lost income that comes when your farm can't operate. Without these add-ons, you might think you're fully covered, but a single unexpected event could leave you vulnerable.

For example, a standard farm property policy might not cover canned exotic fruits stored on shelves. By adding a rider for inventory, you ensure that your product is protected. A business interruption rider can replace income if your farm is temporarily closed due to a covered event. And a livestock rider can protect your goats, chickens, or bees, which might not be included under a basic policy. Riders aren't optional extras but rather tools that allow you to tailor insurance to your farm's unique risks and assets. They make sure that your labor, creativity, and income are safeguarded so that you can farm boldly without fear that one disaster will wipe out everything you have worked to build.

How to Start Getting Covered

Getting insurance for your farm can feel overwhelming at first, but it doesn't have to be. The most important thing to remember is that you don't have to go it alone. There are professionals who specialize in farm insurance and can guide you through the options that make sense for your operation. To get started, the first thing you want to do is to identify your farm's needs. Take stock of what you want to protect: your land, buildings, tools, equipment, harvested crops, livestock, and any value-added products. Think about the risks you face such as fire, theft, extreme weather, disease, or unexpected interruptions in your operations. Don't forget to consider your income: Would you want coverage if something happened that kept you from earning money?

Once you know what you need, it's time to find a farm insurance agent. The USDA's Risk Management Agency keeps a list of approved crop insurance agents, and you can search by state or county. Local farm co-ops, extension offices, or farming networks can also be invaluable sources of referrals. And don't forget to ask other farmers for insurance agency recommendations. When you speak to potential agents, look for experience with small-scale, specialty, or organic farms. Not every agent understands the realities of a boutique or micro farm, and that knowledge can make a big difference.

When you meet with an agent, ask questions. What policies do they offer that cover both crops and livestock? Can you add riders for inventory, business interruption, or specialized equipment? How do premiums, deductibles, and payouts work for small farms? Do they offer bundled coverage that simplifies managing multiple policies? The more informed you are, the better decisions you can make for your farm. It's also crucial to document your farm thoroughly. Take photos of buildings, equipment, crops, and livestock. Keep receipts, invoices, and production records. Good documentation can make filing claims faster and smoother if disaster strikes.

You don't have to insure everything at once. Many farmers start with general liability and property insurance and add coverage for crops, livestock, or business interruption as the farm grows. Start where it matters most, then layer protection over time. For Black women farmers, insurance is more than

Real Talk

If people are eating, drinking, or using your products on their skin, you need insurance. Period. One accident could cost everything you've built. General liability, property coverage, and crop or revenue protection aren't optional; they're your shield. Being insured lets you farm boldly, take risks, and protect your dream.

a line on a budget—it's a tool of empowerment. It protects your labor, your creativity, and your income, giving you the confidence to take risks and grow your farm on your own terms. Showing up prepared with coverage is a statement: You are serious, professional, and ready to claim your space in agriculture. List what you're doing, not what you plan to do. Cover what's active, not what's aspirational. Start with high-risk exposure: If you're putting products on bodies or inviting people to your land, cover that first. Ask for bundled policies or phased coverage. Let your agent know your budget and growth plan—many farm insurers will tailor it to your current scale and adjust as you grow. Your dream deserves to be sustainable and secure. Insurance may feel like an extra cost, but it's also your peace of mind. In a world where one accident or false claim can shut down a small business, being uninsured isn't just risky—it's reckless. So let's keep our farms fruitful, yes—but also protected.

CHAPTER 7

Visuals and Voice

Telling Your Boutique Farm's Story

If there's one thing I've learned in life, it's the power of using your voice.

—MICHELLE OBAMA

Here's the thing about boutique farming: Small moments can become big ones depending on how you present them. Whether you're growing heirloom tomatoes, microgreens, cut flowers, or pasture-raised chickens, how you tell your story is just as important as what you grow. We've all heard the saying that a picture is worth a thousand words. Well, that's especially true in boutique farming, where values, identity, and experience drive customer loyalty just as much as product quality.

In one of my signature and most popular workshops, The 5 V's of Farm Branding, I teach attendees about Values, Vision, Visuals, Voice, and Validity. You get the benefit of that full framework here in this book, whether you're new to farming or shifting your business to something more intentional, aligned, and sustainable. We've already talked about values and vision; now let's explore visuals and voice, two powerful tools in shaping how your farm is seen and remembered.

Branding, Marketing, or Advertising?

When I graduated with my marketing degree, I quickly realized that what many employers said they needed and what they actually needed were often two very different things. Some organizations were seeking branding support. Others were looking for advertising help. Still others really wanted sales expertise, even though they advertised the position as "marketing." It was a little disorienting at first, especially because my undergraduate program had been heavily

focused on market research—not on creative campaigns, branding, or sales funnels. Like many people eager to build their careers, I accepted positions that didn't always align directly with my academic training. What they did offer me, however, was something just as valuable: the opportunity to broaden my real-world experience in communications. Over time, I developed the skills to lead entire communications departments, bridging the gaps among strategy, storytelling, and execution.

For the purposes of this book, and because these terms often get used interchangeably when they shouldn't be, I want to take a moment to break down the differences among branding, marketing, and advertising. Each one plays a different role, but together, they create the foundation that helps your boutique farm grow a loyal and engaged community.

Branding Is Who You Are: It's the heart and soul of your farm. Your branding includes your visuals (like your logo, colors, and packaging), your values (what you stand for), your tone (how you speak to your audience), and the emotional experience people have when they interact with your business. Branding is what makes someone feel connected to you beyond just the products you sell. It answers the question: Why should I care about this farm/business?

Marketing Is How You Tell People Who You Are: Once you know your brand, marketing is the process of sharing it with the world. This includes your messaging, your storytelling, and the channels you use to reach your audience—whether that's social media, newsletters, live events, your website, or collaborations. Good marketing communicates your brand clearly, consistently, and in a way that resonates with the people you want to serve.

Advertising Is How You Amplify That Message to a Broader Audience: While marketing can include organic efforts (like posting regularly on Instagram), advertising specifically refers to paid efforts to promote your farm. This might mean running digital ads on Facebook or Google, sponsoring posts to get in front of more people, printing flyers for an event, or even buying a billboard. Advertising boosts visibility, but it's most effective when it's rooted in strong branding and supported by clear marketing strategies.

Your Digital Presence

Your digital presence is the online reflection of who you are and what your farm stands for. It's not just about being seen—it's about being understood, remembered, and trusted. For boutique farms, where every decision is often rooted in intention and care, your digital presence is where your visuals and voice come together to tell your story. Think of your digital presence as a three-part ecosystem.

Your Website Is Your Digital Homestead: It's where people go to learn more, to shop, and to connect with your story in a grounded and uninterrupted space.

Your Email List Is Your Direct Connection to Your Community: It's where you nurture relationships, provide deeper insights, and keep your audience informed and inspired.

An example of branded marketing material.

Your Social Media Is Where You Show Up Daily or Weekly: It's where your visuals and voice meet your audience in their everyday scroll—and where you get to remind them why your work matters. It's also a good place to direct folks to your email list and website.

Each digital component serves a different purpose, but they all work together to build trust, establish credibility, and, most important, express you. When you align your visuals and voice across these platforms, your audience doesn't just recognize your brand—they feel connected to it.

Above all, your digital presence should feel like an extension of your work, not a separate entity that drains your energy. Approach it with the same care, intention, and creativity that you bring to your farm. Each post, email, or website update should align with your values and contribute to the joy you find in your business. When you prioritize your well-being and make your digital spaces work for you, your audience will feel it—and they'll be drawn to your authenticity. So, as you build your digital presence, ask yourself: How can this bring me joy? How can it serve my audience while also serving me? And most important, how can I show up in a way that feels true to who I am and what I stand for? This is your joy factory—in both the physical and digital realms. Protect it, nurture it, and let it grow at a pace that feels right for you.

The Power of Your Email List

In the world of boutique farming, visuals and voice aren't just for marketing—they are the heart of your brand identity. And while it's easy to think of social media as the primary platform for expressing that identity, there's another tool that deserves just as much, if not more, attention: your email list. Email is one of the most powerful ways to maintain a direct, authentic connection with your audience. Why? Because it's permission-based. People on your email list are there because they chose to be. They trust you. They value what you have to offer. And they've given you a direct line of

Real Talk

You don't have to email every week if that's not your style. But do email consistently. Monthly is better than never. Write how you talk. Make it personal. Make it meaningful. Make it useful. When someone sees your name in their inbox, it should feel like hearing from a friend—not just a sales pitch.

FARMER HIGHLIGHT

Patrice Clark, Emerald Roots Farm Collective, Phoenix, Arizona

Tell us a little about your farm and your "why" for farming.

Emerald Roots Farm Collective grows agricultural goodness, and produces aromatic, artisanal, hand-blended body soaking teas and blow bubbles. We are a minority, family-owned, woman-led boutique farm that grows medicinal and edible herbs, flowers, sugarcane, and assorted seasonal vegetables (including black-eyed peas), as well as hosting honeybees. Our "why" is to organically grow ingredients that support wellness and produce products that invoke joy and inspire self-love—the foundation of health—because we deserve it! My big dream is a self-care, wellness, and happiness (pleasure) brand that is the embodiment of experiencing a French Kiss Life. What is a French Kiss Life? It's a metaphor for the demonstration of living intentionally, boldly, and unapologetically, you-niquely taking care of your whole self to live and be well inside and out. Think about it: A French Kiss is different from a "regular" kiss. It's that bold, fierce, passionate extra, intimate/personal ooh la la! It's being positively passionate about your whole self and living life to the fullest with a focus on wellness inside and out.

Photo courtesy of Patrice Clark.

What has been one of the biggest lessons or truths you've learned through your farming journey?

My biggest lesson and truth has been that everyone's journey is unique, and as long as you are taking positive steps forward, you are moving in the right direction. Farming and business are not for the weak or faint of heart. As with all aspects of life, there will be setbacks. Moving forward is key.

What is one piece of advice you would offer to other women interested in starting a boutique farm?

Start small by understanding the soil you are working with. Then plant or grow what you like and what the soil produces based on your climate/region. It's very important to "date your data." Documenting what you do or did, understanding what worked and what didn't work is important as you build and scale.

How do you care for yourself while doing this work? What grounds you?
Touching the soil, tending the plants, and especially creating products from the harvest to share with family and community members elevates my spirit. I also create self-love rituals that include sipping, soaking, and de-stressing with teas, bath salts, and bubbles.

communication—one that's not filtered by algorithms, timelines, or shifting social media trends.

At Green Heffa Farms, our email list is our most prioritized community. It includes our most loyal customers, crowdfunding supporters, brand ambassadors, and community partners. At the time of this writing, Green Heffa Farms and my personal Farmer Cee brand have a combined social media following of almost four hundred thousand—but neither of those platforms compares with the value of our ten thousand email subscribers. I call them my Faves. It is important to note that this email list is the result of seven years of intentional growth. My initial email list consisted of a whopping seventy-six initial subscribers—and seventy of those were family and friends. Unlike social media, where your content may get lost in the scroll, email lets you show up with intention. It allows for meaningful storytelling, exclusive product drops, and genuine behind-the-scenes updates that help deepen your relationship with your audience. You can also share the stories behind your products and explain the crafting and growing process in a longer format. Email becomes an extension of your voice. It's not about blasting sales—it's about nurturing relationships.

Email is also a tool for education. Many boutique farm offerings—like heirloom crops, regenerative practices, or herbal infusions—are new to your audience. Use your emails to really emphasize what makes your offerings unique. You can highlight your commitment to sustainability. People buy from those they trust and understand. Email helps you build both. Start building your list early, even if you're just getting started. Don't wait for a big following. Every subscriber is valuable.

Social Media: Your Creative Expression

Social media is your chance to connect with a broader audience and express yourself creatively. While it can be overwhelming at times, remember that it doesn't need to be. Choose platforms that you enjoy using and that make

GROUNDWORK

Cultivating Your Email List

The purpose of this exercise is to start (or strengthen) your email list by aligning it with your brand voice and visuals.

Step 1: Define Your Email Voice

How do you want to sound in your emails? Friendly? Informative? Soulful? Sassy? Educational? Pick three words to describe the tone you want your readers to feel.

Step 2: Create a Freebie or Lead Magnet

What can you offer in exchange for someone's email address? A downloadable recipe? A seasonal planting guide? A self-care tip sheet using your products?

Step 3: Set a Rhythm

Choose your email frequency (weekly, biweekly, monthly).

Step 4: Generate Some Topic Ideas

Brainstorm three email topics that blend storytelling and value (for example, "The Plant That Changed My Life," "How I Prep for Planting Season," and "Three Ways to Use Our Natural Products").

Step 5: Design Your First Welcome Email

Write a welcoming email (re)introducing your brand and values. Share what subscribers can expect from being on your list (frequency, content, perks), and include a photo or visual that reflects your farm's vibe.

Step 6: Promote It

Add your email sign-up link to your social media bio and captions. Bring a physical sign-up sheet to your next market. Regularly include a call to action to join your email list on your social media. Share your freebie or lead magnet in a post or story. Reminder: Your email list is more than a marketing tool—it's your community. Treat it like the sacred space it is.

sense for your brand. If you don't love Instagram or TikTok, don't force it—focus on platforms where you feel comfortable and can naturally share your message. And don't forget blog platforms such as Substack, Medium, Blogger, Tumblr, and Squarespace if you prefer that format.

Personally, I'm a fan of organic content creation. I draw inspiration from others but rarely chase trends—that's just my style. I enjoy creating original, authentic posts that reflect what's really happening on the farm. That said, if you're someone who loves trends, by all means participate—trending content can carry built-in momentum that's useful for visibility. I know many people

The interior of the farm's herb cabin showcases the farm's vibe. *Photo courtesy of Candice Brown-Murray.*

thrive with structured content calendars, but that doesn't quite fit my personality. I create when I feel inspired, and I believe that inner peace fuels my creativity. For me, social media is a way to show our customers and supporters what we're up to and to genuinely engage. I treat it as a tool, not a destination. My primary goal is to drive people to our website, where the real story, offerings, and connection live.

To me, it's not about the number of followers—it's about the quality of the connection. It is important to make sure your social media usage serves you, not the other way around. Use it as a tool to showcase the work you love, educate your audience, and build authentic relationships. You can establish boundaries, too—just because the platform is available 24/7 doesn't mean you need to be. You do not have to answer every question. Nor should you share every aspect of your business or life. Be mindful of the risks that come with online visibility. There are some people who are bothered by the sight of unapologetically joyful Black women, especially in agriculture. Safety should always be prioritized. Parasocial relationships—one-sided connections people form with public figures—can become problematic.

Your well-being should always come first. If social media becomes stressful, step back and reassess. What do you enjoy about it? What brings you joy in the process? Lean into the aspects that fill your cup, and let go of the pressure to be everywhere, all the time. Set times for content creation and engagement that fit your lifestyle, and allow yourself to unplug when necessary. Determine which areas are off-limits. Quality engagement will always matter more than quantity, so make sure that you have clarified your social media goals. Are you looking to build a community, educate your followers, or sell products? Once you know your purpose, create a posting schedule that feels manageable, whether that's daily, weekly, or somewhere in between. Focus on consistency, not perfection. When it comes to your social media presence, just as with your physical operation, you want to prioritize that this space is an expansion of your customized joy factory. Your approach to social media should be done with your well-being in mind.

Green Heffa Farms' Social Media Strategy: Step by Step

When I earned my undergraduate degree in marketing in the early 2000s, social media wasn't even a thing. By the time it gained traction, I was resistant to learning it. Eventually, one of my best friends convinced me to create a Facebook account, but it wasn't until social media became part of my professional responsibilities—working in higher education communications—that I started to take it seriously.

As a Gen Xer, my approach to technology was different. I was raised by a generation that didn't fully trust it—people who still paid bills with paper checks and were skeptical about sharing personal information online. Because of that, I didn't jump on every new digital trend. Instead, I saw social media for what it is: a tool. A tool to connect with my audience, share information about my products, reiterate my values, and, ultimately, drive people to my website and onto my email list—because at the end of the day, loyal customers are the heartbeat of a boutique farming brand.

I want to share a strategy that makes social media manageable, including how to use technology to streamline your efforts through scheduling, batch content creation, and automation. But first, let's address a common trap: the vanity metrics. It's easy to feel discouraged when comparing your follower count with influencers who have hundreds of thousands, even millions, of followers. Let me tell you something: I know social media influencers with massive followings who are financially struggling, and I know millionaires with fewer than a thousand followers. It's not about the numbers—it's about who you are talking to and whether they are engaged with your brand.

As of this writing, I still manage the social media accounts for Green Heffa Farms and Farmer Cee brands, plus I have personal, private accounts for close friends and family. At some point, I will delegate these tasks to someone else, but for now I enjoy running my own social media. Yes, I create content, but I don't live my life or run my business with content creation as my primary focus. Instead, I see myself as a content generator—I create with intention and selectively share what aligns with my brand and mission. I knew I wanted to grow my social media audience the same way that I grow my plants—organically. While I have on occasion run a few paid ads and sponsored posts to test the waters, I have found the most consistent growth when I have focused on some core principles.

CORE SOCIAL MEDIA PRINCIPLES

These aren't just tips—they're foundational values that guide how I show up online as a farmer, entrepreneur, and steward of story. I've developed them into an on-farm workshop because I believe every grower, maker, and mission-driven brand deserves to feel confident in how they connect with their community. These principles are especially powerful for boutique farm businesses looking to cultivate trust, visibility, and alignment.

Authenticity: Share your real experiences, both the wins and the lessons. Don't be afraid to show your face, your process, your progress. People connect with people, not perfection. Authenticity builds trust, and trust builds community. Let your values speak louder than your filters.

Realistic Consistency: Set a sustainable pace—whether that's weekly, biweekly, or seasonally—and stick to it. Consistency doesn't mean constancy; it means intentional presence.

Selective Platform Use: You do not have to be on every app. Focus on the platforms where your people are and where you can genuinely enjoy creating. Whether it's Instagram, YouTube, LinkedIn, or TikTok, go deep, not wide. Spread yourself too thin and your message gets diluted.

Recycle, Reuse, Revamp: Your content has more life than you think. A caption can become a blog post, a video clip can turn into a reel, a testimonial can be a graphic. Don't reinvent the wheel—refine and repurpose it. Efficiency is part of sustainability, too.

Seeing the Significance in the Seemingly Insignificant: That morning harvest, the way the light hits the herb rows, a customer's kind words, your tea steeping—those small, honest moments are often the most impactful. Beauty and meaning live in the everyday. Don't underestimate the power of showing the work behind the work.

Transparency and Personal Connection: I share my experiences as a Black woman farmer, but with boundaries. I post only occasionally about my team or family, as I respect their privacy. My posts are raw and unapologetic, covering topics like racism, the realities of farming, and entrepreneurship. This transparency builds trust and resonates with my

A product photo of one of our custom herbal blends.

audience. Behind-the-scenes content also does well. I provide an inside look at Green Heffa Farms—harvesting herbs, blending teas, and managing infrastructure. These posts showcase the labor and love behind my products.

Educational Content: People come to Green Heffa Farms for more than products—they come to learn. I post about the herbs I grow, our products, their benefits, and how to use them. This not only positions me as an expert herbalist but also educates my audience on what makes Green Heffa Farms unique. I also produce content about our sustainable farming practices. I share knowledge about sustainable farming, organic techniques, and biodiversity, reinforcing my commitment to environmental stewardship and my 4 E's sustainability framework (Economic Prosperity, Equity, Environment, and Education).

Purpose-Driven Storytelling: I am committed to advocating for Black farmers and women in agriculture. I speak out about the lack of support for Black farmers and amplify conversations around social justice, inclusion, and equity in farming. On the product side of things, I share the story of our unique product development. Each product has a story, from inspiration to formulation. This adds depth to what I sell, making it part of a broader mission.

Engagement and Community Building: I occasionally host interactive Q&A sessions. I engage my audience by answering their questions on herbs, farming, and entrepreneurship. I also try to stay on top of responding to comments and DMs. I interact with my followers to foster a sense of community and connection. Social media shouldn't be a monologue—it's a conversation. The back-and-forth creates a deeper connection.

Empowerment and Inspiration: I share messages of encouragement, especially for women entering farming and entrepreneurship. I also make sure to highlight that Green Heffa Farms is part of a larger movement, so I acknowledge my supporters and collaborators.

Visual and Aesthetic Choices: A big part of my content is focused on rustic nature imagery. My content features the natural beauty of my farm, highlighting herbs, landscapes, and farmwork. My product shots are also clean and simple, often using natural backdrops.

Balancing Business Promotion with Personal Narrative: I frame product promotions within my broader mission, because weaving my story alongside my promotions makes them feel like genuine recommendations rather than sales pitches. Even the names—like ACCOUNTABILITEA, inspired by my legal fight against a major conservation organization, and RESILIENCEE, born from the support I needed after the farm fire—reflect real moments in my story, turning each product into an extension of my lived experience.

Consistency with Adaptability: I post consistently but vary my content—long-form captions, short updates, static images, and video. My content aligns with the farming calendar, keeping it timely and relevant.

Strategic Hashtags and Tagging: I use targeted hashtags like #Herbs, #PlantMedicine, #BlackWomenFarmer, #WomenFarmers, #Herbalist, #WomenInAgriculture, and #SustainableFarming to reach my

Table 7.1. Hashtag Limits by Platform

Platform	Verified Limit/Rule
Instagram	Up to 30 hashtags per post caption
YouTube	Up to 15 hashtags per video
TikTok	5 hashtags
X (formerly Twitter)	No formal limit, but limited by character count
LinkedIn	No documented hashtag limit
Facebook	No documented hashtag limit
Pinterest	20 hashtags per "pin"

community. This makes my content more likely to come up for anyone searching for those topics. Tagging collaborators and fellow farmers also strengthens my network and extends my reach. I suggest creating a list of hashtags and saving them in a note on your smartphone or computer to be able to easily copy and paste.

Simplicity in Production: I avoid trendy, overproduced content, and focus on meaningful messaging. No choreographed dances, no gimmicks—just real talk. My social media strategy is built around authenticity, education, and purposeful engagement. I balance promoting Green Heffa Farms with fostering a genuine connection to my mission, community, and identity as a Black woman farmer.

If you take nothing else from this chapter, remember this: You don't have to be the loudest voice online to be impactful. You just need to be the right voice for the right people. Social media should serve your business, not the other way around. Make it work for you.

Photography: Telling the Story Through Your Lens

You don't need fancy equipment to build a strong visual identity. A good phone, natural light, and consistency can go a long way. You'll likely need photos for your website, social media, email marketing, and packaging and printed materials. Photograph your farm in all seasons, your harvests or products, your tools, process, daily work, and, most important, you! People connect with people. Show your face, your hands, your joy. Posting photos of myself on the farm allows me to share the full story of being Black and

Green Heffa Farms' brand color palette.

being a woman in agriculture and entrepreneurship—not just the work but the joy, skill, creativity, and resilience that come with it. It brings visibility to our presence and expertise, and I hope it inspires others who might hesitate to show themselves online to step into their own confidence and share their journeys.

Whether you're producing pasture-raised eggs, growing sunflowers, or cultivating edible mushrooms, being consistent is key. A strong, consistent brand presentation can increase revenue by up to 33 percent, according to 2020 research by Lucidpress (now Marq). Customers are more likely to trust and support farms that feel reliable, recognizable, and aligned. When someone sees your logo, your brand colors, or your social posts, they should think, "Oh, that's her farm—I love her work!" Fun fact: People need to see your brand around five to seven times before it becomes memorable.

Using Your Phone

Listen, if you've got a recent iPhone or Android with a good camera, you're already working with more than enough to create beautiful, engaging content. Don't sleep on your phone—it's a powerful visual tool.

TIPS FOR STRONG SMARTPHONE SHOTS

- Use natural light. Early morning and late afternoon are best—hello golden hour!
- Clean your lens. (Yes, sis, we see that fingerprint smudge.)
- Tap to focus and adjust the exposure by dragging that sun icon up or down.
- Use portrait mode for depth.
- Try angles from above (flat lay), below (hero shot), and level with your product.
- Avoid filters that distort color—stay true to your brand's palette.

More on professional photographers in a moment, but if you're not ready for a full shoot, consider using:

- DIY lightboxes. There are some great ones available for less than $50.
- Poster board or contact paper backdrops for clean looks.
- Editing apps like Snapseed or Lightroom Mobile for quick cleanups.

There will come a time in your journey when you'll want to elevate your visuals, especially when you're pitching to retailers or publications, updating your website, launching a new product line, or creating media kits or lookbooks. You will need consistent, branded product photos. Here's a case where a good photographer will bring out the mood, message, and mission behind

Photo courtesy of Candice Brown-Murray.

your work. You're not just paying for photos—you're investing in how your brand is seen and remembered. Hire a photographer who understands or respects your aesthetic. I recommend creating a visual mood board beforehand. Include yourself—yes, you—in some shots. We are not erasing the Black woman from the land again. Be sure to ask for both styled and clean background product shots.

Photography shouldn't be an afterthought in your farm's marketing—it should be a core part of your strategy. Visual storytelling is a powerful way to connect with your audience, showcase your work, and build your brand. Instead of scrambling for photos when a newsletter is due or a product launch is coming up, build photography into your regular marketing rhythm. I recommend starting by dedicating one day each month to batch your photos. Use this time to capture the behind-the-scenes of your farm, product shots, lifestyle moments, and anything else that represents your mission. This habit not only keeps your content fresh but also reduces stress when you need visuals on the fly.

Organize your photos into a reusable asset folder. These images can be repurposed for newsletters, social media, press kits, or pop-up flyers. A well-maintained photo bank makes it easier to respond to opportunities quickly—whether it's a media feature or a last-minute vendor event. Don't forget to lean into the seasons. Seasonal content—like spring planting, summer blooms, fall harvests, and winter preparation—offers a natural rhythm for your storytelling and keeps your audience engaged throughout the year. And if you have upcoming launches, product bundles, or events, plan your photo needs ahead of time. A little forethought goes a long way in making your visuals feel intentional, not like scraps pulled together at the last minute.

Working with AI—Your Digital Brainstorm Partner

I know, I know, I know. Some of you are distrustful of artificial intelligence (AI). I get it, and I respect it. I am not trying to persuade you to think otherwise. For those who are receptive to AI, tools like ChatGPT or DeepSeek can be useful for boutique farmers—helping with writing, brainstorming, planning, and even marketing. Think of AI as a super-sharp assistant that's available 24/7. But just like any assistant, it works best when given clear instructions.

My best friend, Candice, a communications guru, taught me a game-changing way to talk to AI. Start your prompt with "Imagine you are . . ." and follow with a detailed description of the role you want the AI to take on. This gives the AI a "persona" and purpose, which makes the results more relevant and creative.

Some of you may be wondering how to balance the usefulness of AI with the reality of its environmental impact. These systems run on massive amounts of energy and water, and some AI centers are placed near communities of color. They leave a heavy footprint on the same environment I am trying to help heal with my farm. So, it would be remiss of me to suggest using

An example of a specialty product from Green Heffa Farms. *Photo courtesy of Candice Brown-Murray.*

Prompts for Working with AI

Here are some prompts you might feed to your AI program of choice to help with various boutique marketing needs.

For Writing Product Descriptions

"Imagine you are a copywriter for a sustainable beauty brand. Write a short, engaging product description for my herbal facial steam using calendula, lavender, and rosemary."

For Creating Social Media Content

"Imagine you are a social media strategist for a Black-owned herbal farm. Give me five Instagram post ideas for May that highlight herbs in bloom, give tips for using them, and offer behind-the-scenes looks at the farm."

For Planning an Email Newsletter

"Imagine you are a marketing expert writing a monthly email for my farm's subscribers. Draft an outline for a May newsletter that includes a featured herb, a quick recipe, and a reminder about our market days."

For Brainstorming Names or Taglines

"Imagine you are a branding consultant. Give me ten unique name ideas for a tea blend targeted at women seeking stress relief that includes hibiscus, lemongrass, and peppermint."

To get the best results, be specific about the tone, audience, and purpose. Give context when possible (what your farm is about, who your customers are). And don't be afraid to refine and ask for tweaks! AI won't replace your voice, your story, or your wisdom—but it can help you express them more clearly, consistently, and creatively. Treat it like a collaborator, not a crutch. Its role is to accentuate your creativity—not to be the source of it.

AI without also naming its costs. I am very intentional when I use AI and do my best not to use it casually. Again, it comes back to balance. In boutique farming we respect both the abundance and the limitations of the land, and the same approach should be applied to technology. If you use AI, do so mindfully. Use it only in situations that can truly add value or help you tell your story more effectively. And continue to use your own voice to advocate for a greener, more responsible infrastructure.

You may also opt to not use AI at all, which is perfectly understandable. Throughout your journey, you will encounter more instances when you will confront the decision between taking advantage of tools that can help in some way and also remaining accountable to our planet. Do your best, sis.

GROUNDWORK

Cultivating Your Digital Voice

Before you post, you plant. Use this exercise to root your social media presence in purpose, clarity, and authenticity.

Step 1: Define Your Digital Identity

Return to the last Groundwork exercise ("Cultivating Your Email List" on page 95) and your notes on your newsletter voice. Will your broader digital identity be different? How so? Write two or three sentences that describe your farm's unique personality online. Think about how your tone and voice will reflect your values and attract your ideal audience.

Step 2: Clarify Your Purpose

What are the top four goals of your social media strategy? For example, do you want to build community, sell products, educate about products, attract partnerships, or something else? Write them down.

Step 3: Identify Your Core Pillars

List three to five content categories (or "pillars") you want to focus on regularly. These should reflect your brand and help keep your content consistent and intentional. For example, you could share behind-the-scenes glimpses of the farm, herbal education and tips, Black agricultural history, product spotlights, or quotes and inspiration.

Step 4: Know Who You're Talking To

Your ideal *customer* is the person most likely to buy your product or service. Your ideal *follower*, on the other hand, may not buy from you (at least not right away), but they're drawn to your voice, your visuals, your values—and they help shape your visibility. Followers build your platform; customers build your business. Sometimes the right follower becomes the right customer—but not always. Create a quick profile of your ideal customer. Who are they? What do they care about? Why would they buy your product? Write it down. Now create a quick profile of your ideal follower. Who are they? What do they care about? Why would they follow your farm? Write this down, too. This exercise is meant to be a living document—return to it often as your farm grows and your voice evolves.

CHAPTER 8

Building Sustainable Relationships

I don't have to ask permission to be myself.

—VICTORIA SANTA CRUZ, Afro-Peruvian poet, activist, and choreographer

From seed suppliers, to media contacts, to government agencies, your network can often determine the resources you have access to, the opportunities that come your way, and the resilience you build into your business. Relationships are the quiet infrastructure that sustain you when funds are low, when guidance is needed, or when the weight of doing it all yourself gets heavy. In this chapter I will discuss the government agencies and other relationships that will be key to establishing your boutique farm, and I will provide guidance for building your team.

Key Agricultural Agencies

When you're starting out as a boutique farmer, you're not just tending to plants or livestock. You're also navigating a complex network of agencies, policies, and funding opportunities that will impact every aspect of your business. Understanding and engaging with key agricultural agencies can be one of the most powerful tools in your toolbox—if you know how to leverage these relationships to your benefit.

For many farmers, these agencies offer a lifeline of resources, technical assistance, and financial support. But as a beginning farmer—especially if you're a Black woman or someone running a non-traditional farm—navigating these systems can feel like an uphill battle. The language, the bureaucracy, and even the unspoken cultural norms can be intimidating. Yet if you are intentional about making connections and taking the time to build relationships, you can unlock a wealth of opportunities for your farm. Let's talk about the most essential agencies you'll likely engage with, how to build effective relationships, and some of the challenges you may face along the way.

Farm Service Agency (FSA)

The FSA is a division of the USDA that primarily deals with farm loans, disaster assistance, and farm income stabilization programs. For beginning farmers, the FSA is often the go-to for securing operating loans, farmland purchase loans, and even microloans designed specifically to help new and smaller-scale operations.

CHALLENGES

Complex Application Process: FSA paperwork can be overwhelming, with long application forms, stringent requirements, and multiple rounds of reviews.

Bias and Discrimination: Many farmers of color, especially Black farmers, have reported feeling marginalized or facing outright discrimination when working with the FSA. Historical bias has led to a deep distrust of USDA agencies among many Black farmers.

STRATEGIES FOR SUCCESS

Start by identifying your local FSA office and setting up an initial meeting to introduce yourself and your farm. Come prepared with a detailed business plan. While this won't eliminate bias, it positions you as a serious business owner. Document everything. Keep records of your communications, your submissions, and the decisions made by FSA representatives. Build relationships with local FSA employees by attending local agricultural events and meetings where you can connect outside of the office environment. Ask questions, be visible, and show them that you're proactive and committed.

Natural Resources Conservation Service (NRCS)

The NRCS assists with conservation practices, helping farmers protect and improve soil health, manage water resources, and implement sustainable farming techniques. Many boutique farmers overlook the NRCS because they think it's more relevant to large-scale operations, but there's a lot of support available for small farms as well.

CHALLENGES

Understanding Technical Jargon: NRCS programs often use complex terminology and have technical requirements that can be confusing, especially for those new to farming.

Program Fit: As a non-conventional farmer, you might struggle to find programs that seem tailored to your unique needs.

STRATEGIES FOR SUCCESS

Build a relationship with your local NRCS representative by inviting them to your farm. Let them see firsthand what you're working on and ask them to suggest specific programs that might support your efforts. If a program doesn't seem to fit, work with your NRCS contact to adapt your proposal. Boutique farmers often have to be creative in framing their needs to align with NRCS program goals. Learn the language. The more familiar you are with conservation practices and terms, the better you can advocate for yourself.

Local Soil and Water Conservation Districts

Soil and water conservation districts (SWCDs) are typically county-level agencies focused on promoting soil health and water conservation. They offer funding, technical assistance, and workshops that can be particularly beneficial for small, sustainable operations.

CHALLENGES

Lack of Awareness: Many beginning farmers don't realize how valuable these local agencies can be. They might seem small or inconsequential compared with the USDA, but they often have a hand on the pulse of local resources and opportunities.

Resource Constraints: Smaller SWCDs may have limited funding, making the competition for grants more intense.

STRATEGIES FOR SUCCESS

Attend SWCD workshops and public meetings. These events are a great way to meet the staff and other local farmers, which can lead to collaborations and shared resources. Volunteer or join a committee if your schedule allows. This not only helps you learn more but also establishes you as a contributor to the local farming community.

Agricultural Extension Service

Your local ag extension is a treasure trove of information, offering free or low-cost workshops, soil testing, pest management advice, and more. They also serve as a bridge between the USDA and the farming community, providing research-based guidance tailored to your state or county.

CHALLENGES

Lack of Diversity in Outreach: Extension services have traditionally focused on conventional farming methods and may overlook the needs of niche operations like yours.

Perceived Gatekeeping: As a new farmer, it's easy to feel intimidated or dismissed if your farm doesn't fit the mold of what the extension staff considers a "real farm."

STRATEGIES FOR SUCCESS

Be proactive. Schedule one-on-one time with your local extension agent. Share your farm's story and your goals and ask them for specific recommendations. Request site visits. Extension agents can provide more personalized advice when they see your farm firsthand. Don't be afraid to ask for help in navigating their services and resources—extension agents are supposed to serve the entire community.

As a boutique farmer, your relationship with these agencies will be one of your most valuable assets. It's not enough to just apply for a program or show up to a workshop. You have to be intentional about building trust and rapport with these agencies. Developing a strong network within these organizations means you're more likely to get support, be informed about new opportunities, and receive the benefit of the doubt when things get tough.

To help facilitate these relationships, I suggest that you create and maintain a detailed contact list that includes the names, titles, and contact information of key people at each agency. Take notes on your interactions, including meetings, advice received, and follow-up tasks, and record the dates of contact and any commitments made by either party. This isn't just

Farmer Cee (*center, standing*) with members of the Detroit Black Farmer Land Fund (DBFLF).

about bureaucracy—it's about cultivating a support system that sees you as a valued community member rather than just an applicant. And, yes, it is about maintaining records as well in case you ever need to show some "receipts."

When dealing with bureaucracy, whether you're applying for a loan, seeking technical assistance, or just trying to understand the regulations, the relationships you build can either smooth the path or add more roadblocks. Be intentional, be patient, and, most important, be persistent. You belong in these spaces just as much as anyone else, and the more you assert your place, the more these agencies will evolve to reflect the diversity and creativity that small, boutique farms like yours bring to agriculture.

Other Key Relationships

In addition to the previously mentioned bureaucratic relationships, you may also need to establish connections at the following:

County Planning and Zoning Departments: Especially critical if you're starting on raw land or offering experiences on your farm.

Local Health Departments: For product safety requirements and kitchen certifications.

Small Business Administration (SBA) and Local SBDCs (Small Business Development Centers): For business planning, grants, and loan navigation.

Don't just make contact when you need something. Reach out early. Introduce yourself. Let them know you're building something rooted in purpose.

Media Relationships

Media exposure can help you reach more customers, attract partners, and build your platform. Cultivate relationships with local journalists at newspapers, radio stations, and TV newsrooms. Local coverage is a great place to start getting media attention. Reach out to bloggers and digital writers who cover farming, food justice, or wellness, along with magazine editors (local or national) in your niche. These days, podcasters and YouTubers are an important part of the media landscape. Look for those who align with your mission and see if they'll have you on for an episode to talk about your business or farm.

Send thoughtful pitches, not mass emails. Show how your work ties into a broader story—and why it matters right now. Keep a running list of all media you've been featured in. Update it quarterly. It helps with credibility, grants, and partnerships. You can also add it to your website and share your media coverage with your email list.

Farmer Cee (*front row, left*) with fellow boutique farmers and agricultural advocates at SOWTH 2025.

Farmer and Maker Communities

Build with people who get it. A few meaningful relationships with other boutique farmers, herbalists, florists, chefs, and eco-conscious product makers will make you feel less isolated. It's also a good idea to get to know your local market and co-op managers. These folks can become collaborators, cross-promoters, or just people to call when you need to talk it out. Community isn't a bonus—it's a lifeline.

Service Providers You Can Grow With

These may not seem like relationships at first, but your plumber, handyperson, bookkeeper, accountant, graphic designer, web developer, and lawyer—if they understand your vision and values—can become part of your extended team. Don't just look for affordable help; look for people who get your mission for a sustainable working relationship.

Challenges for Black and Non-Conventional Farmers

Being a Black woman or a farmer from an underserved or marginalized community adds layers of complexity to this work. Not only might you face bias and discrimination, but there's also the weight of historical mistrust between Black communities and agricultural agencies. If you're farming outside the standard row-crop or livestock operations—such as herb, mushroom, or flower growing—you might also feel dismissed or misunderstood by agency staff accustomed to dealing with conventional farms.

GROUNDWORK

Cultivating Your Relationship Ecosystem

Relationships take time to grow—but like soil, they get richer with intention and care. Use this exercise to begin identifying, organizing, and nurturing the key connections that will support your boutique farm's journey.

Step 1: Map Your Current Network

Make a list of people or organizations you've already connected with or that you know could support your farming vision. If you don't have many names yet, that's okay. You'll add as you go. Organize them into the following categories (use a notebook, spreadsheet, or your favorite digital tool):

- Government and local agencies
- Funders and financial allies
- Media and story amplifiers
- Farmers, entrepreneurs, makers, and collaborators
- Service providers and specialists

Step 2: Identify Five Relationship Priorities

From the list above, identify five specific relationships you want to grow in the next three months, and develop goals. For example, reach out to your local agricultural extension agent, or set up a meeting with a local co-op rep to learn how their store partners with vendors.

Step 3: Draft Your Connection Messages

Write one outreach message to each of the five people or organizations. It doesn't need to be perfect—it just needs to be you. Keep it simple, and tell them who you are, what you're working on, and why you're reaching out. You could also share something you admire or make a small ask (like a fifteen-minute chat).

Step 4: Schedule Your Relationship Time

Add thirty minutes to your calendar once a week to follow up, check in, or introduce yourself to someone new. Relationship building isn't something you do after the farm—it's part of building it.

Step 5: Revisit Quarterly

Every season, revisit your ecosystem map. Who have you connected with? Who do you need to follow up with? What new people have come into your orbit? Use this exercise like crop rotation—to refresh your soil and keep everything in balance. Relationships are seeds: Plant with intention. Water with gratitude. Harvest with humility.

Do your best to be visible and vocal. Make it a point to show up at community meetings, workshops, and public hearings. Let them see your face and know your name. However, be selective. Your time is valuable. And you are

Farmer Cee (*center*) with members of the South Carolina Black Farmers Association.

not required or expected to show up in places that are hostile or unwelcoming. Not everyone deserves your presence. Seek out those you can learn from and other farmers who have successfully navigated these systems. They can provide insights and support you.

Know your rights. Familiarize yourself with organizational nondiscrimination policies, and don't hesitate to speak up if you feel mistreated. The more knowledgeable you are, the harder it will be for someone to dismiss your questions or applications. Bureaucracy can be exhausting and demoralizing, especially if you feel like the deck is stacked against you. Celebrate your small wins, keep your bigger vision in mind, and don't take rejections personally. They are the ones missing out.

Picking the Right Team

In the early days of Green Heffa Farms, I thought passion was enough. I believed that if someone shared my excitement for herbs, healing, and the mission behind the farm, we'd be good to go. But here's what I've learned: Passion helps, but it's not a substitute for clarity. Building the *right* team requires structure—clear roles, strong boundaries, expectations, and, yes, paperwork. It means drafting job descriptions, signing contracts, and being up front about pay, timelines, and decision-making authority. It also means being ready to have the hard conversations when things don't go as planned.

Photo courtesy of Cliford Mervil.

Loyalty should never outweigh competency. You can appreciate someone's heart and still realize they aren't the right fit for your team. That doesn't make them a bad person—it just means their strengths may lie elsewhere. Hiring or keeping someone simply because they were there from the beginning can quietly stall your growth. A strong team is aligned with your *current* needs and future vision—not just your past. Ultimately, the right team will grow *with* you, not weigh you down. That doesn't mean they'll never challenge you—in fact, the best team members will—but it does mean they'll move in rhythm with your mission. They'll take initiative, offer solutions, and show up when it counts. And in return, they deserve your clarity, consistency, and leadership.

When it works, working with friends and family can be incredibly rewarding. There's an innate trust and a level of commitment that can give you confidence and keep you going through the tough days. But when it doesn't work, it can strain relationships. I can't tell you how many times I've heard, "Hey, just call me if you need anything." But when the real work starts, sometimes the dynamic changes. The warmth and familiarity that felt comforting at first can introduce a set of challenges you'd never face with a stranger or a paid professional. You're not only the boss or the co-founder; you're also the person who might have to hold them accountable, offer criticism, or even end the working relationship if it's not working out. These scenarios are a lot harder when there's personal history on the line.

There are many ways to build your team: local bulletin boards at feed stores or libraries, rural newspapers, organization listservs like Carolina Farm Stewardship Association (CFSA), social media, and colleges or universities. I've partnered with graduate students before, including one who developed a 3-D rendering of our farm's visionary design that became pivotal in the campaign video for our first crowdfunding effort. I also collaborated for a semester with students from the North Carolina State College of Design, who tackled real farm challenges and presented creative solutions. This experience helped me better understand the roles and skills needed on the farm, and informed future hiring.

It's also important to understand the different ways to bring people onto your team. Many small farms start by working with W-9 contractors rather than W-2 employees. W-9 contractors are self-employed individuals who manage their own taxes and often work on a project or freelance basis, offering flexibility for small operations. W-2 employees, on the other hand, are hired as staff and require tax withholding, benefits, and more structured employer obligations. I work with a number of incredible service providers—my graphic designer, CPA, and grants administrator, for example—who are

Photo courtesy of Maddy Gray.

all independent contractors. They're not employees, but they are essential to how Green Heffa Farms runs. Building your team can—and should—reflect the scale and spirit of your boutique operation.

Important Roles

Starting out, your core team will likely be small—and in many cases, you may be the *only* team member. Most boutique farm owners begin as solopreneurs, wearing all the hats: farmer, marketer, bookkeeper, customer service rep, product packager, and social media manager. It's a lot, and it's normal to feel stretched in those early stages. But as your resources grow and your business begins to generate consistent revenue, you'll want to think about which roles are worth delegating first—not just to lighten your load, but to allow the business to grow beyond you.

One of the most important early hires you can make is someone to support farm operations. This person becomes your right hand—your go-to for the daily, on-the-ground work that keeps your farm functioning. Think crop planning, planting, watering schedules, pest control, harvesting, and general upkeep. Even if this role starts as part-time, seasonal, or paid in produce, having someone who knows your land, understands your goals, and can work independently allows you to step back and shift your focus to higher-level decision making. You can't build a business if you're buried in every bed of basil and batch of compost.

Closely connected to operations is order fulfillment—a role that becomes essential once your products are ready to be packaged, sold, or shipped. Turning raw herbs into polished, shelf-ready goods is time consuming. Someone who can assist with making, labeling, packing, and preparing products for farmers markets or online sales frees up valuable time and helps maintain quality and consistency. This role is often overlooked in the beginning, but as orders increase, having a fulfillment helper can prevent burnout and customer service issues.

Next is sales and marketing, and let me tell you—this is where many small farms struggle. You can have the most beautiful products in the world, but if no one knows about them, they won't move. You need someone who can help you craft your message, engage your audience, and position your products where your ideal customer is already looking. This doesn't mean hiring a full-time marketing director right out the gate. It could be a contractor who helps with social media, email newsletters, or content creation just a few hours a week. The key is consistency and clarity—your marketing should reflect your brand's values, story, and vision. Now, I'll admit—I have a bit of an advantage here. My background is in marketing, so I actually enjoy managing this part of the business. But even if you don't, you can still be successful. There are amazing books, YouTube channels, local workshops, and free resources from your county extension office or small business associations that can help you strengthen your skills until you're ready to bring someone else on board.

Lastly, don't underestimate the value of finance and administrative support. This might look like a freelance bookkeeper, a virtual assistant, or even a savvy relative (as long as you have a clear, written agreement) who can track expenses, send invoices, and keep your systems organized. As your business grows and you start applying for grants, working with distributors, or expanding your product line, having someone to help manage the numbers and paperwork becomes more than a convenience—it's a necessity. Clean books mean fewer surprises, fewer missed opportunities, and less stress when it's time to file taxes or apply for funding.

When you're building a boutique farming business, every role matters—but that doesn't mean you have to hire all at once. Start small. Prioritize where you need the most support. As your business continues to evolve, you can expand your team to include more specialized support: customer service, logistics and fulfillment, website and tech support, or even someone focused solely on grant writing and funding research. Growth doesn't have to be rushed or overwhelming—it should be intentional and paced to match your capacity and cash flow. Start with what you *need*, not what you think a business "should" have. Add roles gradually, and choose people who understand your mission and are aligned with your farm's values.

There will also be people you need on your team who might not see your vision right away. The agricultural field has plenty of skeptics, especially when they don't fully understand boutique farming or if they question your unconventional approach. Convincing people to come aboard can require a lot of energy, but the key is clarity and transparency. Lay out your vision and show them where they fit into it. And know that sometimes people need time to be won over. Not everyone will be as ready to take the leap as you are.

Setting Expectations

It's tempting, especially when you're working with people you know, to keep things informal. But without documented agreements, misunderstandings are nearly inevitable. These misunderstandings can be minor, like someone misinterpreting their responsibilities, or they can be major, like disputes over pay, time commitments, or even ownership. Sometimes people literally never speak to each other again because they lacked a clear understanding in writing. The key is honesty—keep everything up front and in writing. I can't emphasize enough how much clear paperwork matters, even if it feels awkward in the beginning. You need documentation of roles, expectations, and what happens if things don't go as planned. When things are put on paper, there's less room for hurt feelings down the line because you've both agreed on your expectations. If you're sharing profits or giving someone a percentage of revenue, formalize it with a contract. Same goes for defining roles and performance expectations. Paperwork isn't about mistrust; it's about protecting everyone involved. You can still shake hands—after the paperwork is signed.

Sexism and racism are real challenges in agriculture. Even though I'm the CEO of Green Heffa Farms, some people still expect me to step into traditional roles just because I'm a woman. I've been expected to clean the bathrooms or restock the fridge with cold drinks—tasks that no one would have asked of a male leader. This kind of subtle (and sometimes not-so-subtle) sexism isn't uncommon, especially in male-dominated industries like agriculture. You have to be prepared to speak up for yourself and to stand firm in your role.

Racism is an equally real, if not more insidious, challenge. As a Black woman in a field dominated by white men, I have faced countless assumptions about my competence and my right to be in the room. Often, people expect me to prove my knowledge and expertise in ways they wouldn't ask of others. It's a challenging road to walk, but knowing what you're up against makes it easier to set boundaries and protect your mental and emotional well-being. Surround yourself with allies and support systems who respect your leadership, and do not tolerate those who undermine it. Set boundaries around your role—and honor them. If you're the CEO, act like it. That doesn't mean you're above pitching in when needed, but it does mean your energy should be focused on driving strategy, vision, and long-term success. Delegate the tasks that don't require your expertise—cleaning, organizing, managing the inbox—and resist the urge to micromanage. You're not here to uphold outdated stereotypes of what women, or Black women in particular, are "supposed" to do. You're here to build something that lasts.

Creating a healthy work environment begins with clear expectations. Foster a culture where everyone—from volunteers to paid staff—understands that mutual respect is the standard. Boundaries, communication, and inclusivity are non-negotiable. When people feel safe, respected, and seen, they show up more fully. Don't forget to check in with yourself, too. Running a boutique farm is labor-intensive and emotionally demanding. When you're balancing entrepreneurship, land stewardship, and your own well-being—as a woman, and especially as a Black woman—that load can get heavy. Make it a practice to pause and ask: What's working? What's wearing me down? Where do I need help? There's no shame in adjusting. There's wisdom in it.

At the heart of it all, building your team is one of the most important investments you'll make. With defined roles, shared values, and mutual accountability, you'll create a space where everyone can contribute and thrive—and you'll free yourself up to lead with intention.

CHAPTER 9

Grow Slow So You Don't Owe

I had to make my own living and my own opportunity. But I made it! Don't sit down and wait for the opportunities to come. Get up and make them.

—Madam C. J. Walker, first self-made female millionaire in America

In numerology, the number nine is often associated with completion, wisdom, and fruition—the final stage before something new begins. It carries the energy of lessons learned, cycles closed, and purposeful transitions. The number nine embodies the spirit of generosity and humanitarianism, encouraging us to build with intention, not impulse. These associations come from spiritual traditions that explore the symbolic meanings of numbers across cultures, including elements of Western esotericism, Eastern philosophies, and sacred geometry.

Farming, especially when you're doing it on your own terms, isn't about quick wins—it's about rooted resilience. It's easy to feel pressured to grow fast: to buy more land, take on debt, and scale up before you're ready. But you determine your pace. And I believe in growing at the pace of your peace. Debt can be a burden that robs you of freedom before you even have a chance to breathe in abundance. This chapter is about building a financially and energetically sustainable farm. Not just a business that survives, but one that supports your values, your community, and your well-being. If you've made it this far, you're stepping into a more complete understanding of what it means to be the CEO of your soil. You've done the planting—now let's focus on the harvesting in ways that honor your vision and your future.

Early on, I made a conscious and deliberate decision to grow slow so I wouldn't owe—financially, mentally, emotionally, spiritually, or psychologically. This wasn't just about money. It was about protecting my peace. About staying whole. About preserving the sacredness of a dream I held dear. Just because you're not borrowing big doesn't mean you can't earn big.

I chose to build slow because I wanted full ownership, full autonomy, and full clarity. I noticed that many who wanted to invest in my business only paid attention to the definition of equity that fattened their pockets—even many who made claims to care about sustainable agriculture or underrepresented entrepreneurs. I didn't want to owe money, but I also didn't want to owe someone else my direction, my joy, or my peace of mind. That meant I had to be patient, intentional, and creative. I had to build what I could with what I had, trusting that slow didn't mean small—it just meant sustainable.

I've owed before. Owed bills I couldn't pay. Time I didn't have. Energy I couldn't spare. I know the weight of that kind of burden—how it creeps into your chest at night, squeezes your creativity, clouds your judgment, and turns passion into pressure. So, when it came to building Green Heffa Farms, I chose to take my time. I knew I had a lot to learn—how to care for the land, how to grow the plants, how to extract and explain their benefits, and how to run a boutique farming business and brand in a way that felt aligned with my values and my sanity.

I didn't want to move so fast that I lost sight of why I started. I didn't want to be so busy "scaling" that I skipped the part where I learned. And I especially didn't want to end up beholden to anyone—not a lender, not an investor, not even an ideal I no longer believed in. Now, let me be real: You may choose differently. And that's okay. Many folks launching a business pursue outside funding. That can look like loans, venture capital (VC), or social impact funding. Let's break those down:

Loans are borrowed money that must be paid back, often with interest. Whether it's from a bank, a government program, or a micro-lender, a loan puts a clock on your business decisions. It can help you move faster, but it can also add a layer of stress—because lenders want their money back whether you're ready or not.

Venture Capital typically comes from private investors who are looking for high-growth businesses that will bring big returns. They're not just giving you money—they're usually buying a piece of your business. This often comes with strings attached: equity, control, and pressure to scale quickly. VC can be transformative, but it can also change the very DNA of your company.

Social Impact Funding or Grant Money—which might come from philanthropic organizations, mission-driven funds, or government programs—is usually aimed at businesses that promise to create some kind of positive change. These can be less predatory than traditional funding models, but they still often require performance metrics, impact reports, or strict deliverables.

Each path has its place. Each comes with trade-offs. The key is to know what kind of growth feels right for you and what you're willing to give up in order to get it. Don't forget you can always layer resources. In fact, that's the smartest move you can make. I'll give you an example from Green Heffa Farms. A couple of years ago, I launched a crowdfunding campaign with a $50,000 goal to fund our high tunnel. The campaign initially gained traction, raising over $6,000, but it hit the plateau that many grassroots efforts do. Then came a new opportunity: I was named the inaugural 2025 Good Farmer US Awardee by Davines Group and the Rodale Institute.

The $10,000 award was applied strategically. Combined with the $6K from the campaign, I purchased a high tunnel measuring 30 feet by 98.5 feet (a total of 2,955 square feet) at a cost of $11,675. (I negotiated free freight shipping for a brand mention in my newsletter plus used the farmer tax exemption benefit for a total savings of $5,000 off the original price.)

Because I had already done the planning work and had an approved EQIP (see page 138) contract in place (more on that in a bit), I qualified for reimbursement at a rate of $5.21 per square foot—up to 3,839 square feet. Since the tunnel was 2,955 square feet, that could have equaled $15,402.55. But

Farmer Cee visiting the Rodale Institute's European Regenerative Organic Center as part of the 2025 Good Farmer Award US. *Photo courtesy of the Rodale Institute.*

EQIP reimburses based on the lesser of the flat rate or actual cost, so the maximum reimbursed was $11,675, the documented cost of the structure. I already know where that money is going: straight toward a zero-turn mower to keep our land in shape. This is what it looks like to layer your resources: crowdfunding, award funding, and cost-share reimbursement—each one serving a specific purpose in a broader strategy. By being resourceful, proactive, and intentional, you can layer available resources. Every dollar has a job. Every opportunity gets leveraged. And none of it happens by accident.

If you're looking to pursue grants, loans, or impact investment, build relationships before you need the check. Make a list of funders (like those focused on Black women, sustainable agriculture, food justice, or the like). Follow their work and attend their webinars or events, or reach out with a warm intro—not an ask. And keep them updated as you grow (short updates with wins, new launches, or collaborations go a long way). Let's get into all the possible outside funding sources.

Venture Capital

Here's something else you need to know, especially if you're a Black woman reading this: Investment dollars are not evenly distributed. In fact, according to a McKinsey report, in 2022, women-founded teams received 1.9 percent of

Green Heffa Farms' first structure was a high tunnel turned into a greenhouse.

venture capital funds, and only 0.1 percent went to Black and Latinx women founders combined.

Further, a *TechCrunch* article noted that in 2022, Black founders overall received just 1 percent of all venture capital funding, amounting to approximately $2.3 billion out of $215.9 billion. According to Project Diane, a landmark study on Black and Latinx women founders, Black women raised an average of just $42,000 in venture capital—compared with $2.1 million for the average start-up. That's not a funding gap. That's a funding canyon.

So, when people tell you to "just get investors," remember—access is not equal. And too often, we're pressured to contort ourselves or dilute our mission just to seem "fundable." That's not freedom—that's performance. Now, there are some funders out there who are doing great work, so do your research; the field and opportunities are always changing. Here are a few venture capital and impact investors that I would suggest looking into:

Backstage Capital: Founded by Arlan Hamilton, this venture capital firm has invested around $20 million in nearly two hundred start-ups, focusing on underrepresented founders, including Black women.

Fearless Fund: Co-founded by Arian Simone, this fund is dedicated to investing in women-of-color-led businesses, providing capital, mentorship, and resources.

Wocstar Fund: Led by Gayle Jennings-O'Byrne, this venture capital firm invests in women of color and diverse inclusive teams, aiming to empower women-of-color-led start-ups.

Impact X Capital: Based in the U.K., this firm focuses on investing in underrepresented entrepreneurs, particularly people of color and women, across Europe.

Acumen: This nonprofit impact investment fund focuses on investing in social enterprises serving low-income individuals, including those in agriculture sectors.

Camelback Ventures: A nonprofit accelerator that supports underrepresented founders and fund managers through coaching, community, and access to capital, with a strong focus on closing opportunity gaps in entrepreneurship and education innovation.

Potlikker Capital: An impact-driven investment firm focused on deploying catalytic capital to support sustainable food systems and historically underinvested communities, particularly in the American South.

Let your growth be organic. Let it be aligned. Let it come from a place of clarity, not desperation. Your farm, your business, your brand—it deserves to be built on your terms.

Slow is not a setback. It's a strategy.

Let's Talk About Grants

If only I had a dollar for every time someone asked me about the "magic grants" that would supposedly fund a Black woman starting a farm . . . Look, maybe at some point the government paid for certain people to start farms. I wasn't there. But today? The likelihood that a government grant will pay to start your farm from scratch is slim. However—and this is key—there are grants that, used strategically, can help you grow, strengthen, and expand your farm. At Green Heffa Farms, I've written successful grant proposals that helped us move our mission forward. Our very first grant helped fund our first structure.

So, once you start—even small—you'll be amazed at how fast you can build momentum. Start where you are. Plant your seeds—literally and financially—and watch the doors begin to open. When used the right way, grants can be a powerful tool in your financial tool kit.

Boutique farming requires clarity of direction and the wisdom to pivot when needed.

But first, let's be clear: Grants are not guaranteed. They are not easy money. And they are almost never fast. Grants are often competitive, strategic, and specific. They come with rules. They come with reporting. And sometimes, even after you've crossed every *t* and dotted every *i*, things can still shift—especially when you're dealing with government grants (ask me how I know). I've seen firsthand how a change in administration or political priorities can pull the rug right out from under a project that was fully aligned just a year earlier. Still, grants can be worth it—if you understand what they are, how they work, and how to use them to supplement (not substitute for) the foundation you are building.

In this section, I'm going to share the different types of grants you might encounter, where to find grant opportunities (popular and lesser-known sources), how to know if a grant is a good fit for your farm, and tips for writing winning grant applications. Plus, I'll pull back the curtain on what it's really like to navigate government, foundation, and corporate grants as a Black woman farmer. While I, Farmer Cee, have not personally received funding through all the resources shared, it's important to keep them on your radar—others have successfully navigated those systems even if I haven't.

Here's the reality: As a Black woman, especially in agriculture, navigating the grant space can feel like entering a room you weren't invited to. We are underrepresented in decision-making spaces, and too often, our labor and impact are overlooked or undervalued in funding conversations. Some grant reviewers may have never even imagined a Black woman owning and operating a boutique farm, let alone branding products, running education programs, or practicing regenerative agriculture. This can create a subtle, but real, barrier. It often means there is an expectation that we over-explain, over-credential, and work twice as hard to prove legitimacy.

That's why your story matters. Funders are increasingly recognizing the importance of equity and representation in agriculture. More grants are asking about cultural relevance, community impact, and sustainability—areas where many Black women farmers shine naturally. There may be an opportunity to center your identity, your unique lived experience, and your community impact as strengths in your application. You are not a side note to this movement. You are the future of farming.

Applying for grants can be a game changer for your farming operation, providing essential funding to support growth, innovation, and sustainability. However, grants should not be relied upon as your primary income stream—they are best leveraged as supplements to your broader business strategy. Think of grants as accelerators rather than foundations for your farm's success. Grants may vary in their restrictions. Some may be unrestricted, allowing you to use the funds as needed, while others may be tightly controlled, requiring detailed reporting and proof of specific uses. It's critical to thoroughly understand the expectations and requirements for each grant you pursue. When used strategically, grants can provide much-needed resources to build and expand your boutique farm while preserving your independence and long-term vision.

Key Considerations Before Applying for Grants

Before diving into the world of grant applications, there are a few crucial points to understand. When you are reviewing a grant application, pay close attention to the fine print. The moment you realize you do not meet a key eligibility criterion, move on. Eligibility criteria are legally binding. Grant makers are legally obligated to uphold the requirements they publish. If they say you must have a three-year business history, and you don't—applying is a waste of your resources. Focus your efforts on grants where you are truly a match. Grant writing is labor-intensive and better spent on opportunities where you have a real shot at success.

Understand what areas of your farm operation can be considered fundable. For instance, if your farm has technological needs, look for technology grants that can assist you in upgrading your equipment or improving your processes. Take inventory of the challenges you face and the areas where funding would be most beneficial. This could include infrastructure improvements, sustainable practices, educational programs, or community engagement initiatives.

Most grants require that the applicant be a registered legal business entity (LLC, S corp, et cetera). Very few grants are awarded to individuals. Some grants are exclusively for nonprofit organizations. However, plenty of opportunities exist for for-profit boutique farms, especially those committed to sustainability, education, health, or community development. It's important to only pursue grants that align with your business model and mission. Chasing every opportunity can spread you thin and waste valuable time and energy. Last, partnering with other farmers or organizations can make your project more appealing to funders and increase your chances of securing larger grants.

Grants come from a wide variety of sources. Knowing where to look can greatly improve your chances of finding the right fit.

GOVERNMENT GRANTS

- Local (city or county programs supporting agriculture and small businesses)
- State (agricultural development, rural business development)
- Federal (USDA programs like the Value-Added Producer Grant, NRCS conservation programs)

FOUNDATION GRANTS

Public Foundations (for example, community foundations supporting food security initiatives) are nonprofit organizations that receive funding from multiple sources (government, individuals, or corporations) and often run their own programs or grant them to other organizations. Public foundations are accountable to a broad community of donors rather than a single family or individual. An example is the Ford Foundation, which receives funding from many donors and supports initiatives in social justice, human rights, and poverty alleviation.

Private Foundations (for example, family foundations funding educational or agricultural projects) are nonprofit organizations typically funded and controlled by an individual, family, or corporation. Private foundations generally make grants to other charitable organizations rather than running their own programs. An example is the J. M. Kaplan Fund, which operates grant programs focusing on the environment, heritage conservation, and social justice.

Family Foundations (often smaller but highly mission-driven) are a type of private foundation specifically created and controlled by a family. Family members usually serve on the board and guide grant-making decisions. An example is the Shumaker Family Foundation, which allocates funds to support endeavors in social justice, education, and environmental justice.

CORPORATE GRANTS

- Corporations often fund grants that align with their business interests (for example, organic food companies funding regenerative agriculture projects). Many corporations have affiliated foundations that distribute philanthropic dollars (such as Patagonia's grant programs).

Sowing Grant Success

Securing grants requires careful planning, research, and alignment with funder priorities. By understanding the types of grants available, being creative in your research, identifying your fundable needs, and effectively positioning your farm in applications, you can significantly enhance your chances of receiving funding. As demonstrated by my own journey, persistence and strategic alignment can lead to successful grant applications that propel your farming operation forward.

As we learned in chapter 8, building relationships with funders and other grant recipients can lead to valuable insights and opportunities. Attend networking events, workshops, and seminars to connect with individuals and organizations that can help you navigate the grant landscape. But be selective about what you attend. Do not become a serial conference or event attendee

Farmer Cee receiving the Good Farmer Award US in 2025. *Photo courtesy of the Rodale Institute.*

or a constant course enroller. I see it happen all the time—people end up becoming parts of cliques disguised as community but never really move closer to their dream.

When applying for grants, remember this: It's okay to ask questions. In fact, it's smart. Grant program officers are there to help ensure that applications are complete, eligible, and competitive. Don't be afraid to reach out for clarification if something is unclear. A thoughtful, well-prepared inquiry not only helps you submit a stronger application but may also make your name more familiar to the person reviewing it. That's not a guarantee of funding, of course, but professionalism and clear communication go a long way in building a positive impression.

That said, make sure your questions are genuine and substantive. Read the grant guidelines thoroughly before you reach out. You want to demonstrate that you respect their time and have done your homework. Avoid asking things that are already clearly stated in the materials. The goal is to engage, not annoy. In this space, being memorable for the right reasons matters.

Never use a generic template to just copy and paste information into applications. While you can certainly revamp existing content, always customize your answers to the specific funder's mission and language. With that said, there are some solid components that you can have developed in advance, such as your organizational overview, relevant résumés, and the like. Here are some other tips to keep in mind:

Tell a Compelling Story: Funders fund people and stories, and not just projects. Even government grant applications are often reviewed by people. The ability to paint a vivid picture of who you are, your farm's journey, and the community impact of your work will prove invaluable.

Focus on Outcomes: Funders want to know what their money will achieve. Make sure your outcomes align with their goals. Be specific about the outcomes you will deliver, not just the activities you will complete.

Stay Organized: Maintain a spreadsheet or project management board that tracks application deadlines, requirements, amounts, contacts, and notes.

Collect Your Documents Early: A grant can require that you include a business plan, tax documents, documents verifying your business structure, budgets, letters of support, and certifications. Have these ready in advance.

Show Your Work: It's always helpful to share examples of previous funding or projects that were successful—in my case, the initial $5,000 from Gaia Herbs for a greenhouse, which laid the foundation for our operations.

Budget Carefully: Your proposed budget should be realistic, detailed, and clearly tied to the goals of the project. Never inflate or guesstimate numbers. Try to prevent ambiguous budget lines such as "contingency" unless the grant specifies it is allowable.

A Juneteenth event hosted by Farmer Cee and Green Heffa Farms featured small plates sourced from Black farmers across Afro-Carolina. Events like this are part of Green Heffa's story and mission.

Proofread Meticulously: Typos and careless mistakes can make funders question your attention to detail. Always have someone else review your application before submission.

Meet Every Deadline: Late applications are usually disqualified automatically. Set internal deadlines earlier than the final due date.

Be Prepared for Reporting: Winning a grant often comes with reporting obligations. Be ready to track your progress and provide updates as required.

It's always a good idea to start grant application drafts early. Rushed applications rarely win, so give yourself plenty of time. Always attach letters of support from partners or community organizations if allowed. It shows funders that you are part of a broader ecosystem. And if you win, treat the grant as a partnership. Funders want to feel like partners in your success. Stay transparent and keep them updated on your successes.

Do the Deep Research—It Matters

Here's another important truth: Never chase money that isn't aligned with your mission. It's tempting, especially in the early stages, to apply for any grant that seems remotely applicable. But don't bend your vision to fit funding. Shifting your farm's goals just to secure a grant can pull you off course and create more stress than success. The administrative burden, required reporting, and deliverables that come with funding are real—and if the money isn't supporting your core values, you'll feel the strain.

Project Management

Consider using a project management platform like Asana or Trello. These tools are great for visual thinkers and help you break big goals into actionable tasks. Whether you're planning your editorial calendar, tracking a product development timeline, or mapping out a seasonal event, they keep everything in one place and give you that satisfying feeling of checking something off when it's done. If you want a more flexible, all-in-one space, Notion is a fantastic option. It combines notes, databases, task lists, and calendars into a single workspace. You can use it to outline your yearly vision, document your growing practices, organize recipes, or keep track of vendor contacts. The key is choosing a system that fits how your brain works, then sticking with it long enough to make it a habit.

Instead, focus on opportunities that strengthen what you're already doing or where you authentically want to grow. Let your mission be your compass. When you apply for funding that's in harmony with your purpose, your passion shows, and your proposals are stronger because of it. Trust that the right money will meet you where you are when you lead with clarity and intention.

One of the most overlooked but powerful strategies in grant writing is targeted research. Don't just look for grants broadly related to agriculture—dig deeper into opportunities that prioritize you. Seek out grants that support your identity, community, or geographic region. For instance, there are grants specifically for Black women entrepreneurs, beginning farmers, veteran-owned operations, or Indigenous growers. If you hold any of these identities, those are potential lanes of funding where your story and mission are especially valued.

Also, pay close attention to regional or place-based funding opportunities. A grant aimed at improving access to healthy food in the southeastern US, for example, could be a perfect match if your farm supports community wellness or food justice efforts. These kinds of grants not only align with the broader goals of your farm but often include outreach, education, or community development—things you might already be doing. Local foundations, regional agricultural nonprofits, city and county government initiatives, electric co-ops, even your local conservation district may offer funding that's tailored to the needs of your community. These programs are often less competitive than national grants and may offer more flexible funding terms, shorter applications, and better access to support staff.

Strong research lays the foundation for a winning grant strategy. Set aside regular time to search through agricultural funding databases, community bulletins, and newsletters from organizations like USDA, Appropriate Technology Transfer for Rural Areas (ATTRA), or your local extension office. Follow relevant organizations on social media and subscribe to their mailing lists—you'd be surprised how many smaller, time-sensitive opportunities are shared there first.

The more intentional and strategic you are in researching grants, the more likely you are to find funding that truly fits—and to avoid wasting time chasing money that doesn't. When searching for grants, think outside the box. While there are specific agricultural grants, many other funding opportunities may align with your farm's mission and needs. Look outside of agriculture. Boutique farmers can qualify for grants in sectors beyond farming, such as:

- Technology (use of farm management software, irrigation innovations, and so on)
- Education (workshops)
- Small business development
- Environmental conservation

- Health and wellness (especially if you're growing medicinal herbs or organic produce)
- Food security and access
- Social justice and community empowerment
- Workforce development

In the next few sections, we'll cover how to write winning grant applications for both government and corporate/foundation grants. Here are some trusted online resources to explore some of the grants out there:

Grants.gov: The primary portal for finding and applying for federal government grants, it's ideal for USDA, conservation, and small business grants: www.grants.gov

USDA Grants and Loans: Specifically targeted to agricultural businesses, including small farms, organic farming, rural development, and food access initiatives: www.farmers.gov/fund

Foundation Directory Online (FDO): A massive database of foundations and the grants they've awarded (a subscription is required, but some libraries offer free access): fconline.foundationcenter.org

Local Extension Services: Your local cooperative extension office often shares grant opportunities relevant to your state or county; search "[your state] cooperative extension"

Small Business Development Centers (SBDCs): These offer free resources and can guide you toward grants for small business and agriculture-related ventures: www.sbdcnet.org/find-your-local-sbdc-office

Black Farmer Fund: A funding resource designed to nurture community wealth and health by investing in agricultural systems in the Northeast: www.blackfarmerfund.org

I would also recommend exploring these lesser-known places for opportunities that might be less competitive:

JustFund: A platform designed to make philanthropy more equitable, where grassroots groups (including farms) can find funding opportunities: www.justfund.us

SARE (Sustainable Agriculture Research and Education): Offers grants directly for farmer-led research and sustainable farming initiatives: www.sare.org/grants

LISC (Local Initiatives Support Corporation): LISC funds a wide variety of community-based enterprises—including farms and food projects—particularly in underserved areas; they often partner with local governments or banks to offer grant opportunities, technical assistance, and loans: www.lisc.org

New Voices Fund: New Voices is committed to funding businesses owned by women of color, especially in wellness, beauty, and lifestyle sectors; if your boutique farm creates value-added herbal products or has a wellness-focused brand, this could be a strong fit: www.newvoicesfund.com

The FruitGuys Community Fund: This nonprofit offers small, accessible grants (typically under $5,000) to small farms focused on sustainability, food justice, and ecological resilience; they fund real things—from fencing and hoop houses to pollinator hedgerows: fruitguyscommunityfund.org

Patagonia Environmental Grants: If your farm has a strong environmental or land stewardship component, Patagonia funds grassroots work: www.patagonia.com/actionworks/grants/

Amber Grant for Women: Monthly $10K grants are awarded to women entrepreneurs—and boutique farmers definitely qualify: www.womensnet.net

Resourceful Communities Program (North Carolina–specific but a good model): This program supports grassroots projects in rural communities, particularly Black- and Indigenous-led farms and food initiatives: www.conservationfund.org/our-work/resourceful-communities

Sky High Farm Grants: An annual grant program that awards funding to individuals or organizations working in agriculture, food justice, and land sovereignty: www.skyhighfarm.org/grants

Also note that many counties and cities have community foundations that quietly give small grants to local businesses and projects. Your local or regional community foundation could be one of the most overlooked sources of support. Many offer small business or community impact grants that align with your work—especially if you're creating jobs, improving food access, or stewarding land in underserved communities. Search by county, region, or state—then sign up for their newsletters, attend events, and build relationships.

Writing Winning Government Grant Applications

When it comes to government grants, you have to master the art of developing compelling, data-driven content. This is not just about being clear and concise—it's about understanding how to present your farm in a way that is credible, impactful, and aligned with public interests.

Government agencies fund solutions to problems they have identified. Don't just talk about what you want to do—talk about why it matters. Instead of: "We want to expand our herb production," say: "There is a 35 percent year-over-year increase in consumer demand for medicinal herbs (American

Where to Find Great Data for Grant Applications

If you need reliable data for a grant application, I recommend the following sources:

- USDA Agricultural Census (race and gender breakdowns)
- City or county economic development strategies
- USDA, Economic Research Service (ERS), and National Agricultural Statistics Service (NASS) data sets
- Academic research reports on agriculture and minority producers
- Market trend reports (such as IBISWorld and Mintel)—often available free through your library

Botanical Council, 2023), but BIPOC-owned farms represent less than 2 percent of the suppliers. Expanding Green Heffa Farms' herb production will help meet this growing demand while diversifying local agricultural economies." Good data makes your grant application believable and fundable. Always tie your ideas back to real numbers from credible sources.

Government agencies love numbers because numbers can be audited. Use quantitative language instead of qualitative. For example: "We will increase herb production by 25 percent within eighteen months, expanding our reach to two hundred additional customers," is measurable, whereas "our customers will feel more connected to our farm" is a nice sentiment but not measurable. Similarly, objectives should be specific, measurable, and achievable—not vague dreams. Language like "we hope to grow our farm" is a flimsy way of describing your goals. Instead, use strong language to state your intentions. For example, "Green Heffa Farms will install a new 500-gallon rainwater catchment system within six months, reducing our reliance on our electrical well by 30 percent."

Finally, government grants often restrict what you can spend money on. If professional services (grant administration, accounting, legal) are allowed, budget for them. It's also important to pay attention to limits on salaries, construction, equipment, or land acquisition. Many grants might prohibit using grant funds for these categories.

Corporate and Foundation Grant Applications

Corporate and foundation grants are a different game—and you need a slightly different strategy. Corporations and foundations want to fund projects that align with their brand values or philanthropic goals, so as you look for compatible grants, it's a good idea to emphasize mission alignment. For example, if a company's focus is on sustainability, highlight how your regenerative practices reduce soil erosion and build biodiversity.

Unlike government grants, corporate and foundation funders often want to feel something, so it's important to tell a powerful story. Personalize your application by weaving in your journey, your community and economic impact, and your vision. For example: "As a Black-woman-owned farm in rural North Carolina, Green Heffa Farms is building a regenerative agriculture model that not only produces premium herbs but also reconnects our community to its ancestral plant knowledge."

Even though you should be emotive, don't skimp on the numbers. Foundations need data to justify the grants to their boards. For example, "With grant support, Green Heffa Farms can expand our pollinator garden, increasing native bee populations by 40 percent within two seasons (source: USDA Natural Resources Conservation Service)." Finally, many corporate and foundation grants have tight word counts. Get to the point, make it easy for them to understand your impact, and outline clear, trackable outcomes.

Subgrants Are a Smart Play

Let me be real with you: Not every boutique farm wants to carry the weight of writing and managing a grant. And we shouldn't have to. Also, for those of us with businesses based on values, there is often alignment with the work of nonprofit organizations. That's where subgrantee relationships come in—a smart and strategic way to access funding without taking on all the administrative burden.

At Green Heffa Farms, we partnered with a nonprofit that was awarded a federal grant. They brought us in as a sub-awardee written directly into their

Real Talk

Writing a successful grant isn't about sounding fancy. It's about making a clear, convincing, data-backed case that you are the best investment for that funding. Grant writing is both an art and a science. It's about strategic alignment, excellent communication, and persistence. You will not win every grant you apply for—and that's okay. Every application is a learning opportunity, helping you sharpen your vision, your pitch, and your farm's path forward. Remember: You are not just asking for money. You are inviting someone to invest in your dream—and that's a powerful thing.

proposal. Our role? To create original educational and social media content that supported the goals of the grant. They handled the paperwork and reporting; we handled the messaging, content, and community connection. We were compensated fairly and didn't have to manage the entire grant process ourselves. That's what I call a strategic alignment. But let me also say this: Just because you're a subgrantee doesn't mean you should be silent, sidelined, or shortchanged.

Many grant-funded spaces still have a distance to go before they are truly inclusive. There are grantors, funders, companies, and "partners" out there that will smile in your face; use your image, name, or numbers to check a "diversity" box; then turn around and exclude you from real decision making or fair compensation. Underrepresented voices are often brought in as "community partners" but not given the same level of respect or pay as institutional or corporate collaborators. That's why relationship building and accountability matter. You need to know who you're working with. Before you agree to be written into anyone's grant, ask the hard questions: How are decisions made? What is the compensation structure? Will we be co-branded, white-labeled, or green-washed? Will my voice be valued—or just used?

It's okay to expect transparency. It's okay to walk away if it doesn't feel right. And it's absolutely okay to hold organizations accountable, especially when public dollars are involved. When you're looking for potential partners, start with alignment: Reach out to nonprofits, HBCUs, co-ops, and community health organizations that share your values. Educate them on how your farm's work intersects with their mission. Ask to be written into grants before the proposal is submitted. That way your contribution—and compensation—are baked into the budget.

Make sure expectations, deliverables, and payments are clearly outlined in writing. Verbal agreements can get lost when the grant checks start flowing, so have your own lawyer review subaward agreements if you can. And once you've been awarded a grant, don't just show up for the check. Show up to the table. Participate. Stay visible. Build trust—and demand reciprocity. We are not sidekicks in this work. We are leaders. And subgrants, when done right, can help you show up in your full brilliance without carrying the whole load. So yes—know your worth. Guard your time. And never let gatekeepers keep you from the garden.

Cost-Share Programs

Let's talk about one of the most overlooked resources available to farmers, especially new, small-scale, and underserved ones: cost-share funding. Cost-share programs allow you to share the cost of implementing a project or practice with an agency—most often a government entity like the USDA. Cost-share funds are reimbursed after you've paid out-of-pocket and completed the work. This means you need to front the money initially and navigate some paperwork, but the payoff can be substantial. These programs are rooted in the idea of public investment in conservation, soil health, and sustainable land management. And while I don't walk around with a mindset of entitlement, I fully believe that if a resource exists—especially one funded by public dollars—then Black women farmers deserve equitable access as a rightful share.

Keep in mind that cost-share programs are not a silver bullet. There are trade-offs. You need up-front capital, the paperwork can be time consuming, and reimbursements aren't immediate—they may take several months. But if your goal is to build something sustainable without burying yourself in debt, cost-share is one of the most powerful tools available.

EQIP: Environmental Quality Incentives Program

Remember how I got reimbursed for my high tunnel? One of the most well-known cost-share programs is EQIP, run by the USDA's Natural Resources Conservation Service (NRCS). EQIP supports farmers who want to adopt conservation practices, and it's designed to help reduce environmental

EQIP in Practice: Timeline and Numbers

Sample Timeline (based on Green Heffa Farms)

- January—Meet with NRCS, get initial farm visit
- February—Complete your conservation plan
- March—Submit your EQIP application
- May—Get approved and sign your EQIP contract
- Summer—Complete project (for example, build your high tunnel)
- Fall—Submit documentation for reimbursement
- Winter—Receive funds, reinvest into next infrastructure need

Sample Cost Breakdown

- High tunnel kit (30 × 98.5 feet): $11,675
- Site prep: $2,000
- Labor : $2,500
- Permits/miscellaneous: $500
- Total investment: $16,675
- Expected reimbursement from EQIP: $11,675

impact while increasing long-term sustainability. Practices supported under EQIP include installing high tunnels, improving irrigation, managing nutrients, building composting systems, planting pollinator habitats, and more. To qualify for EQIP, you'll need:

- A farm number, which you can get through your local USDA FSA office
- A conservation plan, which you create with your local NRCS agent
- Documentation proving ownership or lease of your land
- Clear goals that align with EQIP conservation practices

If you're a beginning, socially disadvantaged, limited-resource, or veteran farmer, you may receive higher cost-share rates or priority consideration—an important reason not to count yourself out.

Other Cost-Share Opportunities

EQIP isn't the only game in town. At the time of writing this, there are a few more programs worth exploring:

CSP (Conservation Stewardship Program): Supports ongoing conservation improvements on working lands

REAP (Rural Energy for America Program): Assists with energy efficiency and renewable energy systems

State and Local Programs: Many local governments offer their own conservation cost-shares via soil and water conservation districts

Nonprofits and Foundations: Some organizations offer private cost-share or matching-fund models for underserved growers

You don't have to be perfect. But you do have to be prepared. Cost-share programs reward planning, intention, and follow-through. Keep your records tight, communicate with your NRCS contact, and document everything. When done right, these programs can help you take real steps toward building the farm you envision—on your terms, and in your own voice.

Crowdfunding: Letting Community Invest in Your Vision

I want to talk to you about something that's been both humbling and empowering in my journey as a boutique farmer: crowdfunding. When I first launched Green Heffa Farms, I knew I would need some support with early infrastructure—things like irrigation, fencing, and basic supplies that add up fast. Instead of going straight to the bank or applying for loans I wasn't quite ready for, I decided to try a crowdfunding campaign on IFundWomen. My goal was to raise $5,000.

By the end of the campaign, we had brought in over $11,000.

Now, let me tell you something real. I've raised millions of dollars before—for causes, organizations, missions that promised to make the world a better place. I know what it takes to tell a compelling story, to write a winning pitch, to make the right ask. So, stepping into crowdfunding for my own business, I thought I was ready. But nothing prepared me for how different it would feel. Why? Because I'm a Black woman farmer. And this society still struggles to fully value Black people, women, and especially farmers. This is not a victim mentality. This is the cold, hard truth. As a Black woman farmer, you're working uphill in a landscape where people don't always see the worth of what you're building—even when you lay it out plain. I had to adjust my own expectations.

I'm not willing to beg. I'm not going to lie or scam to raise funds. And I'm definitely not going to commodify my pain to make folks feel more generous. What I am willing to do is show up, be honest, share the vision, and keep pushing—because the people who are meant to support you will. And their support means more because it comes without strings, shame, or spectacle.

Crowdfunding isn't just about the money—though the money helps. It's also about letting your community participate in what you're building, offering a debt-free way to grow your business, and giving folks a chance to invest in something good—sustainable products, food, healing, land, and equity. Creating a story-based connection can turn crowdfunding supporters into lifelong customers. It invites people to become co-dreamers, even if all they can give is $10. That connection is invaluable—not just for your farm but for your spirit.

There's an art to crowdfunding, especially for a business. It's not about putting on a performance. It's about sharing your "why" in a way that invites people into your purpose. Tell your story—not the polished version you think funders want but the real one. The one with soil on your hands and hope in your voice. Realness resonates. When people sense authenticity, they are far more likely to contribute—not just with their dollars but with their hearts.

Plan your outreach. A successful campaign doesn't live on social media alone. Use email, texts, phone calls, your website, and any networks you're part of. Don't assume people saw the post. Follow up with kindness and clarity. Be visible. Be consistent. Be courageous enough to remind people that they can help grow something powerful. Don't forget to celebrate every single contribution. Whether it's $5 or $500, someone chose *you*. That deserves acknowledgment and gratitude. It can be as simple as a shout-out, a DM, or a thank-you video in your garden. People remember how you made them feel, and small farms thrive on genuine relationships.

Offer rewards that reflect your values and your work. These can be products, handwritten notes, behind-the-scenes updates, or special experiences like virtual herb walks or a thank-you garden planted in supporters' names. The goal isn't to overextend yourself trying to produce merch—it's to share a meaningful piece of your farm's soul.

Pace yourself emotionally. Crowdfunding can stir up all kinds of feelings: vulnerability, self-doubt, even exhaustion. Asking for support, even when fully justified, can be emotionally taxing—especially when you've been conditioned to feel like you have to do everything on your own. But here's the truth: Crowdfunding isn't begging. It's brave. It's one of the few financial tools where you get to set your own terms, lead with your values, and build capital in community. You're not just raising funds; you're raising awareness. You're showing the world that boutique, Black-woman-led farming is not only viable—it's vibrant. Every yes is a reminder that what you're growing matters. It's one of the few spaces where you get to invite people to stand beside you as you build something from soil and soul—and every time they say yes, it's a reminder that what you're growing is worth it.

Let me also say this: I don't use GoFundMe for my business. That's not to knock anyone who does—GoFundMe can be a lifeline for emergencies and personal hardship. But for my farm, I want people to understand they're not giving to a charity case. They're investing in a business rooted in values, purpose, and legacy. That's why platforms specifically created for crowdfunding for businesses work better for me. They let me tell a full story—one that centers possibility, not pity. For a list of these platforms, see "Resources" at the end of this book.

Miscellaneous External Funding

In addition to cost-share programs and grants, you should be aware of a few other ways to get outside investment or save money on your farm. First, farmer-specific tax exemptions can make it easier to afford some essential farm inputs. And second, donor-advised funds (DAFs) and program-related investments (PRIs) are less traditional routes but worth exploring as your farm matures or if it takes on nonprofit or mission-aligned elements.

Farmer-Specific Tax Exemptions

Tax exemptions can save real money. Depending on your state, farmers may be exempt from paying sales tax on items used directly in agricultural production—such as seeds, feed, fertilizer, equipment, and even utilities. This can add up quickly and significantly lower your operating costs. To qualify, you typically need a farm number or agricultural exemption certificate and proof that your

Real Talk

Subscribe to newsletters from grant databases, nonprofit associations, agricultural alliances, and even social justice or environmental organizations. Many share grant alerts that you might not find otherwise.

purchases are for qualified farm use. I also recommend keeping clean, detailed receipts. If you're ever audited, proper documentation makes the difference between owing and saving.

Some states also offer property tax relief or income tax deductions for qualifying farm operations. Be sure to check with your state's department of revenue or agriculture to understand what exemptions are available to you and how to apply. These tax benefits aren't loopholes—they're designed to support food production and farming sustainability. Don't leave them on the table.

Donor-Advised Funds

Think of DAFs as charitable savings accounts that wealthy individuals or companies set up. They can direct funds to causes donors care about—including agriculture, equity, and sustainability—if they are made aware of your work. You can find DAFs through community foundations, financial institutions like Fidelity Charitable or DAFgiving360, or donors who prioritize values-aligned giving. Relationships with these foundations or donors can open these doors. Impact donors often support individuals they discover via media, social campaigns, or word of mouth. Sharing your farm's journey, mission, and successes makes it easier for DAF holders to connect with your work. My advice is: Tell your story publicly.

Program-Related Investments

PRIs are a way foundations invest in for-profit businesses that serve a social purpose—like food justice, environmental impact, or rural revitalization. The returns are often lower than traditional investments, but that's by design; foundations are prioritizing impact over profit. PRIs often come with mentorship, network access, and long-term support, making them ideal for farms building scalable, mission-driven brands. Some foundations offer both PRIs and grants, so cultivating relationships with foundations that have PRI programs can be a dual opportunity for funding and strategic guidance. Of course, you can also do an internet search on both DAFs and PRIs to learn of available funding opportunities.

CHAPTER 10

Planting Profitability

It is important to build your own lane and not wait for permission.

—Rihanna

There are so many ways to generate revenue as a boutique farmer or wellness-focused entrepreneur—ways that align with your lifestyle, values, and vision. The main categories are the sale of products (digital and physical), social media and brand partnerships, and events and hosting.

Digital Products

For many small farmers, the introduction of digital products has become a critical piece in diversifying revenue. These products provide a way to generate income with minimal overhead, leveraging your expertise and passion for farming to create value beyond what's grown in your fields. My first successful digital product was the Big Hemping course, a comprehensive training program for small-scale farmers looking to enter the legal hemp industry. I later added a digital course on grant writing for small farmers and even digital yard signs I created on Canva.

This yard sign offered by Green Heffa Farms is an example of a digital product.

The key to creating a successful digital product is focusing on a niche that combines your expertise with a market need. Each digital product has been a layer of support for our farm's growth and sustainability, giving us more tools and knowledge while also strengthening Green Heffa Farms as a center for education and empowerment. Digital products are not only scalable but also allow you to share your unique story and expertise far beyond your farm's physical footprint. They are an excellent way to expand your impact and revenue without being tied to the limitations of farming seasons or in-person events. You do not need to reach millions. You only need to reach those who want what you have to offer. Creating a successful digital product for your boutique farming business includes:

Identifying the Pain Points: What challenges or gaps in knowledge do you constantly see your community struggling with? For me, it was the legal complexities and start-up nuances of hemp farming.

Designing a Solution: The heart of any successful digital product is a clear, step-by-step curriculum that addresses the key pressure points your audience faces. Here's a little tip for organization: I love incorporating acronyms or number-and-letter combos. For example, in Big Hemping, "BIG" stood for Branding, Infrastructure, Growth. Another framework I use is the 5 V's: Values, Vision, Visuals, Voice, and Validity. These simple structures help learners remember core concepts and keep the curriculum focused.

Building Credibility: It was essential to establish myself as a trusted voice, and that required being transparent, sharing my own mistakes, and illustrating my wins.

The best part about digital products? The possibilities are unlimited, and start-up costs are usually nominal.

Physical Products

Creating and selling physical products can deepen your connection to customers by allowing them to experience your farm's mission tangibly. But it can also be a high-risk endeavor. Choosing the right product, managing production costs, and understanding your market

Farmer Cee wearing farm-branded merchandise. *Photo courtesy of Nate Burrows.*

are critical. The sale of physical products is the most common—and often first—source of income for boutique farms. You may have some products in mind already if you've already developed your farm concept, but below are some product ideas to jump-start your imagination if need be.

HERBAL AND BOTANICAL GOODS

- Dried herbs (culinary or medicinal)
- Herbal tea blends
- Salves, balms, and body butters
- Tinctures, tonics, and syrups
- Aromatherapy oils or rollers
- Herbal smoking blends

NATURAL SKINCARE AND BODY PRODUCTS

- Handmade soaps (goat's milk, herbal, charcoal)
- Sugar or salt scrubs
- Facial masks or toners
- Lip balms, deodorants, or moisturizers
- Bath bombs or soaks (with botanicals, salts, clays)

Assorted blooms, herbs, and veggies at Emerald Roots Farm Collective.

PRODUCE AND PANTRY GOODS

- Fresh produce boxes or curated veggie bundles
- Canned or preserved items (pickles, jams, sauces, chutneys)
- Infused vinegars, oils, or honeys
- Dried fruit, herbal snack blends, or granola
- Fermented goods (kimchi, krauts, herbal sodas)

FLORAL PRODUCTS

- Fresh-cut flower bouquets (seasonal or themed)
- Dried flower bundles or wreaths
- DIY bouquet kits (flowers plus greenery plus instructions)
- Flower crowns (for events, weddings, photoshoots)
- Botanical confetti or bath florals

FIBER AND CRAFT PRODUCTS

- Raw fleece or roving
- Naturally dyed yarns
- Botanical-dyed fabric pieces
- Handmade apparel (hats, scarves)
- Craft kits (dye-your-own, fiber art kits, pressed flower art)

GARDEN AND HOME GOODS

- Seed packets or garden starter kits
- Seedlings, potted plants, or houseplants
- Plant potions or compost teas
- Herbal sachets or bug repellents
- Natural materials decor (wood, stone, dried goods)

BRANDED MERCHANDISE

- T-shirts, totes, and mugs with your farm logo or slogans
- Illustrated farm maps, journals, or stickers
- Calendars or postcards featuring your farm photography
- Recipe cards or how-to zines bundled with products

Every Product Tells a Story

Start small with a signature product line—something that's both effective and meaningful to you, something you can sustainably grow, source, or make—and build from there. My first physical product was Brenda's Balm, named in honor of my late mother, who passed away during my early days of farming. This wasn't just any product; it was a holy basil and hemp–infused balm crafted to help ease pain and promote relaxation. Launching it during the COVID-19 pandemic was a gamble. With supply chains in chaos and customers tightening their wallets, it seemed like a crazy idea. But this balm was more than a product; it was a tribute, a source of healing, and a message that small Black-owned farms could create something beautiful and beneficial even in the hardest of times.

Since its launch, Brenda's Balm has evolved into one of our signature products. It taught me several key lessons about developing physical products. For starters, begin small, know your ingredients, know your market, and tell a good story. I didn't start by trying to create a full line of body care products. I started with one item that I poured my heart into. I knew that sourcing and formulating with organic farm-grown herbs would set me apart in a crowded wellness market. I was able to purchase hemp from a USDA-certified organic nursery that produced excellent flower but did not have an outlet from which to sell it. Naming the balm after my mother gave it a story that resonated.

When people buy Brenda's Balm, they're not just buying a product—they're supporting the story.

Here is the thing: My mom and I had a troubled relationship for most of my life until she unexpectedly died in her mid-fifties. At the time, we had finally gotten to a relatively peaceful period. We were getting to really know each other. My mother had a beautiful green thumb. Plants adored her, and she loved growing them. I went through a period of literally resenting the idea of growing plants due to my unhealed mother wound. So, the creation of Brenda's Balm was healing to my soul in addition to being a healing blend. The artwork is inspired by both of my parents, Clarence and Brenda. And yes, that is how I got the name Clarenda.

In addition to our teas and herbs, we also have branched into the branded merchandise arena. Again, using many of my "Heffaisms," I have been able to generate additional revenue for my farming business while also spreading awareness. There is no better billboard than a happy supporter. Previously, I purchased the inventory up front and was responsible for its distribution, which resulted in my farm receiving a larger percentage of the profits. However, this also required more work on my part as I was responsible for maintaining inventory records, as well as packaging and shipping the orders. I also had to make more of an up-front investment, paying for the screen print setup and merchandise. Because I try to use eco-friendly options, that meant even more of an up-front investment, but again, it also meant I was able to keep more money in my pockets. Currently, as I am writing this, I am working with a third-party vendor to handle drop shipping. Sites such as Printful, Bonfire, and Printify are able to print merchandise on demand and ship it to your customer, saving you the hassle of handling inventory. While you receive a smaller percentage of profits, it also requires essentially no additional effort on your end. Of course, if you have local printing and fulfillment options, I encourage exploring those as well.

Developing physical products requires careful planning, especially for farmers who have limited time and resources. But when done well, it provides a lasting income stream and a tangible piece of your farm's identity for your customers to cherish.

From Product to Profit: Understanding COGS

Farming is a labor of love—but it's also a business. And like any business, it comes with unpredictable variables: bad weather, pest outbreaks, supply chain hiccups, or sudden price spikes in jars or compost. Having a solid handle on your numbers can help you build a boutique farm that's not just surviving but thriving. When you know what each product truly costs to produce, you can price with confidence, plan for profit, and weather financial storms with more ease.

You've poured your heart into creating physical products. Now it's time to make sure they're not just beautiful but also financially sustainable. That's where understanding COGS (cost of goods sold) comes in. COGS is the total direct cost to make a product. On a boutique farm, this includes everything from seeds and soil to jars and labels. COGS tells you how much money you've spent to produce the things you sell. This number is essential when setting prices, calculating profits, or applying for grants and loans. Let's break this down using two examples: dried herbs (which you may grow or purchase), and a value-added product like tomato sauce.

Example 1: Herbs—Grown Versus Purchased

In the first scenario, you grow your own herbs, so you'll need to calculate the cost per ounce based on:

- Seeds or plant starts
- Inputs (compost, fertilizer, amendments)
- Labor (sowing, harvesting, drying, processing)
- Utilities (water, drying equipment)
- Land use or depreciation
- Drying and storage materials

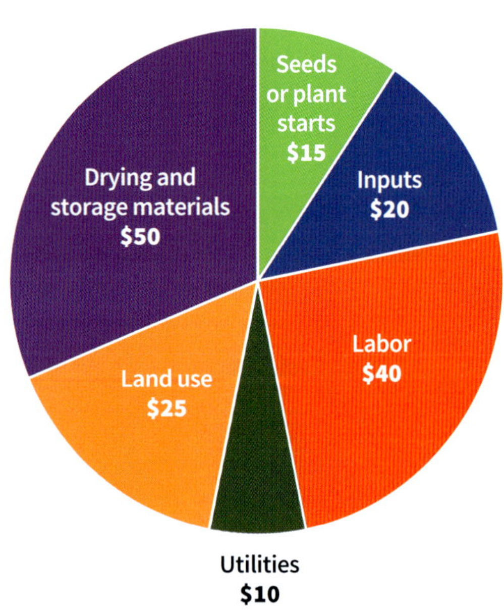

Cost breakdown of growing and processing 160 ounces of lemon balm. Total cost = $160.

In this example, say you sell 160 ounces of lemon balm at $10/ounce, giving you a total revenue of $1,600.

Subtracting the total costs of growing and processing the herbs ($160) leaves a gross profit of $1,440. You can use part of that gross profit to pay yourself. The remaining profit can be reinvested into the farm—for seeds, equipment, marketing, or future crops. By tracking your COGS and pricing strategically, each product you sell builds a foundation for both personal income and business growth. If instead you buy the herbs, you have to factor in:

- Base price from supplier
- Shipping
- Taxes/duties
- Bulk order minimums

Let's say you buy 5 pounds (80 ounces) of dried chamomile for $125, for a total of $1.56/ounce of chamomile. Round up slightly to account for handling or loss. You might use $1.75/ounce in your costing spreadsheet.

The reality of COGS is often more complicated than these examples, because there are tons of variables in farming. If you grow some herbs yourself and buy others from suppliers, the cost per unit will be different for each. Using a weighted average helps you calculate a single "average" cost that accounts for how much of each herb you have. For example:

You grow 100 ounces of lemon balm at $1/ounce	**→**	**cost = $100**
You buy 50 ounces of peppermint at $2/ounce	**→**	**cost = $100**
Total combined = 150 ounces		**total cost = $200**

Weighted average cost per ounce

= Total cost ÷ Total ounces = $200 ÷ 150 ounces = $1.33/ ounce

Premium-quality hemp flower is one of the three dozen specialty crops grown on the farm.

This ensures that your pricing and profit calculations reflect the mix of grown and purchased herbs, rather than treating them all as if they cost the same. Track losses—from mold, pests and bad drying days. Record everything you used, even "free" items you grew on your own time. Time, tools, and land aren't free.

Example 2: Value-Added Product—Basil Tomato Sauce

Let's apply raw material costing to a more complex product: a 16-ounce jar of Farm Fresh and Fancy Basil Tomato Sauce. You grow your heirloom tomatoes and basil, and buy the rest: olive oil, garlic, spices, jars, labels. The COGS breakdown becomes:

If your selling price = $16, then $16.00 – $10.21 = $5.79 gross profit per jar (see table 10.1). You now have a clear snapshot of your real costs. And if the basil gets wiped out in a storm and you have to buy it next season? You already know how that impacts your bottom line.

Knowing your COGS helps you price your products profitably and in accordance with their quality. It's critical data to have to make smart decisions about which products are worth scaling, shifting, or tweaking without guessing at margins. Having your COGS figured out also means you can navigate grant applications and business plans with real data, which is especially useful for government grants.

Paying Yourself a Salary: Valuing Your Time

Paying yourself a salary is huge. It's one of those things that can make or break the financial sustainability of your farm, and yet it's often overlooked in

Table 10.1. COGS Farm Fresh and Fancy Basil Tomato Sauce

Item	Cost
Tomatoes (grown, internal cost)	$1.20
Basil (grown, internal cost)	$0.40
Olive oil (purchased)	$1.80
Garlic, spices (purchased)	$0.60
Jar and lid (purchased)	$1.10
Label	$0.40
Labor (blending, cooking, jarring, cleanup)	$4.00
Utilities (water, stove use)	$0.71
Total COGS	**$10.21**

early planning. When I initially started, I was still working a full-time job, so I did not pay myself a salary. This allowed me to pour more into the farm. However, I eventually had to figure out how to factor my own labor into my farm costs and when it was feasible to actually take a salary. Figuring this out early on will save you headaches down the line.

Let's start with COGS. We know this includes everything it costs to produce your product: seeds, soil amendments, packaging, processing, and labor. If you hire employees, their wages are part of COGS. If you're doing the work yourself, you can—and should—factor your own labor into those costs. This isn't just accounting; it's a way of understanding the true cost of production and valuing your time appropriately. For example, say you're producing 10 pounds of herbs. The materials and additional labor might cost $60. If you want to pay yourself $50 per hour and it takes three hours of your time, that's $150. When you add that to your $60 in materials, your total COGS becomes $210. This approach ensures you're not undervaluing your labor when setting product prices. When you calculate COGS, include your hourly labor costs, set retail prices to cover materials and overhead, and subtract projected expenses from expected revenue to see what amount of salary is realistic. It is common to start with a smaller salary and increase it over time as the farm grows.

Next, let's talk feasibility. Begin by adding up your monthly expenses—both personal and farm-related. Compare that total with your projected farm revenue. Will your farm consistently cover operating costs and your salary? Having a realistic picture of your finances helps you plan for growth, and here's where personal brand revenue can be a game changer. I generate income through speaking engagements, consulting, and other opportunities outside the farm, and this revenue covers my living expenses, which allows the farm income to be focused on building infrastructure, expanding production, and reinvesting in equipment. Personal brand income acts as a cushion, giving the farm breathing room while ensuring I can still pay myself fairly for the work I do on the ground.

The Real Deal on Retail and Wholesale

So, you've made something beautiful—produced with care, crafted with intention. Now you want to get it on a shelf. That moment when a buyer says yes? When your jar, your bundle, your bar, your blend is sitting proud under a store light? That is a big moment. Celebrate it. But understand this: Behind that shelf placement is a system. Behind that yes is a whole new level of work. Especially for us: Black. Women. Producers. Farming in a country that still acts like equity is a threat. Selling in a market that wants our magic but not always our leadership. That shelf can be a blessing—but it can also be a burden.

In a boutique farm business, selling is building relationships, not just revenue. Whether retail or wholesale, selling is about far more than pricing, margins, and shelf space. At the core, it is about relationships. Behind every order placed or purchase made is a person—a buyer, a stock clerk, a distributor, a co-op volunteer. These are people with inboxes full of pitches and shelves full of choices. What sets you apart isn't just the excellence of your product. It's your presence. People remember how you made them feel. Were you respectful of their time? Did you follow through? Did you show up with clarity, confidence, and care? This isn't just a placement—it's a partnership. So, bring your full self into the room. Your values, your story, your joy. But also: Protect your energy. Not every door is yours to walk through, and that's okay. Be clear. Be kind. Be consistent. And above all—communicate. Follow up. Don't ghost people who showed interest. But also—don't shrink. You're not asking for a favor. You're offering an opportunity—to carry a product rooted in purpose, grown with care, and crafted with integrity. Believe in the value of what you've created, and others will, too.

Start where you're already valued. Target sales channels that understand boutique farming and wellness from the soil up:

- Co-ops and independent grocery stores that care about local sourcing
- Local apothecaries and wellness boutiques that speak your language
- Holistic shops, yoga studios, and indie bookstores that build lifestyle around values

Wholesale Terms 101

These are the terms you'll come across when you sell your products wholesale.

Payment Terms

Net 30 / Net 60: The buyer pays thirty or sixty days after receiving an invoice. You front the cost.
COD (Cash on Delivery): Paid when the goods arrive.
Prepaid: The buyer pays up front. This is safer for small or new producers.
50/50: Half up front, half before shipment—a good compromise.

Shipping Terms

FOB (Freight on Board): The buyer pays shipping from your location.
Delivered Pricing: Your wholesale price includes shipping.
Drop Shipping: You ship directly to the buyer's customer.
Consignment: The buyer only pays you if the item sells. Risky, but sometimes strategic.

Order Terms

MOQ (Minimum Order Quantity): The smallest quantity a buyer can purchase.
Case Packs: Orders must be made in specific batch sizes.
Lead Time: How long it takes to prep and ship your order.

- Gourmet food stores that celebrate small-batch and handmade
- Farmers markets, where stories matter as much as products

Look for shelves that welcome your energy—places where your story can breathe, and where your product doesn't have to shout to be seen. And when they support you? Support them right back. Send your customers their way. Tag them in posts. Share their wins. Celebrate their shelves. Let it be mutual. Let it be community—not just commerce. This is the kind of selling that sustains not just profits but people. Wholesale can be a beautiful thing when it aligns with your values and your margins. Here's what it can do for you:

Consistent Revenue: When you price and plan it right, wholesale can help level out the feast-or-famine cycle. Instead of chasing every single sale, you've got orders coming in like clockwork.
Bulk Orders: One wholesale order for a hundred units? That's way less labor than packing and shipping a hundred individual orders. It saves time, energy, and packing tape.

Brand Visibility: Landing on the right shelf puts your product in front of people who may never have found you online. It builds recognition, trust, and the kind of exposure you don't have to buy with ads.

Operational Efficiency: When you're producing in larger batches, you can streamline your process and cut waste. You're not scrambling every week to fill onesies and twosies.

Market Reach: Wholesale opens doors in cities and communities you couldn't afford to target solo. Suddenly your farm-grown tea is on shelves in places you haven't even visited—and that's powerful.

Now let's be real. Wholesale ain't all dreamy purchase orders and shelfies. There are some real trade-offs—and for Black-owned, woman-led farms like ours, those trade-offs can cut a little deeper. To start, price pressure. Retailers want their margin. Period. That means they're coming for yours. If you're not careful, you'll end up working harder for less money. Do the math and make sure your prices leave room for you to profit, too. Payment terms are often a bad

What Is a Line Sheet?

A line sheet is your wholesale résumé, the document you will give to potential stockists. No fluff, no filler. Just the facts. This is what makes you easy to do business with. Make it clean, professional, and aligned with your brand vibe. But remember: Clear always beats cute. A well-done line sheet tells them you're serious and ready. It's not about fancy design or elaborate storytelling. It's about precision. Wholesale buyers are often managing hundreds of SKUs and dozens of vendors. Your line sheet helps them understand your product offerings at a glance and makes it easy for them to say yes. At a minimum, a good line sheet should include:

- Your business name and contact info
- Your logo and product photos (optional, but high-res images help)
- Product name and SKU (Stock Keeping Unit for inventory tracking)
- Short description (just one or two sentences per item)
- Wholesale price and suggested retail price (SRP)
- Case pack size (for example, "sold in packs of 6")
- Variants (size, scent, flavor, et cetera)
- Minimum-order quantities (MOQs)
- Lead times ("5 business days," say, or "made to order")
- Ordering instructions (how to place an order—portal, email, what have you)
- Payment and shipping terms

deal for the producer. For example, the terms *net 30* and *net 60* mean *you* front the cost. You've bought the materials, done the work, shipped the goods . . . and now you're just waiting to get paid while they sit on your inventory.

These days, there's also a lot of performative partnerships. Some shops want to check a "diversity" box. They'll post your face on their feed during Black History Month, then quietly ghost when the social trend shifts. As we saw in the aftermath of George Floyd's murder, followed by the second Trump presidential term, priorities and commitments can change fast. When pursuing partnerships, ask: Do they move like they value the partnership, or just the optics? And let's not pretend. The current climate has made some companies bold in their DEI backpedaling. There's a growing resistance to equity, and many buyers are playing it safe—which often means bypassing Black brands altogether. That's not just discouraging; it's strategic exclusion.

If your product ends up on a crowded shelf with no context, it can get lost. Or worse, it'll be compared with some mass-produced junk with no soul. Your story is your value. If the store's not telling it, is it even the right shelf? Bottom line: Wholesale can work for you, but don't let it work you. Choose partnerships rooted in respect. Set your terms. Protect your margins. And never forget: Your brand is more than a product. It's a purpose.

Not every partnership is a good partnership. And just because they want your product on their shelves doesn't mean they've earned the right to carry what you've built. So, before you say yes, ask yourself: Do they align with my values? Do they uplift Black brands with integrity, not just optics? Are they committed to mutual respect—or just to retail trends? Your product is sacred. It came from your soil, your sweat, your story. You're not just selling your farm's products—you're selling something that holds your legacy. Protect it accordingly.

Let me say it plain: You don't get what you don't ask for. Don't just accept what they offer. You have the right to negotiate. I recommend asking for:

- Lower minimum-order quantities
- Faster payout terms (due immediately or net 15 instead of net 60)
- Co-marketing support (like featuring you in their newsletter or social media)
- Coverage of shipping costs

If they want your partnership, they should also invest in the relationship. Negotiation isn't being difficult; it's being intentional. Here's the truth: Some buyers have never worked with a farm-based, Black-woman-owned brand. If they're open, you *can* help educate them on your product, your process, and why your margins matter. But that's a gift, not a requirement. You don't owe them that labor. If they're unwilling to learn, keep it moving.

Remember, COGS is not just a business term—it's your boundary. Know what it costs you in full to produce what you sell: labor, ingredients, packaging, time, land, shipping, everything. If the wholesale price doesn't give you room to breathe—and a profit—it's not worth the squeeze. No partnership should leave you burned out and barely breaking even.

One major lesson I had to learn when we entered the retail space was the importance of UPC codes and SKU (pronounced "skew") numbers. I'd worked in retail before, so I'd heard the terms, but I didn't fully understand how these identifiers functioned behind the scenes. When we received our first major wholesale order from Thrive Market, they asked for both. And I had a moment of panic—like, "Wait, what now?"

A UPC (Universal Product Code) is the barcode you scan at checkout—it's required for most retail and third-party sales. A SKU (Stock Keeping Unit), on the other hand, is your internal way of tracking specific products—variations in size, scent, formula, or packaging.

While I won't go deep into all of this in this book, I do want you to know these systems matter. And knowing what they are—and how to set them up—can make or break your ability to sell with confidence and clarity. UPCs are issued by GS1, the nonprofit organization that manages global product identification standards. They are twelve-digit numbers consisting of a manufacturer prefix, a product identifier, and a check digit. UPCs are accompanied by a scannable barcode that allows for quick product lookup at checkout. If you plan to sell in major retail chains or on e-commerce platforms, you'll need a UPC for each product. To get your UPCs, register with GS1. Visit www.gs1.org and purchase a UPC prefix. Each unique product,

One of Green Heffa Farms' product labels, showing the UPC as well as certification logos.

A Note for Right Now

Let's name what's happening. We're living in a time when DEI is being slashed, diversity is being politicized, and Black-owned brands are being deprioritized. Some buyers are backing away from equity—not because you've changed, but because their courage has. If you're a Black woman in this work, they may label you a "DEI brand" whether you claim it or not. That label can be used to uplift or to dismiss. But you are not the label.

Your brilliance doesn't need a justification. Your farm is not a checkbox. Your value is not up for negotiation. You don't have to perform. You don't have to contort yourself to make others comfortable. Some doors will stay shut. That's not a reflection of your worth—it's a reflection of their readiness. And it's okay. You're not for everybody. And that's exactly the point.

including variations (size, scent, formulation), needs its own UPC and barcode. Ensure the barcode is visible and scannable on your product label.

You create your own SKUs based on a system that makes sense to you, so they're flexible and tailored to your business. Commonly, folks use an alphanumeric code, typically eight to twelve characters long and structured to provide product details (category, variant, size). If you sell a 2-ounce jar of Soothing Lavender Salve, your SKU might be: SALV-LAV-2OZ. Starting with a clear SKU system will help you stay organized, whether you're fulfilling orders from your website or managing stock for an upcoming farmers market. You can use inventory management software (like Shopify, Square, or QuickBooks) that supports both SKUs and UPCs for seamless tracking.

Events, Education, and Agritourism

Offering experiences on your farm is another powerful way to generate revenue and engage your audience. As much as people love digital and physical products, nothing beats the opportunity to connect with the land and the people behind the brand. One of the most exciting ventures we're working on is transforming our farm into a destination for immersive learning and relaxation. This includes developing a tiny house on the property, which will serve as an Airbnb-style rental for guests who want to experience life on a working farm. We also offer herbal workshops and guided farm tours; in the future we'll add wellness retreats where visitors can learn more about sustainable

Setting the stage for an on-farm workshop focused on connection and sharing (*top*). Setting the table for a joyous Juneteenth celebration in 2025 (*bottom*).

agriculture, herbalism, and the daily rhythms of boutique farming. Creating these experiences wasn't just about adding another income stream; it was about fulfilling our mission to educate, inspire, and empower others. When people stay on the farm, they leave with a deeper understanding of what it means to farm ethically, sustainably, and in a way that honors both the land and the people who work it. This diversification into farm-based experiences provides three key benefits:

Income Stability: Experience-based revenue is less dependent on seasonal variations, making it an excellent supplement during off-peak production months.

Brand Loyalty: Visitors who have a meaningful experience on your farm become lifelong supporters. They're more likely to purchase your products, support your campaigns, and share your story.

Personal Fulfillment: There is immense satisfaction in seeing people connect with your farm in a hands-on way. It's an opportunity to extend your impact beyond what you can grow and sell.

Offering on-farm experiences also requires a significant investment in safety, infrastructure, and programming. Be sure you read the information about insurance in chapter 6, do your research, and talk to the appropriate permitting offices before you start hosting folks on your farm. As I continue building out this aspect of Green Heffa Farms, I'm learning how to balance the demands of farming with the expectations of guests to ensure that each visitor leaves with a memorable and transformative experience. Here are some great resources that can help you navigate the complexities of on-farm hosting:

WWOOF (World Wide Opportunities on Organic Farms): links visitors with organic farmers, promoting educational and cultural exchange and building a global community conscious of ecological farming practices: wwoof.net

Food Animal Concerns Trust (FACT) has created a helpful resource, "Host a Farm Day: A Farmer's Toolkit," which is available on their website: www.foodanimalconcernstrust.org

Social Media and Brand Partnerships

Social media isn't just a marketing tool—it can be a revenue stream all on its own. With thoughtful and consistent use of platforms like Instagram, TikTok, YouTube, Substack, and even Pinterest, you can monetize your content and grow a loyal following that supports your farm's mission. For instance, you can earn income from:

Ad Revenue: Through YouTube, Facebook, and Instagram (especially for creators with high engagement).
Sponsored Content: Posts, videos, or reels created in partnership with brands.
Affiliate Marketing: Earning a commission when followers purchase products using your custom link.
Collaborative Product Lines: Co-branded teas, skincare, or merch.
Subscription Options: Platforms such as Facebook, Instagram, Substack, and Patreon allow supporters to pay for exclusive content.

Social media also provides an opportunity for revenue through brand partnerships. Your audience will trust you more—and be more likely to buy—when your endorsements feel authentic. I've collaborated with brands that reflect Green Heffa Farms' values of sustainability, herbal wellness, and small-scale farming. These collaborations can take many forms: paid sponsorships, affiliate promotions, product collaborations, or storytelling campaigns. It's not about promoting just anything—it's about advocating for what you believe in, and getting paid for it. For boutique farmers, especially Black women building values-driven businesses, authenticity is non-negotiable. The best partnerships reflect your purpose, uplift your voice, and respect your labor.

As I mentioned previously, one of the most meaningful collaborations I've been a part of has been with Dovetail Workwear, the world's largest woman-owned workwear brand. As part of their Maven ambassador program, I've partnered with them not just to model clothes but to share what it really means to be a Black woman stewarding the land. Dovetail created a dedicated page highlighting my work and published an in-depth profile on their blog, celebrating my journey as a farmer, entrepreneur, and advocate. They also created an affiliate discount code for my supporters that generated additional revenue for my farm in addition to the compensation I received for creating original content. And they provided me with many of the stellar images included in this book. This partnership wasn't about selling an image—it was about elevating a story.

That's what makes a brand partnership powerful. It's not just about posting a product photo; it's about storytelling, visibility, and compensation that honors your experience. Some collaborations are paid; others offer exposure, product, or creative freedom. But all of them should feel aligned. Your audience doesn't need to be massive. You don't need a hundred thousand followers. You need a community that sees you, supports you, and trusts you. That's what brands are looking for—real engagement, not just reach.

So don't just be flattered by free products or exposure. Ask yourself: Is this advancing my business? Would I do this if I weren't getting free stuff? If the answer is no, it's probably not aligned. I have structured multiple brand partnerships in ways that serve both my farm's mission and its bottom line. Through collaborations, I have received free merchandise, paid sponsorships, affiliate commissions, and even creative control over image rights. Here's my advice to make sure you make the most of these partnerships and don't get taken advantage of for your platform:

Image Access: Always ask for the right to use professional photos taken during the partnership. These images are valuable assets you can repurpose for your website, social media, media kits, and grant applications.

Free Products Versus Value Exchange: Free gear might be nice, but ask yourself: Does it serve your business, or just the brand's goals? For example, I once partnered with a solar battery company to feature a portable power station on the farm. I wasn't paid cash, but I did receive

Farmer Cee leaving the fire-damaged herb cabin wearing Dovetail attire.

Real Talk

Regardless of which revenue streams you choose to pursue, one piece of advice I would offer is to document everything. The journey, the successes, the failures, and everything in between. There is somebody out there who will need to learn from your experiences. What may seem insignificant today could be the story that inspires someone else. Who knows? It may even turn into a book one day.

over $5,000 worth of solar equipment. In exchange, I created one dedicated YouTube video, one mention in another video, and four social media stories. No fluff, no overextending—just clear deliverables for clear value. This equipment has been invaluable in supplying power all over the farm and during outages.

Affiliate Codes: These can generate passive income if you have an audience that trusts your recommendations. I have used affiliate codes to earn extra funds from products I truly use and believe in.

Paid Content: Whether it's an Instagram post, a short video, or a workshop, your time and expertise are worth compensation. Don't be afraid to set your rates and negotiate.

When structuring a partnership, clarify the deliverables on both sides. What exactly are you being asked to do—and what are you getting in return? Is it product, payment, visibility, content rights, or all of the above? Draft a simple agreement if the brand doesn't provide one. Professionalism protects everyone. Well-structured partnerships can uplift your brand and create new streams of value—but only if you stay rooted in your purpose and firm in your worth.

Customer Versus Client: Expanding Your Boutique Farm's Revenue Streams

As a boutique farmer, your revenue potential is only as limited as your imagination. While land and labor are essential to your business, so is understanding the full scope of how your work can generate income. One of the most empowering mindset shifts you can make is recognizing the difference between customers and clients and learning how to serve both in ways that align with your mission, values, and lifestyle. While customers buy your products, clients invest in your knowledge. This section is included in the diversification of revenue discussion because revenue streams are not just about what you grow or make, but also how you share your gifts with the world. Knowing who you're serving and how expands your ability to generate income intentionally and sustainably.

Customer Service Boutique-Style

Customers are those who purchase your physical products. At Green Heffa Farms, our customers seek high-quality herbs and thoughtfully crafted herbal products that support their well-being—whether mental, emotional, physical, psychological, or spiritual. They are not just consumers; they are investors in our growth, connected to our story, values, and brand ethos. Every aspect of our packaging, branding, and product variety is designed with them in mind.

This level of connection doesn't happen by chance. It takes clarity and consistency. When you understand who your customers are, you can tailor your offerings to meet their needs through product curation, storytelling, and an immersive brand experience. Boutique means you are not growing or creating for everybody, and that's a good thing. You are not Amazon; nor do you want to be. You are not a big-box store. You are building something specific, intentional, and rooted in your values. Your customer service should reflect that. Attracting the right customer means being clear about what you offer, how you offer it, and what kind of experience you're curating. Your marketing, packaging, policies, and, yes, your tone are all part of the message you're sending. Your goal isn't just to make sales; it's to create alignment. That way, the people who find you are more likely to be the people who get you. Many boutique farmers make the mistake of trying to serve everyone. But when you try to reach everyone, you often end up resonating with no one. Your ideal customer buys your products and shares your values. They are drawn to your story, mission, and farm-based lifestyle. You find your ideal customers by asking yourself: What problem does my product solve for them? Where do they shop? What do they value?

At Green Heffa Farms, our customers know: If you want prime quality, you will not get Prime delivery. And that's by design. We grow and process with intention. We ship when things are ready, not rushed. Our people give us the grace to give them our best—and we absolutely do. We love adding in gifts and samples and handwritten notes and cute stickers. I personally respond to many customer emails. I don't argue over refunds—though they're rarely requested. And yes, I have fired a handful of customers since launching in 2018, because let's be clear: The customer is not always right. Not when it comes to disrespect, entitlement, or energy that doesn't align with our house rules. That's the beauty of boutique—you get to set the tone. You get to manage expectations. You get to decide what excellent service looks like on your terms.

GROUNDWORK

Cultivating Your Customer Culture

Your farm, your vibe. Let's start building a customer service philosophy that fits your mission—not just a default policy copied from somewhere else. Use the prompts below to start shaping the experience you want to create for the people you serve.

Step 1: Envision the Customer Experience

List three things you want customers to feel when they buy from you. Go beyond "satisfied." Think about emotion and connection. For example, I want my customers to feel nurtured, respected, and inspired.

Step 2: Write a Sample Customer Service Manifesto

This is a short paragraph (three or four sentences) that reflects how you intend to serve. Make it real. Make it you. For example, I respond with grace, but I do not accept disrespect. I aim to educate when needed, offer resolution when fair, and always center mutual respect. I serve people, not egos.

Step 3: Set Your Boundaries

These are the non-negotiables—what you will not tolerate in your customer relationships. For example, I do not accept rude or demeaning messages. I do not explain my pricing. I do not rush harvest or shipping schedules for convenience. Write down two or three of your non-negotiables or boundaries.

Step 4: Define Your Boutique Value

What makes your product or service worth it to the right people? For example, every tea blend is grown, handpicked, and processed on land that is tended with love and intention. What we offer is rare and sacred—and we price accordingly.

Save these responses somewhere you can revisit as your business grows. This becomes the soil for your customer service policies, email language, refund rules, and even your packaging tone. When you know your values, your boundaries can stand firm and soft at the same time.

Clients: Service-Based Revenue

Clients engage with your expertise. They seek services like consulting, workshops, educational programs, or speaking engagements. For me, this has included consulting with new herb farmers building product lines, advising wellness brands on ethical herb sourcing, and leading workshops on sustainable farming. Client services are typically higher-value, require more of your time, and are relationship-driven. These are powerful opportunities to diversify income without relying solely on physical goods.

Your ideal client is someone who seeks your guidance. They see you as a leader and are ready to invest in your time. You'll find your clients by asking yourself: What expertise am I uniquely qualified to offer? Who benefits from my knowledge? What service delivery model works best—one to one, group, online?

Many of your customers can grow into clients. For example, someone who buys your tea may want to learn to grow their own herbs. Someone who follows your agritourism events may want you to help design one for their venue. But it's important to remember that not every customer is an ideal client. At Green Heffa Farms, I had to learn this the hard way. People would book me for encouragement or planning sessions—but not everyone was ready to actually get to work. Now I only accept clients who are clear, committed, and respectful of the value of my time. My ideal client doesn't negotiate my rate. They come prepared, having done their homework, and they know what they want to accomplish.

There are too many folks out here overcharging with little substance, especially in natural wellness or self-care. You don't need to follow that model. Instead, assess the true value you bring, set your prices accordingly, and stay aligned with your own ethics. When this book launches, my consulting rates will rise. I'll be focusing more on speaking engagements and workshops. Those events bring in more for my brand and give me time back—plus, let's be honest, I love getting "flewed out" to share knowledge and make impact at scale. Align your service-based revenues with your desired lifestyle. Build streams that protect your peace. If it doesn't feel good, it's not worth it. You should never feel like you're scrambling to make a buck doing something you resent. Here are ways you can turn your expertise into income:

Workshops and Classes: Create ticketed events for local communities or online audiences, like sessions on herbs, farming, or entrepreneurship.

Speaking Engagements: Accept invitations to speak at conferences, schools, and events. Get paid to share your story and elevate your brand.

Consulting Services: Offer one-to-one or small-group coaching or advising, build packages or retainers for long-term clients, or create member-based learning communities.

Whether you are growing flowers, hosting retreats, making delicious chocolate alternatives with tree nuts (yes, I know a farmer doing this, and it's delicious!), or producing high-quality duck and quail eggs, your offerings are your opportunity to be more than just a farmer—you are also a trusted voice, guide, and change maker. That deserves to be compensated. When you design your revenue streams with care, clarity, and creativity, you create a boutique farm that supports your joy, your mission, and your bottom line. Customers and clients are both part of your ecosystem—and when you nurture both intentionally, your boutique farm can bloom in ways you never imagined.

Are you picking up what I'm laying down? Perhaps your target market is boutique hotels. If they are a wedding destination, you could work with them to offer experiential showers for bridal parties, each guest leaving with a special favor and more awareness of your brand. The key thing to remember is that you need to be clear on who your ideal client is. I realized early on that when it came to consulting, many people who booked time with me wanted me to plan out their farm or to consistently encourage them. I learned the importance of defining my boundaries and managing expectations. Currently, I am very selective about the consulting clients I agree to work with. My ideal clients are clear on their goals and willing to put in the work. They do not argue about price, but they do expect their money's worth. They come to the conversation with some well-thought-out questions that let me know they have been doing their research. They take their investment in my services seriously.

When it comes to pricing, you really need to do the work in truly understanding the value of your time balanced with the value you are bringing. There are some people out here who are downright scamming others, playing on vulnerabilities and in many cases naïveté. I see it happen a lot in the natural wellness or the women's self-care space. For your boutique farm to be your customized joy factory, you need to feel good about the services you provide and the compensation you receive. When you stay in tune with the quality of life you truly desire, you will build your revenue streams accordingly. They will support your peace, not detract from it. You won't feel like you are in a money grab where you are trying to make money any kind of way that you can—even agreeing to things that you do not enjoy doing. That is *not* the goal here.

Boutique farming extends beyond growing and selling. By balancing products, services, and strategic partnerships, farmers can establish a financially sustainable business, deepen community connections, and create lasting impact. Embracing creativity and innovation ensures success while staying true to the farm's mission and values.

CHAPTER 11

From Verified to Valued

Establishing Trust in Your Boutique Brand

When we grow with intention, we grow with direction. That's how legacy is made—not by accident, but by alignment.

—JAMILA NORMAN, urban farmer and host of *Homegrown* on Magnolia Network

As Black women building boutique farm brands, we often enter spaces that weren't designed for us—but that doesn't mean we don't belong there. It just means we move differently. We build with intention. We lead with integrity. And we understand that while we don't need external permission to claim our power, strategy helps us protect it and grow it. This chapter is about how to build credibility and visibility on your terms—through certifications, verifications, continued learning, and meaningful recognition. Not to prove your worth, but to protect your work, amplify your mission, and connect with communities and opportunities that nourish your growth.

A Deep Dive into Certifications and Verifications

How you choose to grow your crops or raise your livestock doesn't just impact the quality of what you produce—it shapes your entire brand story. Your farming methods set the tone for how you can market your products, and, more important, they communicate your values to your customers. When you hear me use words like *artisanal*, *premium*, *organically grown*, *sustainably harvested*, *regenerative*, and *oppression-free*, they are not just buzzwords. They represent a holistic approach to farming that prioritizes environmental stewardship, worker well-being, and the empowerment of marginalized communities. These terms not only reinforce our core values but also help attract customers who share those values and are intentional about where they spend their dollars.

At Green Heffa Farms, our approach to farming is intentional and deeply rooted in a commitment to ethics, which is why we've pursued and achieved certifications that reinforce these values. My farm is already a Certified B Corp, which means we meet the highest standards of verified social and environmental performance, public transparency, and legal accountability. And by the time this book reaches your hands, Green Heffa Farms will have attained its organic certification and Soil and Climate Health Initiative Verification as well—milestones that ensure we adhere to strict standards that foster soil health, biodiversity, and natural ecosystems while avoiding synthetic inputs. But we don't stop there. We also sustainably harvest our crops, which means we are mindful of how we interact with the land. This goes beyond certifications—it's a deep respect for the Earth and ensuring that what we take, we give back.

The differences among terms like *organic*, *regenerative*, *sustainable*, and *fair-trade* matter when you're building your brand. Each one speaks to a distinct set of principles and practices, but they all have one thing in common: They communicate that your farm is about more than just products. It's about producing in a way that respects the Earth and its people. *Organic* focuses on natural growing processes, avoiding synthetic pesticides and fertilizers while maintaining the health of the soil. *Regenerative* goes further, emphasizing practices that restore and enhance the environment, contributing to long-term ecological balance. It's about healing the land, not just

avoiding harm. *Sustainable* ensures that you are producing in a way that can continue indefinitely without depleting resources or damaging ecosystems. It's about longevity and balance. *Fair-trade* is about ensuring fair wages and ethical treatment of everyone in your supply chain, with a focus on equitable practices for workers, especially in traditionally exploited regions.

These labels are more than just marketing tools; they are promises to your customers about your commitment to integrity, quality, and ethical production. And as a Black woman farmer, owning these certifications and principles means I'm pushing back against centuries of exploitation and exclusion in agriculture. By embodying these values, I'm reclaiming the narrative—demonstrating that Black women not only belong in this space, but that we can lead with intention, sustainability, and respect for both the Earth and our communities. Below, I'll walk you through the certification processes, what they mean for your business, and how to leverage them in building a boutique farming brand that resonates with conscious consumers. Whether you're at the beginning of your farming journey or further along, understanding these distinctions will empower you to market your products with authenticity and clarity while ensuring that your farming practices align with your values.

Let me be transparent right now: I have been a title pursuer for many, many years. Since elementary school, where I was labeled as gifted and even skipped second grade, I've been motivated by winning. I wanted the blue ribbon, the trophy, the title—because winning meant recognition. And recognition meant people were nice, they paid attention, they listened. I have healed from feeling that I need to win to feel valued, and I have learned to be selective about whose praise makes me preen. In the past, I might have tried to chase every certification like a prize, but now I know to be choosier. Some certifications are time-intensive. Many are so involved that an entire industry of consultants exists to assist farmers in acquiring them, often for a hefty fee. I totally understand those who feel that the entire certification space is a racket. I get it.

Certifications are often seen as essential markers of credibility and sustainability in farming. However, not all certifications are created equal, and not all of them serve the best interests of small-scale, Black-owned, or boutique farming operations. Many common certifications were not designed with farmers like us in mind. The systems favor larger, white-dominated farming operations, and often, these certifications serve as economic barriers rather than equitable opportunities. They weren't created to include small-scale, Black, Indigenous, or other farmers of color, nor do they take into account the ways we have been farming regeneratively, organically, and ethically for generations—before a certification even existed.

Before investing time and money, it's essential to evaluate whether a certification aligns with your business goals, values, and market strategy. You do not have to pursue certifications. Your farm's success is not dependent on a stamp of approval from an outside organization. However, whether or not to pursue certification should be a business decision—not an emotional one. There are a number of questions to consider. Was the certification created with small, independent, and culturally rooted farms in mind? Or does it force you into a framework that doesn't reflect your heritage, your farming traditions, or the way you do business? Does it align with your farm's values and community?

I only focus on certifications that serve a purpose—otherwise, they're just expensive decorations. We find that some labels assist us in leveling the planting field. Being strategic about which certifications to pursue can make a difference for a boutique brand. Certifications can be a tool to fast-track consumer trust—especially in markets where customers rely on third-party validation. They can open doors to wholesale or export markets that require specific verifications or they can differentiate your brand in a crowded field where customers seek assurance of quality, sustainability, or ethical sourcing. Choose what is best for your business. There is no one-size-fits-all approach.

Let's break down some of the most common certifications, their realities, and how they may—or may not—work for you. Your options include USDA organic, regenerative, and sustainable certifications, Ethical and Fair Trade, Animal Welfare, Specialty Crop, a range of local certifications, and Certified B Corporation. USDA organic is often seen as the gold standard for clean, sustainable farming, but is it the best fit for every farm? The movement toward regenerative agriculture is growing, but who controls the narrative? Many large corporations that historically harmed land and people now dictate the standards. Certifications like Fair Trade USA and Fair for Life claim to ensure fair wages and labor conditions—but who truly benefits? For those raising animals, certifications like Animal Welfare Approved (AWA) and Certified Humane promise better treatment of livestock. For herbalists, tea growers, and value-added product makers, certifications like Non-GMO Project Verified, Good Agricultural Practices (GAP), and FDA Current Good Manufacturing Practices (cGMP) can seem important—but do they serve your business?

B Corp certification verifies that a business meets high standards of social and environmental responsibility. Currently, no US state offers B Corp (Benefit Corporation) as a legal business structure in the way that they offer LLCs or C corps. However, many states offer a legal designation called a Benefit Corporation—which is distinct from a Certified B Corporation, the private certification issued by B Lab US & Canada. A Benefit Corporation is a legal business structure or status available in many US states that legally requires a company to consider social and environmental impact in decision making. A Certified B Corporation is a third-party certification granted by B Lab that evaluates a business on social and environmental performance, transparency,

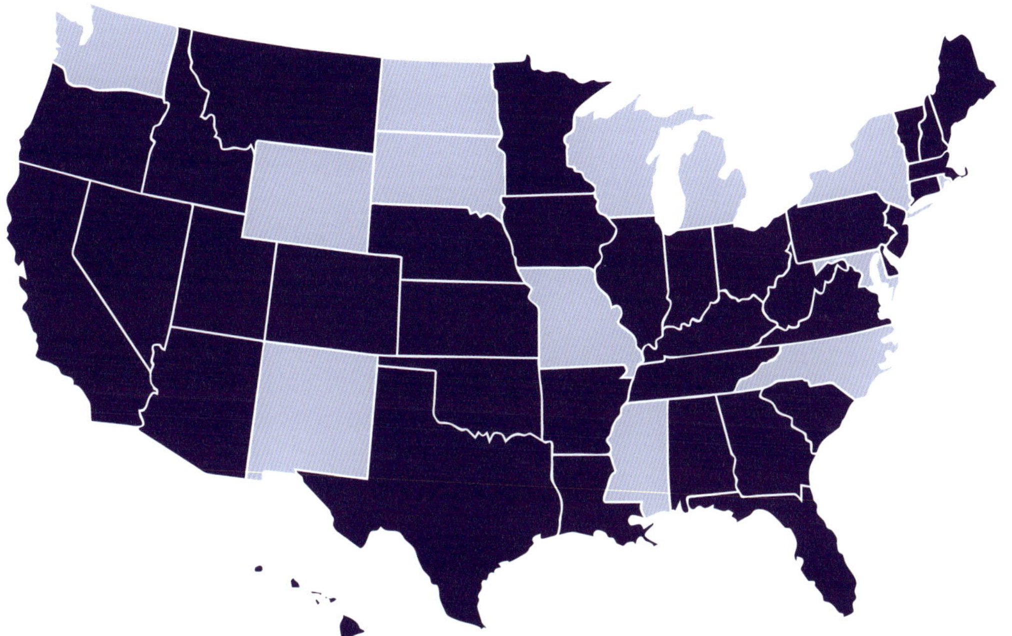

Dark purple states recognize the Benefit Corporation as a legal business structure, distinct from Certified B Corp, which is a third-party certification and available nationwide. *Illustration by Tunisa Rice.*

and accountability. You can be certified regardless of your state's corporate laws, and without being a legally designated Benefit Corporation. So, let's look at the advantages and disadvantages of each certification.

Organic Certification

ADVANTAGES

Consumer Trust: Many shoppers recognize and trust the USDA organic label.

Access to Premium Pricing: Certified organic products often command higher prices.

Market Access: Some retailers and distributors require USDA organic certification.

Environmental Standards: Prohibits synthetic fertilizers and genetically modified organisms (GMOs).

DISADVANTAGES

High Costs: Certification fees range from $700 to $1,500-plus annually, not including compliance costs.

Administrative Burden: Extensive record keeping and inspections favor large-scale farms.

Not Pesticide-Free: USDA allows certain organic-approved pesticides that may still harm soil health and pollinators.

Green-Washing Risk: Large corporate farms can afford certification while smaller farms practicing true organic methods get overlooked.

CONSIDER AN ALTERNATIVE

Certified Naturally Grown (CNG): Follows organic principles but is designed for small, independent farmers. It's peer-reviewed, community-based, and more affordable.

Regenerative and Sustainable Certifications

ADVANTAGES

Regenerative Organic Certified (ROC): Combines organic farming with regenerative principles like soil health and fair labor practices.

Demeter Biodynamic Certification: Requires crop diversity, composting, and holistic farming methods.

DISADVANTAGES

Barriers to Entry: ROC requires USDA organic first, making it inaccessible for many small farmers.

Eurocentric Bias: Demeter Biodynamic's framework often overlooks African and Indigenous agricultural knowledge.

Limited Application: Some regenerative certifications prioritize ranching over diversified farming.

CONSIDER AN ALTERNATIVE

Tell your own story. You don't need a certification to prove regenerative practices—use transparency, customer education, and direct marketing.

Ethical and Fair Trade Certifications

ADVANTAGES

Consumer Confidence: Many customers seek out fair-trade products.

Fair Labor Standards: Aims to protect workers and ensure ethical sourcing.

International Recognition: Helpful for selling in global markets.

DISADVANTAGES

Prioritizes Imports: Focuses on farms in developing countries, often excluding US farmers.

High Certification Costs: Can be too expensive for small farms.

No Guarantee of True Fairness: Some brands use fair-trade certification as a marketing tool without making real change.

CONSIDER AN ALTERNATIVE

Your pricing, sourcing, and storytelling should reflect your ethical business practices. Build customer trust through direct relationships and radical transparency.

Animal Welfare Certifications

ADVANTAGES

Animal Welfare Approved (AWA): Stricter than USDA organic on animal welfare.
Consumer Trust: Many shoppers actively seek humane-certified meat, dairy, and eggs.
No Cost for AWA: Unlike other certifications, AWA is free for qualifying farms.

DISADVANTAGES

Paperwork and Inspections: Time consuming for small farmers.
Market Limitations: Not all customers understand or seek out these certifications.

CONSIDER AN ALTERNATIVE

Educate your customers on your ethical farming practices instead of relying on a label.

Specialty Crop Certifications

ADVANTAGES

GAP (Good Agricultural Practices): Required for selling to grocery chains and distributors.
FDA cGMP (Current Good Manufacturing Practices): Ensures product safety for herbal supplements and teas.
Non-GMO Project Verified: Appeals to consumers avoiding GMOs.

DISADVANTAGES

Expensive and Bureaucratic: Non-GMO Project Verified and FDA cGMP compliance are costly and time-intensive.
Not Always Necessary: If you sell direct to consumers, many of these certifications may not impact sales.

CONSIDER AN ALTERNATIVE

Instead of chasing expensive certifications, clearly communicate your farming and processing methods. Customers value trust and transparency more than a label.

State and Local Certifications

EXAMPLES

- Certified SC Grown (South Carolina)
- Homegrown by Heroes (for veteran farmers)
- State-specific organic programs

CONSIDER AN ALTERNATIVE

Check your state's agriculture department for local programs that better support small-scale and Black-owned farms.

Certified B Corporation (B Corp)

ADVANTAGES

Brand Recognition: Consumers trust B Corp as a marker of ethical businesses.

Accountability: Requires companies to consider social and environmental impact.

Market Advantage: Some retailers prefer working with B Corps.

DISADVANTAGES

Expensive and Time Consuming: The application process can take six to twelve months and cost $1,000 to $50,000, depending on revenue.

Not Built for Farms: Originally designed for corporations, making the standards challenging for agricultural businesses.

No Specific Focus on Black Farmers: Doesn't directly address land reparations or food sovereignty.

CONSIDER AN ALTERNATIVE

Instead of a certification, focus on clear messaging, ethical sourcing, and community-driven business practices.

Sometimes a well-crafted story and ethical business practices are more valuable than a costly label. Certifications are tools—not necessities. Choose wisely. They should serve your business, not the other way around. Before

The B Corp Level Program

When Green Heffa Farms attained its Certified B Corp status, I didn't just see it as a personal and professional victory—I viewed it as an opportunity to make it easier for other BIPOC women- and women-identifying-led businesses to become Certified B Corporations. Becoming a Certified B Corp is no small feat, especially for small, boutique farms and businesses owned by women of color. The process is complex, rigorous, and often inaccessible to entrepreneurs due to the expenses, lack of access to resources, and systemic inequities in the certification industry.

Unbeknownst to me, B Lab US & Canada, the nonprofit that managed this certification, was undergoing an internal transformation, led by Andy Fyfe, to make the certification process more accessible. A white man with a man bun, Andy was a bit of a surprise. Recognizing the need for more representation in the B Corp movement, I worked closely with Andy and B Lab to help establish what would become the Level program—a groundbreaking initiative to make the B Corp certification process more accessible, supportive, and equitable for BIPOC women and women-identifying entrepreneurs in agriculture and beyond. The program offers tiered support based on where you are in your business journey, allowing you to level up toward full certification at a pace that suits your business needs and capacity.

One of the biggest challenges I faced in getting B Corp certified was the financial investment required. Between application fees, compliance costs, and auditing processes, the financial burden can be overwhelming, particularly for smaller operations without deep pockets. With the Level program, BIPOC-women-owned businesses can access grant funding, sliding-scale fees, and low-interest loans to cover the cost of the certification process, making it more attainable for farms and businesses of all sizes. Beyond financial support, the Level program also provides one-on-one mentorship and guidance from established BIPOC-women-owned Certified B Corporations and consultants, so you're not navigating this process alone. The goal is to ensure that more women of color are not just gaining certification but also thriving once they have it, using their platform to attract values-aligned customers, partners, and investors.

Farmer Cee with aspiring and new B Corp–certified business owners.

you apply, ask yourself: Does this certification help my business reach my ideal customer? Does it align with my values, or does it force me into a system that wasn't built for me? Will the cost of certification be outweighed by increased revenue or opportunities? If a certification will increase your revenue, build credibility, or open new doors—go for it. If it's just for clout, save your money and put that energy into your farm and your customers. Boutique farming is about building something sustainable on your own terms. Certifications are strategic tools for increasing the economic value of your farm's products, but they aren't the only tool. They can serve as proof that you are committed to high standards, and they may provide a level of assurance that builds trust with your customers. In boutique farming, where the scale may be small but the impact is big, having certifications can make the difference between staying local and expanding into larger, more lucrative markets.

Certifications and verifications are important. They show that your business meets standards, and they help build trust with customers, funders, and partners. But let's be honest: For Black women in agriculture, being "qualified" doesn't always mean being respected or included. We've often had to prove ourselves multiple times over just to be granted what others are given with ease. That's why brand building isn't just about credentials—it's also about presence. About being seen, heard, and respected in spaces that influence the future of farming. But showing up must be done with care. Not every room deserves your energy. Not every platform is safe or supportive. And not every opportunity is worth the emotional labor.

Conferences, Trade Shows, and Investing in Education

As a Black woman building a boutique farm brand, you carry more than a business on your shoulders—you carry legacy, resilience, and often the weight of representation. Learning and growth are essential, but so is protecting your peace. Conferences, courses, and trade shows can open doors, expand your network, and sharpen your business—but they can also drain you if the space isn't inclusive, affirming, or aligned with your values. So, before you sign up, ask yourself: Will I feel safe and respected here? Are they centering marginalized voices or tokenizing them? Will this experience pour into me—or pull from me? Give yourself permission to be selective. You do not have to be everywhere. You do not have to exhaust yourself to prove that you belong. Your worth is not tied to visibility in spaces that don't make room for you with dignity.

The right community can be a powerful catalyst for growth, offering encouragement, shared resources, and collective wisdom. But not every group that calls itself a community operates with that spirit. Some spaces are more like cliques—exclusive, performative, and rooted in social validation rather than genuine connection. It's important to seek out inclusive environments where newcomers are welcomed, questions are encouraged, and knowledge flows freely. Be mindful of hype-driven spaces that prioritize popularity over substance—if people only show up when there's something in it for them, it's likely not the kind of support network that will serve you long-term. True community is built on reciprocity. When you show up and contribute with intention—by sharing insights, offering help, or simply being present—you not only gain value but also help shape the culture of the space itself. And most important, don't lose yourself trying to fit into circles that don't reflect your values. Stay grounded in your mission, and remember: You're building a business, not chasing belonging.

Conferences

When you do choose to show up, do it with intention—and a plan for rest. Pack boundaries with your business cards. Make space for recovery after the event, especially if you've had to navigate microaggressions or perform emotional labor on top of professional engagement. Once you decide to attend, make the most of your experience. Choose events that provide tangible takeaways. Have a plan. Review the schedule ahead of time and identify must-attend sessions and key people to connect with. Ask questions, take notes, and introduce yourself to speakers and fellow attendees. Don't just collect business cards—have meaningful conversations and follow up afterward. And when you go home, implement what you learn. Knowledge without action is wasted.

Trade Shows

Trade shows can be a significant investment, but they can also offer unmatched opportunities to grow your business. If you're sourcing materials or suppliers, trade shows allow you to meet vendors face-to-face, ask questions in real time, and inspect products or packaging options up close. These interactions can lead to better pricing, custom solutions, and stronger supplier relationships that may be hard to develop via email alone.

Trade shows can also help you connect with your target market. If your ideal customers, retailers, or wellness professionals are attending, showing up with a branded booth or well-designed samples can increase awareness, generate buzz, and drive direct sales. Even if you're not exhibiting, walking the floor and talking to attendees can build your presence and gather valuable feedback. Trade shows can also be a useful industry networking opportunity. Some of the most valuable moments happen

Real Talk

Investing in learning—whether through conferences, trade shows, or courses—can be a game changer for your boutique farm brand. Be selective, intentional, and proactive about applying what you learn. Surround yourself with a community that genuinely supports your growth, and always ensure your investments align with your long-term business goals. Certifications and awards can open doors that racism and bias try to keep closed. They signal credibility to buyers, funders, and media who might not "get it" until someone else stamps it. They help us stand out in crowded markets, access premium pricing, and build trust with folks who still underestimate Black excellence in agriculture. Bottom line: They're not required to be legit—but they can be powerful tools for visibility, leverage, and legacy. Use them on your terms.

outside of formal programming—conversations in hallways, over coffee, or during workshops. Trade shows often attract thought leaders, distributors, and media, offering a chance to make connections that can shift your business trajectory.

Before you commit, calculate the full cost: registration, travel, lodging, shipping, booth setup, printed materials, and your time. Develop a clear return-on-investment plan, and set realistic goals: Will you gain five wholesale accounts? Build a supplier relationship? Gather a hundred leads? If the potential return outweighs the spend—and you have a plan to follow up—attending can be a smart investment.

Course Buying Guidance: Avoiding the Hype

Online courses can be powerful tools for learning and growth—but in a crowded digital marketplace, it's easy to get caught up in the hype. Flashy marketing, countdown timers, and promises of six-figure success can distract from what really matters: Does the course actually help you build skills and move your business forward? Before you invest your time and money, here's how to make sure a course is worth it:

Research the Instructor: Look beyond the slick landing page. Does the person teaching the course have real-world experience doing what they teach—or are they mainly known for selling courses? Authentic expertise is rooted in practice, not just polished branding.

Look for Honest Reviews: Seek out feedback from past students, ideally outside the course's own website or social media. Pay attention to reviews that mention what was actually learned, how applicable the content was, and whether support was available. If reviews are overly vague or feel like copy-and-paste praise, proceed with caution.

Assess the Content for Practical Value: Does the course outline include actionable strategies and clear takeaways? Or is it filled with vague mindset advice, hype language, or generic information you could easily find in a blog post? A solid course will help you actually move forward, not just feel inspired.

Check the Refund Policy: A trustworthy course provider stands behind their work. Look for a clear, fair refund or satisfaction guarantee. If there's no way out once you buy—or worse, if the refund process feels shady—that's a red flag.

Not all digital learning is created equal. The best courses empower you with tools, not just talk. Be intentional and let alignment—not urgency—guide your decision.

Awards: Recognition as a Resource

Recognition often opens doors that were previously locked or invisible. Behind that shout-out might be a grant invitation. Behind that award might

Farmer Cee at the 2025 Good Farmer Award US reception. *Photo courtesy of the Rodale Institute.*

be a mentorship or a collaboration that shifts your whole trajectory. These are the spaces where relationships are formed, where partnerships bloom, where your name is spoken in rooms you haven't even stepped into yet. But let's keep it real: It's also political. As Black women farmers, our labor has long been overlooked, and when the spotlight finally lands on us, it can feel both affirming and complicated. When I was named the 2019 Featured Farmer for Hemp History Week, I was proud—but I was also clear-eyed. I saw how few Black women were visible in those spaces. I knew that if I was going to be put on a pedestal, I needed to turn that visibility into something real—funding, partnerships, opportunities. Not just photo ops.

So, by the time I received the 2025 Good Farmer Award US from Davines Group and the Rodale Institute, I was more rooted in my purpose and intentional about how I used the recognition. It wasn't just symbolic—it came with a $10,000 cash award, national media exposure, a trip to Italy to visit the European Regenerative Organic Center, and connections to a global network of sustainability leaders. But the award wasn't just for me—it was for every other Black woman out here building something beautiful, impactful, and regenerative on her land. These moments matter. But not just because of the title or attention. Awards are tools. Strategic tools. Use them to gain support, to shift the narrative, to remind folks—and yourself—that you belong in this industry, on your terms. Let me also say this: Don't let awards define you. And don't let the absence of them derail you. The most important recognition is the one you give yourself—when you lie down at night knowing you farmed with purpose, integrity, and care.

Real Talk

Don't let a lack of recognition make you question your value. Some of the most brilliant, most radical, most revolutionary work is being done without a hashtag or a headline. In the quiet. In the soil. In the sweat. And don't let accolades define you, either. Awards can affirm your brilliance, but they don't create it. You were brilliant before the ceremony. Before the article. Before the applause. Let recognition be a mirror, not a measuring stick. Let it reflect what you already know. Let it expand your reach. But don't chase it at the expense of your peace, your mission, or your truth. The land sees you. Your community sees you. *You* see you. And that, sis, is more than enough.

GROUNDWORK

Root Your Brand in Trust

Verification may open the door, but *value* is what keeps people coming back. This exercise helps you explore how trust is cultivated—not just through external certifications but through clear values, consistent communication, and authentic relationships with your customers and community.

Step 1: Define What Trust Looks Like for Your Brand

Trust isn't abstract—it's built through behavior. Think about the specific ways people engage with your farm: online, in person, through products, or in your storytelling. What does trust mean in the context of your farm? What qualities or actions make you trust a brand? Using the following prompts, write a few sentences in your notebook:

- *"Trust, to me, looks like . . ."*
- *"I want my customers to trust me because . . ."*

Step 2: Go Beyond the Seal

Do you have certifications (organic, regenerative, Soil & Climate Initiative, B Corp, et cetera)? Great—but how do you explain what they *mean*? And if you don't, how do you show your values through your actions? Using the following prompts, write about how you communicate your values to your customers, with or without certifications:

- *"I communicate my farm's integrity by . . ."*
- *"Even without formal certifications, I show alignment with my values through . . ."*

Step 3: Share the Story Behind the Product

People don't just buy products—they buy into stories, values, and experiences. Choose one of your products and write a few sentences in your notebook reflecting on how you currently share its journey from soil to shelf.

Step 4: Reflect on a Trust-Breaking Moment

Have you ever made a mistake in your business—or seen another brand lose customer trust? What happened, and how was it handled? Tell that story, and then using the following prompts, write a few sentences about that mistake:

- *"What I've learned about trust through challenge is . . ."*
- *"If I face a trust issue in the future, I will . . ."*

This exercise is about being real, not perfect. Trust doesn't come from polished branding alone. It grows from transparency, accountability, and a willingness to show up as your full, values-driven self.

Last year, despite operating lean and without major funding, we nearly doubled our revenue. Right now, as I write this, most of our website is sold out—a natural result of scaling without debt. But sales are still strong because our customers pre-order in anticipation of harvest. That's the result of trust, quality, and a clear mission. More than anything, the Good Farmer Award affirmed what I already knew: You can farm with intention, intelligence, and integrity—and still win. Recognition like this brought visibility to Green Heffa Farms, new partnerships, new customers, and a broader platform for this work. But it didn't make me. It amplified what I'd already built by centering herbal wellness, prioritizing land care, and being Black-owned, woman-led, and mission-driven. Awards like this don't just shine a light on the individual—they illuminate the entire ecosystem we're part of and they remind the industry that sustainability looks like us, too.

When respected institutions, publications, or platforms acknowledge your work, it's more than a feel-good moment—it's a signal. A signal to customers, partners, and peers that what you're doing is real, that it's valuable, and that it deserves attention. Every piece of recognition adds another thread to your story. It gives you momentum. It helps you stand out in a crowded space. And sometimes, it's the thing that draws in a new customer, funder, or stockist who's looking for exactly what you offer—but didn't know where to find you.

Recognition gives your farm a louder mic. Use it.

CHAPTER 12

The Land Chapter

You can't have food justice without land justice.

—KAREN WASHINGTON, urban farmer and food justice leader

Let's be clear: In this country, land is power. Land is legacy. And land has always been political.

In 1910 Black farmers owned over 14 million acres of land. Today that number has dropped to around 2.5 million acres—less than 1 percent of all US farmland, with Black women owning just a fraction of that. According to the 2022 USDA Census of Agriculture, Black women make up less than 0.5 percent of all US farmers, and the barriers we face in acquiring land are both systemic and sustained. From discriminatory lending practices to heirs' property laws that fractured Black landownership, our access to land has been historically denied, delayed, or diminished.

Sunset over Green Heffa Farms. *Photo courtesy of Taj Cotten.*

But here's the good news: We're still here. We are reclaiming soil. Rebuilding legacy. And redefining what landownership looks like—not just through deeds but also through stewardship, community partnerships, and creative strategy.

This chapter breaks down the many ways you can start or grow your boutique farm, no matter your current acreage. Buying, leasing, joining an incubator, or maximizing the land already under your feet—there's a way forward for every situation and budget.

Let's explore what's out there—and what's already yours.

Whether you're ready to buy your own acreage, lease a plot, or join a land-access program or incubator, there are paths to putting roots down. This chapter will walk you through several ways to gain access to land—including the pros and cons of each—so you can make decisions that are right for your vision, resources, and season. Because access to land isn't just about growing crops or raising animals—it's about growing freedom.

One of the most common misconceptions about farming is that bigger is always better. Many new farmers believe they need dozens or even hundreds of acres to run a successful farm, but the reality is you can grow a profitable business on much less land if you manage it properly. Every boutique farm has different land needs. It depends on crop selection, farming methods, value-added production, whether you'll have livestock, and whether you plan to host events and agritourism. If you grow high-value crops like medicinal herbs, you can produce substantial yields on a fraction of an acre. If you grow row crops or large-scale vegetables, you may need more space. Intensive farming methods (such as raised beds, vertical farming, and permaculture) require much less land than traditional row farming. High tunnels or greenhouses can extend growing seasons, reducing the need for large fields. If you need to process products on-site (like herbal teas or infused oils), you need space for drying, storage, and packaging rather than additional fields. Raising smaller livestock (such as chickens or bees) requires minimal land, whereas goats or cattle require rotational grazing space. If you plan to host workshops, farm tours, or retreats, you'll need land for parking, pathways, and gathering areas.

Buying Versus Leasing Land

One of the earliest and most impactful decisions you'll make as a boutique farmer is whether to lease or buy your land. This choice is deeply personal and situational—it depends on your financial capacity, your business model, and how clearly you've defined your long-term vision. There is no one-size-fits-all answer, and both leasing and buying come with distinct opportunities and challenges. Understanding these nuances will help you move forward with more confidence and clarity.

Leasing land can be a wise and strategic entry point, especially for new farmers who are still shaping their concept, building market relationships, or operating with limited start-up capital. The primary advantage of leasing is reduced up-front costs. You won't need to worry about a down payment or securing a mortgage, which can significantly lower the financial barrier to entry. Leasing also allows flexibility—if your farming direction evolves or you need to relocate, you're not locked into the land as a landowner would be. In some cases, you can even negotiate lease terms that allow you to make certain land improvements or invest in temporary infrastructure.

However, leasing does come with limitations. Because you don't own the land, your ability to build permanent structures may be restricted, which can limit the scale or scope of your vision. There's also the uncertainty of renewal—your lease might not be extended, which can disrupt your operations and force relocation. Additionally, some landowners may place restrictions on what practices you can use, particularly when it comes to chemical inputs, livestock, or the installation of fencing or irrigation. If you go the leasing route, aim to secure a multi-year lease with clear terms and renewal options. Explore local conservation land programs, which may offer farmers access to affordable, lease-based land stewardship opportunities.

Buying land, on the other hand, gives you full control over your operation and the ability to build out your farm exactly as you envision it. Ownership means long-term stability and the opportunity to invest in permanent infrastructure—from barns and greenhouses to value-added processing facilities and living quarters. Landownership can also build equity and generational wealth, especially if the property increases in value over time. As an owner, you may also qualify for USDA loans, grants, and agricultural tax exemptions, which can offset some of your costs and support your development.

But ownership comes at a price. The up-front costs are high—think down payments, mortgage interest, insurance, legal fees, and the closing process. And the financial responsibility doesn't stop there. You'll need to budget for ongoing maintenance, property taxes, repairs, and improvements. Additionally, owning can reduce your flexibility. If your business model changes or you decide to relocate, selling farmland can be time consuming and subject to market shifts. If you choose to buy, be proactive in researching financing programs that support first-time or socially disadvantaged farmers and take advantage of any agricultural tax benefits your state may offer.

Leasing on Existing Agricultural Land

For many new boutique farmers, leasing land on an existing farm or nursery can be a smart, cost-effective option. Leasing means you don't have to make a large up-front investment in land, which can be a major financial relief for new farmers. Instead, you can use your capital to purchase seeds, tools, and other essentials to get your farm up and running. You may get access to established infrastructure, such as irrigation systems, greenhouses, and barns, which can save you significant time and money on setup and allow you to focus more on planting and growing.

If you lease from a more experienced farmer, you can often benefit from their knowledge and mentorship. They may offer advice on best growing practices, pest management, or marketing strategies. Often, existing farms that offer lease agreements are already practicing sustainable farming techniques. This allows you to align with environmentally friendly practices from the start, which can be particularly important if your goal is to run an organic or regenerative farm. Additionally, you may have access to shared resources like equipment or labor, reducing your individual costs.

Leasing allows you to test the waters and scale gradually. If you're not ready for the long-term commitment of purchasing land, a lease offers the flexibility to grow your operation at your own pace. You can expand to more land over time as your business becomes more profitable, or you can switch to a different location if needed.

Buying Land (with Eyes Wide Open)

Buying land is a dream for many farmers—and for good reason. It's a move that offers long-term security, generational potential, and the chance to build something on your own terms. But it's also a significant financial, legal, and emotional commitment—especially for Black women who often face systemic barriers in accessing credit, navigating rural real estate markets, and building trust with lenders or local agencies. Still, it's one of the most empowering moves you can make when the timing and resources are aligned, because ownership = autonomy. When you own the land, you set the rules. That means you can decide how you grow, what you grow, and how your land is used—whether that's farming, hosting events, or building agritourism programs. You're not restricted by a lease or someone else's expectations.

Ownership is a long-term investment. Land tends to appreciate in value over time, especially if it's well maintained and strategically located. Owning property can build wealth and create opportunities for funding—many grants and programs prioritize landowners. Some lenders and grant funders view landownership as a signal of stability, which can open doors to additional funding, insurance, and USDA programs. Being a landowner can shift how institutions view your legitimacy and potential as a business. It also positions you to pass something down to your family or your community.

But buying land isn't just about the down payment. You'll need to budget for closing costs, surveys, soil tests, zoning research, fencing, water access,

Tax Sales with a Plan

Tax sales—which are public auctions where properties with unpaid property taxes are sold by a local government to recover the owed taxes, often at a lower-than-market price—can be a creative strategy to acquire land affordably, but they come with risks. As a Black woman entrepreneur, doing your due diligence is key. You might find a gem of a property for pennies on the dollar—or you might end up with legal headaches. Consider: Are there clear titles? Is the land in a community where you feel safe and supported? Could this purchase connect (or disconnect) you from your customer base? This strategy can work, especially in rural areas where land is underutilized, but it's not for everyone. It works best with legal guidance, local insight, and a clear business vision.

insurance, and taxes. Not all land is ready for farming—especially if it's been stripped of topsoil, been contaminated, or lacks infrastructure. A dreamy piece of land can become a financial drain if you don't know what you're buying.

Many affordable rural properties are located in predominantly white areas where you may be one of the few—or only—Black farmers. That can bring emotional and safety concerns, especially in today's climate. Building relationships with trusted neighbors and regional networks is essential if you're going to plant roots in unfamiliar soil.

How I Acquired My Land

You know I am all about transparency. I share my story not to influence you to do the same but rather to spark innovation and creativity as you develop your own strategy. I want to share with you how I got my land—because it's not a glossy story. I initially got a loan to purchase the land. The mortgage was under my name, using my Social Security number and my credit. But at the time, I was legally married. So, while my then-spouse's name went on the deed, they were not on the mortgage. I was solely responsible for that loan.

I opted to use a credit union that focused on farmers and agribusinesses. Now, let me say that even with a high credit score and the needed down payment, I was still initially denied. It was not until I asked questions about who was getting approved for loans through that credit union that somehow, they found a way to make it work. I looked at their board of directors and the staff who were making decisions. It looked like a group of folks that would say no to a farmer like me. But I pushed back. I advocated for myself. And I got the loan.

Listen—I wasn't under any illusion that my marriage was thriving. If I'm being honest, buying the land was a last-ditch effort. No babies were coming, so the land *was* the baby. The idea was, "Here, let's build a farm. That'll fix it." Spoiler alert: It didn't. Moving forward, I know to protect myself better. When I got legally un-entangled, I had to essentially buy out the other party. From the moment lawyers got involved until the moment I gained full control, I stopped all activity on the land. I didn't invest another dime other than to pay the monthly mortgage. That meant that the land wasn't generating any income—it was actually in the red. But once it was mine, and I could finally pour into it, I invested my time, energy, love, and money. And yes, the value of the business grew, but that didn't happen overnight.

Cleared Land Versus Wooded Land

When purchasing land for farming, one of the first decisions you'll face is whether to buy cleared land or land that's densely wooded and requires clearing. At first glance, buying a plot with trees and clearing it yourself may seem like an attractive option because it's often more affordable. However, cutting down trees comes with several environmental and practical downsides that you should consider before going that route.

Cutting down trees disrupts the local ecosystem. Trees serve as important habitats for wildlife, help prevent soil erosion, and play a crucial role in maintaining air quality by absorbing carbon dioxide. When you remove trees, you're not only displacing animals and insects but also contributing to environmental degradation. From a sustainability perspective, clearing land can contradict the core values of regenerative or organic farming practices, which aim to work in harmony with nature rather than against it.

Clearing wooded land can also be expensive and time consuming. You'll need heavy machinery to remove the trees, and then additional work will be required to remove the stumps and roots. This can delay your planting schedule and significantly increase your start-up costs. Additionally, depending on the type of trees and vegetation, you may have to deal with long-term soil health issues that could limit your initial crop yields. On the other hand, purchasing cleared land allows you to get started more quickly. The land has already been prepped for farming, meaning you can begin planting much sooner. Though cleared land may cost more up front, it can save you money in the long run by avoiding the high costs associated with land clearing and soil rehabilitation. Cleared land also tends to have better soil conditions since it's often used for farming or pasture already, reducing the need for extensive soil amendments.

If you're thinking about borrowing against your assets to acquire land, here's what I want you to hear from me, woman-to-woman: I'm not telling you that you should or shouldn't do it. That's your choice, and it's a big one. But if you choose to borrow from your future, don't give up. Be 1,000 percent sure you're committed to what you're doing with that money. I knew this farm had the potential to be profitable. I knew I was betting on myself. And as a Black woman, I also knew the funding wasn't going to fall from the sky. We don't get handed capital like that. So, if you're going to pull from your future to fund your dream, see it through. You owe yourself that much. Ultimately, whether you lease or buy, the key is to make a decision rooted in your current reality and your future goals. Be honest with yourself about what you can manage financially, how much permanence you desire, and what kind of legacy you want to build through your land.

Land Trust Assistance

Land trusts can play a crucial role in increasing farmland access—especially for those of us who've been historically excluded from landownership. These

Farmer Cee (*center, black boots*) with cohort participants after a workshop in Athens Land Trust's Grow Your Business course.

nonprofit organizations work to conserve land for public or community benefit, often removing farmland from the speculative real estate market and protecting it for agricultural use. I had the rewarding experience of serving on the board of one of our regional land trusts here in North Carolina, Triangle Land Conservancy (TLC), for several years. I also served on the committee for their Good Ground Initiative, a program created to increase farmland access for historically underserved farmers—particularly Black farmers and other farmers of color—while preserving that land for sustainable use.

The goal of the Good Ground Initiative is to identify threatened farmland, conserve it through easements or purchase, and ensure that the next stewards of that land reflect the true diversity and history of agriculture in this country. It's about connecting people to land in a way that's enduring and intentional—not just protecting the land but restoring who has access to it. And yet, in that work, I saw firsthand how even well-meaning institutions can struggle to face historical truth. There was a moment that still sits with me: A white farmer threatened to sue TLC for "discrimination" because the Good Ground Initiative named its intention to prioritize those who had been historically denied land access. Imagine that. A program designed to correct centuries of exclusion was framed as unfair by someone who had never been excluded. The irony is heavy—but sadly, not surprising. It's a reminder of how some folks want to leap over history, pretend it's been even the whole time, and then act shocked when anyone names the truth. But I digress.

Land trusts can be a powerful partner for Black women farmers. Some offer leased land at low or no cost, especially for beginning farmers. Others offer opportunities to purchase land already protected from development. They can offer support for farm infrastructure, conservation easements, and technical assistance. And if nothing else, land trusts provide connection to networks of allies, including other farmers, conservationists, and funders.

Programs like the Good Ground Initiative, or the work of groups like the National Black Food & Justice Alliance, Black Family Land Trust, and Land Loss Prevention Project, show how land trust work is evolving to center equity—when the will is there.

If you're interested in buying or leasing land, contact your regional or local land trust and ask if they have farmland access programs. Better yet, ask how they're working to support BIPOC farmers—and if they're not, let them know why they should.

Farm Incubators

A farm incubator is a training-based program that provides new or aspiring farmers with temporary access to land, tools, mentorship, and infrastructure.

The goal is to reduce the start-up costs and risks of beginning farming while helping participants develop the skills and experience needed to launch independent farm businesses. These programs usually have a defined timeline (one to three years) and may offer business support, markets, and stipends. Think of it as a "starter kit" for farmers—a safe, supported space to learn and grow before farming on your own. A farm incubator is like a supportive landing pad for new farmers. These programs provide temporary access to land, infrastructure, equipment, and often mentorship and business support. Most are designed to help farmers "graduate" into their own land or long-term lease situations.

There are several BIPOC-led farm incubators across the US that provide land access, training, and community support for beginning farmers, especially Black women and other farmers of color. These programs are rooted in cultural knowledge, food sovereignty, and economic justice. They not only provide land access but also offer mentorship, technical assistance, and a supportive community, making them invaluable resources for Black women interested in starting or expanding their boutique farming businesses. Boutique farming is often specialized; incubators allow you to test niche markets while still learning the logistics of growing and selling.

Cooperative Models: Power in Partnership

A cooperative farming model is a long-term, shared-ownership or shared-operation approach where farmers collectively manage land, resources, infrastructure, and/or marketing. Cooperatives can be structured in many ways—from farmers growing separately on shared land to fully integrated collective farming operations. Members make decisions democratically and share responsibilities, risks, and profits. Think of it like a "farming village"—everyone has a stake, voice, and shared commitment to the group's success. If you don't want to farm alone—or if you want to share infrastructure, costs, and land with others—a cooperative model may be your next step. In these settings, land is either co-owned or collectively leased, and members share responsibilities, decision making, and sometimes profits. Some cooperatives operate as shared-use farms, while others support individual businesses working side by side.

A cooperative can be a great model for Black women or beginning boutique farmers. You can reduce costs by sharing equipment, land, and storage, and build community and resilience in a shared mission of reciprocity, care, and sustainability. Some co-ops are also buying land together—so even if you're not ready to own solo, you can still build equity as a group.

FARMER HIGHLIGHT

Patty Lacrete, Bed Head Plant Nursery, East Point, Georgia

Tell us a little about your farm and your "why" for farming.

We specialize in over fifty varieties of organic medicinal and culinary herb starts, alongside freshly harvested herbs for local markets. Committed to transforming Atlanta's food systems, we champion a resilient local foodscape, create diverse agricultural opportunities, and mentor future growers. Our mission centers on providing accessible, organic herbs while empowering communities to cultivate their own food and medicine. By blending education with sustainable farming, Bed Head Plant Nursery strives to make herbal wellness attainable, fostering self-sufficiency and reconnecting Atlanta to the roots of holistic health.

Feeling constrained in my tech career, I envisioned a different path for myself, one filled with soil, seeds, and learning to work with the land. I took a leap of faith in the uncertain economy of spring 2020 and left a steady job to study agricultural science at the University of Georgia. I then managed an invasive plant removal company, and eventually became an apprentice, mastering greenhouse management, permaculture, and plant propagation.

My vision is to plant one million native plants and share the tools of regenerative farming to combat the climate crisis. My commitment is to empower first-time gardeners and herbal enthusiasts through access to fresh

Photo courtesy of Patty Lacrete.

medicinal herbs and the knowledge to use them, putting personal health back into the hands of the people.

I'm inspired by Black woman farmers like Farmer Cee, who is now a catalyst herself—a landowning Black woman farmer demonstrating what's possible. Her work is a living invitation, encouraging other Black women to leap into the agricultural spaces the world so desperately needs. I farm not just to grow plants but to grow possibility, proving that nurturing our ecology and our communities are one and the same.

What has been one of the biggest lessons or truths you've learned through your farming journey?

This work has taught me how to be truly present and to finally, truly honor my body. Before the pandemic and before farming, my life was all go-go-go. As a high-achieving eldest daughter of a first-generation Haitian immigrant, I was taught that perfection and relentless hard work were valued above everything—even if it came at the cost of my own well-being. Farming completely rewired that. Out here, you learn quickly that you are not in control. Crops fail. The Georgia weather absolutely refuses to comply. And through that, I learned that letting go was not a sign of weakness but a necessity for survival.

Therapy has been my anchor through it all, helping me turn inward. I've learned that the only things I can truly control are my own reactions. Cultivating a practice of radical acceptance has become my most vital tool for managing my mental health, especially during those exhausting, unrelenting seasons—working late into the night potting plants, juggling a full-time job, and working farmers markets on the weekend.

What grounds me now is the opposite of what I used to know. It's the feeling of my hands in the soil, a direct connection to something real and patient. It's the quiet mindfulness of tending to each plant, and the profound lesson they teach: that growth requires rest, sunlight requires rain, and strength is found in flexibility, not in rigid perfection. This land has taught me how to care for myself by showing me that I am a part of it, not separate from it, and that to nurture it, I must also nurture the woman who tends it.

What is one piece of advice you would offer to other women interested in starting a boutique farm?

If I could offer one piece of advice to another woman dreaming of starting her own boutique farm, it would be this: Become a detective of your dream. Before you even put a seed in the soil, invest your time in deep, curious research. For me, that meant getting my hands dirty in every way I could. I didn't just read about farming—I lived it. I spent days drenched in sun, from sunup to sundown, doing invasive species removal. That hard work taught me the profound importance of native ecology and land management. I got certified in permaculture design, learning how to truly see a landscape, to understand its rhythms of rain, light, and life. And I completed a two-year plant nursery apprenticeship, where I learned the entire beautiful cycle, from seed to sale. Your research has to extend beyond the field. Go to the farmers markets. Seriously! Grab a coffee and just observe. What's everyone selling? More important, what's missing? Is there a gap you could fill? I also made a point to tour over twenty greenhouse operations across Georgia, my curiosity and notebook in hand. I asked a million questions, and in doing so, I unknowingly built a community of growers who would later become my greatest supporters.

Which brings me to the most important part: Seek mentorship. Once I started my farm, I quickly realized there was a whole world of business knowledge—marketing, consumer demand, pest management, even how to ship a plant safely—that I still needed to learn. I was so fortunate to be surrounded by seasoned farmers who generously shared their wisdom. Social media was huge for me in finding my tribe. Seeing other Black women like Farmer Cee, Cheyenne Sundance of Sundance Harvest, and Jamila Norman of Patchwork City Farms thriving in this space was the fuel I needed. It reminded me that if I could see it, I could absolutely be it. Your community is out there, ready to cheer you on.

How do you care for yourself while doing this work? What grounds you?

One of the greatest truths this path has shown me is that health is the ultimate form of wealth. I've realized that you can't pour from an empty cup, and sustainable agriculture has to start with the sustainable farmer. For me, true abundance isn't just a measure of a plentiful harvest; it's a measure of my own well-being. To be an effective steward of the land, I first have to be a good steward of myself: mind, body, and spirit. That means honoring the basics without compromise: nourishing food, restful sleep, consistent therapy, and moving my body. I learned the hard way that without these anchors, I simply can't show up fully for my plants, my customers, or my purpose. My yoga and meditation practice over the last five years has been a game changer, quieting the noise and helping me tune into the subtle rhythms of the land. And I've finally given myself permission to prioritize recovery, scheduling monthly massages and mental health days to reset from the very real physical and emotional demands of seasonal work.

Most important, I'm learning to embrace play with the same seriousness as work. I'm trying my hand at things I'm genuinely bad at (hello, my lackluster tennis skills), because that discomfort is where the magic happens. Farming is a constant teacher of patience and resilience, and my self-care is how I practice those same lessons on myself. It's a beautiful reminder that I am part of this ecosystem, too. And when I nurture my own roots, everything I cultivate grows that much stronger.

Soil Quality

Once you've secured access to land, the next critical step is understanding the soil you'll be working with. Healthy soil is the foundation not only for successful crop production but also for overall farm ecosystem health, influencing the quality of forage for livestock, the presence of beneficial microbes, and even the safety of water sources.

If your soil is poor, your plants and animals will struggle—even with perfect infrastructure. In addition, certain crops prefer certain soil types. You do not want to plan on growing something in clay soil that actually prefers sandy soils. You want to know not only the soil types but also the nutrient makeup and if the soil has any contaminants and heavy metals. I strongly recommend having soil tested prior to making any land purchases.

One useful tool is the Web Soil Survey provided by the USDA's Natural Resources Conservation Service (NRCS). This free GIS-based platform allows you to identify the soil types on most properties across the US. Simply input your address or map location to view detailed information on soil composition, drainage, and more. Understanding your soil's classification—such as sandy, loamy, or clay-heavy—can guide everything from crop selection to irrigation planning.

To get a more precise understanding of your soil's health and growing potential, soil testing is essential. You have a couple of options. Your local agricultural extension office can provide soil testing services, often at a low cost. These tests range in complexity from basic pH and nutrient levels to more comprehensive analyses that include micronutrients and contaminants. Private soil testing laboratories also offer in-depth testing and may provide more tailored recommendations based on your intended crops. To test your soil, collect samples from multiple locations on your property to get a representative picture. Follow sample collection instructions carefully, then send them to either your extension office or a private lab. Typical results will include pH levels, nutrient content (nitrogen, phosphorus, potassium), soil texture and structure (whether your soil is sandy, loamy, or clay-dominant), and possible contaminants (such as heavy metals or pesticide residues).

If your results indicate poor or imbalanced soil, don't worry—there are practical steps you can take to improve it:

- Incorporate organic matter, such as compost, aged manure, or biochar, to enrich the soil and improve structure.
- Plant cover crops like clover, buckwheat, or winter rye to restore nutrients and improve soil tilth (your local extension office can help you choose the right species for your region and goals).

- Use raised beds or containers if your native soil is severely depleted or contaminated.

These methods offer greater control over your growing medium and drainage. Healthy soil is the literal and figurative ground beneath your farm's success—investing in it pays dividends. To learn more about improving soil quality, see "Resources" at the end of this book.

Growing in Small Spaces or Indoors

Not every boutique farming operation starts with acres of sprawling farmland. In fact, many successful farmers begin by growing in small spaces, whether it's an urban garden, a backyard plot, or even containers. While space might be limited, your creativity and strategy can make a big difference in how much you produce. With small spaces, the focus should be on intensive growing techniques that maximize yield per square foot. Methods like raised beds, vertical gardening, and intercropping (growing complementary crops together) can allow you to grow a surprising amount of produce or herbs in a confined area. For example, herbs like basil, thyme, and parsley can thrive in raised beds or containers, while trellises can support climbing plants like beans or cucumbers in vertical gardens.

Growing in small spaces often requires less water and fewer inputs, which can make your operation more sustainable and environmentally friendly. You also reduce the need for transportation and infrastructure, allowing you to market your produce directly to local consumers or through farmers markets.

While traditional outdoor cultivation remains common, alternative growing methods like indoor farming and greenhouse or nursery production can offer greater flexibility and control, especially for high-value specialty crops. Indoor farming provides the advantage of year-round production in a fully controlled environment. This method is particularly well suited for cultivating premium herbs—like microgreens, culinary herbs, and medicinal plants—as well as crops that require consistent conditions, such as mushrooms and sprouts. The success of an indoor setup depends on thoughtful infrastructure planning, including grow lights (typically LED or full-spectrum fluorescent), ventilation and humidity control to prevent mold, and vertical stacking systems to maximize space (more on infrastructure in the next chapter). However, indoor farming also comes with significant challenges. It can be highly energy-intensive, especially when artificial lighting and climate control systems are running daily. This can lead to higher utility costs and a larger environmental footprint if not paired with sustainable energy practices. Additionally, the initial investment in equipment and the technical know-how required for consistent production can be a barrier for beginning farmers.

Greenhouse or nursery farming offers a balance between indoor and outdoor cultivation by protecting plants from extreme weather while still allowing them access to natural sunlight. Greenhouses are especially valuable for seedling production, extending the growing season, and cultivating herbs or specialty crops year-round. Structure types range from glass and polycarbonate buildings to more affordable high tunnels. Key considerations include proper ventilation, automated temperature control (through fans or vents), and, in some cases, supplemental lighting during winter months. While generally less energy-intensive than fully indoor setups, greenhouses still require careful management of heating and cooling, especially in regions with extreme climates. Up-front costs for construction and the need for routine maintenance are additional factors to keep in mind.

Ultimately, successful farming doesn't depend solely on how much land you have—it depends on how strategically you use the space and resources available to you. Whether you're growing in a converted shed, managing a leased plot, or investing in a greenhouse, aligning your infrastructure with your crop needs, climate, and budget is essential for long-term sustainability and resilience. For more on farming in small spaces, see "Resources" at the end of this book.

CHAPTER 13

Infrastructure and the Investment Behind It

Black women can do anything. We have proven that time and time again.

—TARANA BURKE

Starting a farm from scratch involves a lot more than simply finding a piece of land and planting seeds. I am the first to admit that I grossly underestimated what all was involved in building a farm. I made a lot of expensive mistakes that I hope to help you avoid. The decisions you make in the beginning will shape the success of your operation, so it's important to weigh your options carefully—especially when it comes to land. Whether you're buying property, growing in small spaces, or leasing, each choice comes with its own set of opportunities and challenges.

As you continue on this path, remember that building a successful boutique farm requires ongoing education and adaptability. Engage with your local agricultural extension office or join farming associations to access resources, training, and support. By embracing your farm as a business and following these essential steps, you'll be better equipped to cultivate not just crops but a sustainable and prosperous future for yourself and your community.

One of the most foundational—and often underestimated—aspects of that future is infrastructure. This is not just about having land; it's about what you build on it, in it, and around it to make your farm functional and financially viable. Infrastructure is everything from water access and fencing to storage, processing spaces, power, technology, and internet. Every one of those elements comes with a cost, and many of these systems are intertwined.

I've been intentional about weaving financial conversations throughout this book, because I don't want money to feel like a separate, intimidating topic. It isn't. A healthy relationship with money—knowing where it's going and why—will make your farming journey far more grounded and less stressful. I knew building a farm would take money. That's one of the reasons I've taken a slower, more deliberate path. Growing gradually has helped me avoid overwhelming financial obligations, and it's allowed me to adapt as I learn. When I first started building Green Heffa Farms, it became clear that farming isn't just about seeds and soil—it's about resources. And yes, that includes funding, tools, time, and a whole lot of planning. Before you think about the capital needed to bring your boutique farming vision to reality, it's important to understand what exactly you are creating. What exactly does it take to build your boutique farm—physically and financially? Grounding yourself in that reality is what turns vague dreams into strategic action.

Infrastructure isn't just about what you build—it's about how you plan for what you'll eventually need. Keep in mind the farming model that you have determined from previous chapters. There's no one-size-fits-all budget for building a farm; too many variables come into play. A good place to start is by reflecting on your personal context. Are you working full-time on the farm, or are you building it alongside another job? Will your farm focus primarily on products, experiences, education, or a combination of these? Are you doing most of the labor yourself, or do you plan to hire help? Do you already have tools, buildings, or community resources you can lean on, or are you starting completely from scratch? These questions may seem simple, but your answers will shape the decisions you make about what to invest in first and how to pace your growth responsibly. And that's what we'll dig into next—how to assess your infrastructure needs, prioritize what matters most, and start building (and budgeting) from a place of clarity, not confusion.

These are the core expenses that keep your farm functional: land, water, power, fencing, internet, buildings, storage, and access. Depending on your goals, the cost of putting these systems in place can add up quickly. But here's the thing—you don't need everything at once. You need the right things at the right time. Building with intention—not urgency—will serve you far better in the long run.

Creating a farm plan that focuses on infrastructure helps you avoid unnecessary expenses and delays. This part of your plan should take into account your growing methods, your terrain, your climate, and your access to utilities and water. Infrastructure doesn't just mean buildings—it includes fencing, irrigation systems, storage, drying areas, processing equipment, energy sources, and any tools you'll need for planting, harvesting, and handling crops. Even if you're starting small, mapping out the infrastructure you have versus what you'll need will give you a clear picture of what's required to operate efficiently, safely, and legally. In this chapter, we will discuss the following areas of infrastructure:

Production Setting: Will you grow in fields, raised beds, greenhouses, high tunnels, or indoors? What construction or prep work is needed to establish that space?

Processing: Do you need areas to dry herbs, cure crops, or store tools, packaging, and supplies? Will you be processing any value-added products?

Water Access: What water sources do you have (well, municipal, rain catchment)? Do you need irrigation systems, pumps, or storage tanks?

Wastewater and Sanitation: How will you manage wastewater from washing produce, processing products, and cleaning tools and equipment? Do you need drainage systems, septic systems, or greywater solutions? What sanitation practices and infrastructure are required to meet food safety, product, or livestock care standards?

Electricity and Internet: Is there access to electricity on-site? Will you need solar, generators, or battery systems to supplement or replace the grid?

Structures: What buildings do you have or need (barns, sheds, greenhouses, wash stations, storage units)? Are they up to code and functional for farm use?

Aesthetics: How do you want your farm to look and feel to customers, guests, and/or partners? What elements, such as signage, landscaping, layout, or communal spaces, will reflect your farm's identity and create a cohesive, intentional experience?

Access and Security: What roads, pathways, fencing, or gates are necessary for safety, access, and protection of your land and products?

Tech Infrastructure: What technology systems do you need to support your farm and business operations, such as crop reporting, bookkeeping, sales systems, inventory tracking, customer communications, or monitoring tools? How will you ensure reliable connectivity, data management, and integration across your platforms?

Before you begin designing your processing setup or buying equipment, take a step back and review the previous planning you have done defining your vision and mission. Remember your model. What kind of products are you planning to make? Whatever your goals, they will determine what kind of legal and regulatory paths you'll need to follow. For example, a tea blend intended for consumption will be governed by different rules than a topical salve or a bar of soap. Likewise, raw milk for sale, depending on your state, could be either a complete no-go or allowed under tight restrictions. Your first step should always be to research your local regulations. Start with your state's department of agriculture and health department. Reach out, get names, take notes, and don't be afraid to ask "small-scale" questions. Many states have cottage food laws that allow you to produce certain items from your home kitchen, while others require a certified processing space, even for seemingly simple products like dried herbs.

An herb drying room at Green Heffa Farms.

Once you've thought through the regulations, it's time to get real about your time. Whether you're starting with cleared acreage, converting a backyard, or repurposing an existing structure, your infrastructure decisions will directly shape how much time and labor your farm requires. That naturally leads to a critical consideration: Are you planning to build your farm as a full-time commitment, or are you balancing it alongside another job or responsibility? To help you make that decision with confidence, let's get clear on what your infrastructure will actually demand from you—physically, financially, and logistically. I say that as someone who started with raw land and all the uncertainty that comes with it. In full transparency, I thought I would have a partner to share the responsibility of building the farm. That partnership dissolved before there was even a working well. I had no idea what I was doing. I was in way over my head and, honestly, I thought about quitting at least once a day for quite some time. I'd watch others getting started—often with the help of a significant other or with strong family support—and I'd feel the weight of doing this alone. The demands required to build out raw land are considerable. There's the financial cost, yes, but there's also a steep knowledge curve. I quickly realized that it wasn't just about what I could learn—it was about learning how to find the right people who already had the expertise I didn't.

The larger your production setting, the more complex and costly your infrastructure needs become. Every element—water access, soil testing, grading, trenching, electrical work, drainage—comes with its own set of requirements, timelines, and price tags. These aren't just line items; they are foundational systems that determine how effectively and safely your farm can function. When you're building from scratch, especially without a partner or team, those demands don't just double—they multiply. That's why having a detailed and realistic infrastructure plan is not optional; it's essential. You may not know everything at the beginning, and that's okay. But you do need a working road map that outlines what you're building, the phases you'll take to build it, and the people or services you'll need to fill in the gaps of your expertise. Infrastructure isn't just a checklist of supplies and structures—it's the backbone of your farm's viability. And if you're doing it solo, that backbone must be constructed with strategy, intention, and enough flexibility to accommodate the inevitable hard days when the load feels too heavy.

The larger and more complex your setup, the more labor you will need—not just during planting and harvesting but also the labor required to build your infrastructure, and later on, the everyday maintenance, system checks, and unexpected fixes. If you're planning to manage a high-output operation, you should also be prepared to budget for skilled labor and reliable help. More production space often means more equipment—tractors, implements, irrigation tools, processing setups—all of which require maintenance, storage, and training to use properly. These are not just financial costs; they're management responsibilities. As you scale, your infrastructure plan must also include your plan for people: Who is doing the work, how will they be trained, and how will you sustain the labor needed to keep your farm running efficiently and safely? Building infrastructure is more than construction—it's building capacity. It's about making intentional decisions that align with the type of farm you want, the lifestyle you can realistically support, and the legacy you're trying to grow.

Production Setting

Let's begin with your production or physical setting. In the last chapter we covered raw versus cleared land. Now we will also think about whether your land already has some infrastructure, like buildings or utilities. These factors will impact everything from your start-up budget to your production timeline. Raw land offers a blank canvas, but it also requires a significant investment of time and resources to make it ready for production. On the other hand, a property with existing buildings, utilities, or growing systems can provide a head start, though it may come with its own set of limitations or required modifications.

Think about where and how you plan to grow. Will your production take place in open fields under the sun, or will you use structures like greenhouses or high tunnels that allow for extended seasons and greater environmental control? Some boutique growers even produce entirely indoors, using controlled environments such as converted garages, basements, or purpose-built structures outfitted with grow lights and hydroponic systems. Your physical setting affects not only what you can grow and when but also how much labor, water, energy, and capital you'll need. Each option comes with trade-offs, and understanding those early will help you design a setup that works for your vision, your capacity, and your market.

Processing

Processing doesn't end when the product is made. Storage is where you protect your investment—and your reputation. Heat, light, moisture, and pests can all ruin a perfectly good batch of tea or infused oil. Your storage space should be cool, dry, and free from contaminants. Airtight containers, preferably food-grade or UV-blocking for light-sensitive products, help maintain quality over time. Always label your containers with the name of the product, the date it was made, and a batch number. This isn't just helpful for organization—it's crucial if you ever need to recall a product or trace an issue. And remember, your storage area should be separate from your production area to prevent cross-contamination.

If your farm includes animals, you'll need to plan carefully for how to process and sell their contributions. Eggs and milk are highly regulated products and often require refrigeration logs, clean collection practices, and sometimes a certified facility to be sold legally. Raw milk laws vary widely, and in some places, it's illegal to sell at all—so make sure you know your local laws inside and out.

For meat processing, most farmers will need to take animals to a USDA-inspected facility, particularly if you plan to sell to the public. Some states offer exemptions for small-scale poultry processing, allowing you to butcher on-site under certain conditions. Beekeeping and honey production are often more lenient but still require proper food-safe practices and clear labeling. And don't forget—your animals can contribute to products beyond food. Beeswax candles, lanolin salves, or goat's milk soap are just a few creative and less regulated options that still offer excellent market potential.

Even a small space can support a thriving value-added product line if it's well designed. A dedicated room, a converted shed, or even a small mobile trailer can serve as your micro processing center. Focus on cleanliness, organization, and efficient use of space. Floors and surfaces should be easy to sanitize. Handwashing stations are a must. Good lighting and ventilation help ensure both quality and comfort.

As your farm grows, you may find that shared commercial kitchens, co-packers, or incubator spaces offer the scalability you need. But in the beginning, start small, stay legal, and focus on doing a few things really well. Processing is where your creativity and your business acumen meet. It's where you turn herbs into healing, milk into magic, and your farm's abundance into offerings that nourish your community. Do your homework, respect the regulations, and invest in infrastructure that supports your long-term vision. Above all, make it yours. Your process, your products, your path.

Water Access

Water is pretty essential to a boutique herb farm. After acquiring full ownership of the Green Heffa Farms land, I realized that the well that I thought had been paid for in full had not been. I also didn't know that the person who digs the well is not necessarily the same person who installs the pump. I found this out the hard way when I arrived at the farm expecting to see a fully functional well—only to discover there was no water because there was no working pump. Turns out, the well pump guy hadn't been paid. And not only had he not been paid, but he also hadn't connected the pump yet. He was ready to pull it if I didn't come up with $900—immediately. With the well pump finally in place, I thought I was in the clear. Water should be flowing any minute now, right? If I could insert a side-eye emoji here, I absolutely would.

Because—fun fact—you need electricity to make a well pump work. Ha! WHO KNEW??? Certainly not me. Now I had to figure out how to get electricity to the farm—an entirely separate and costly process. But in the meantime, I was pretty proud of my progress, so I decided to have an entire photoshoot because I had done so . . . well. I couldn't resist.

Farmer Cee, showing off her nearly completed well. *Photo courtesy of Tunisa Rice.*

Water is a non-negotiable necessity, no matter what kind of farm you're building. Whether you're growing herbs, raising animals, or creating value-added products, your success hinges on a steady, clean, and reliable water source. In the beginning, it's easy to overlook water infrastructure, especially when the excitement of selecting crops or building greenhouses takes center stage. But water—or the lack of it—will quickly become the most urgent part of your operation if not thoughtfully addressed up front. I don't want you to repeat my mistakes, but here's the thing: Had I not gone through all of that, I wouldn't have the knowledge to share with you. Every setback presents a learning opportunity. Every unexpected challenge is a piece of wisdom earned.

If you're creating value-added products, water quality and safety move front and center. Water used in product preparation—especially anything that's ingested or applied to the body—must meet food-grade or cosmetic-grade standards. That may require additional filtration, treatment, or testing, especially if your source is a well or rain catchment system. It's not just about quantity at that point—it's about quality, and ensuring your water meets the legal and health requirements for the type of products you intend to sell. On the other hand, if you're raising animals, daily water needs can add up quickly, especially in warmer months.

The type of water access you choose or inherit depends heavily on your land and your production goals. Municipal water may seem like the easiest option for smaller boutique setups, especially if you're in or near a town, but it comes at a higher cost and often with restrictions on volume, usage, or quality. If you're producing for consumption or manufacturing products like teas, tinctures, or skincare, those restrictions can matter a great deal. On the other hand, drilling a well can provide long-term independence, but it comes with a steep initial investment, ongoing maintenance, and no guarantee that the water table will yield what you need. Then there's rain catchment—a more sustainable and environmentally conscious option, but one that requires serious planning, infrastructure, and local legal compliance. In some places, collecting rainwater is regulated or even prohibited. In others, it's incentivized. Knowing your local regulations and climate patterns is critical when considering rain catchment as part of your system. Also of note, EQIP can provide financial and technical assistance for farmers, ranchers, and forest landowners to implement rainwater catchment systems to conserve water, so please be sure to look into that possibility.

Surface water—ponds, creeks, or streams located on or near your property—can also be used as a water source in some cases. However, this typically involves additional permitting, testing, and specialized pumping equipment, and may be subject to environmental regulations and seasonal fluctuations. While surface water may seem like a cost-saving option, it can pose legal and ecological complications if not managed properly.

No matter your source, the method of delivery to your crops or animals matters just as much. Drip irrigation is one of the most efficient systems available, especially for boutique farms. It delivers water directly to the base of the plant, reducing evaporation and runoff while conserving water and minimizing weed pressure. Drip systems can be scaled up or down, automated or manual, and are particularly well suited for medicinal and culinary herbs.

Installing these systems can be labor-intensive at first, but the long-term benefits in water savings and healthier plants are well worth the investment.

The amount of water you need depends on your crop selection, scale, and climate—but always plan for more than you think. Crops like herbs may require less frequent watering than vegetables, but consistency is key to quality and yield. Your cooperative extension agent can be helpful in planning your water needs.

Securing water access and installing efficient irrigation systems can be expensive, but there are resources to help, such as EQIP. If you meet certain criteria—for example, if you are a new farmer, if you are socially disadvantaged, or if you are a veteran—you may receive a higher reimbursement rate and advance payments. At the time of this writing, it is important to note that DEI efforts are under increasing political attack, which may influence how these programs are emphasized or funded in the future. Applying for EQIP requires a conservation plan, so it's worth connecting with your local NRCS office early to begin that process. Conservation plans are provided at no cost to the farmer, so they are certainly worth looking into.

Water isn't just a resource—it's a lifeline. Without it, nothing grows or lives. As you develop your infrastructure plan, give water the central importance it deserves. Secure your access early, design your systems with intention, and don't hesitate to seek funding support to help lighten the load. Thoughtful water planning won't just sustain your crops—it will sustain your peace of mind. Building your farm with water efficiency in mind from the start can save you money and frustration down the line.

Wastewater and Sanitation

If you're making products on your farm—whether teas, tinctures, infused oils, or bath and body items—wastewater isn't something you can afford to ignore. The moment water becomes part of your production process, you have to start thinking about where that water goes, how it's handled, and what regulations may apply.

Not to mention—you'll need a place to take care of basic human biological functions. For almost an entire year, we either found a tree or drove into town when we needed to use the restroom. That may sound wild, but it was our reality. So trust me when I say: Getting working toilets and handwashing sinks needs to be a top infrastructure priority. Sanitation is not just about comfort—it's about dignity, health, and compliance, especially if you're planning to host guests or process products on-site.

The most common solution in rural areas that are not connected to municipal sewage is a septic system. This includes a septic tank, where wastewater is collected, and a drain field, where that water filters through the soil and is naturally treated before returning to the groundwater. It's a long-term investment and usually the best option if you're adding bathrooms, kitchens, processing areas, or lodging to your farm. But here's the catch: Not all land is suitable for a septic system.

Before installing—or even *purchasing*—land where you'll need to use septic, make sure the property will perc. That's short for "percolate" and means your property must pass a percolation test, which evaluates how well the soil can absorb and filter water. If your soil doesn't perc, you may not be able to install a septic system at all. And without a functioning wastewater plan, your farm operation could hit a wall before it even begins. A perc test is typically required by your local health department before you'll be issued a septic permit, so don't skip this step when considering raw or undeveloped land.

Once septic is installed, you also need to be thoughtful about how you use the land over and around your drain field. Drain fields are sensitive zones that require air, drainage, and minimal soil compaction to function properly. That means no permanent structures, driveways, heavy machinery, or deep digging in those areas. While it may seem like wasted space, it doesn't have to be. Shallow-rooted plants like herbs, grasses, or pollinator-friendly wildflowers can grow there safely while supporting soil health and biodiversity.

However, if you have or plan to raise livestock, your drain field area needs even more protection. Livestock should not be allowed to graze, walk, or rest on top of a drain field. Their weight can compact the soil, and their waste can overload the system or introduce pathogens that undermine its function. Fencing off your drain field—or locating it well away from animal areas—is essential. It's also worth noting that hoof traffic, especially from larger animals like cows or goats, can damage the soil structure and compromise pipes beneath the surface. Your septic and drain field area may be out of sight, but it should never be out of mind. It's one of the foundational systems your farm relies on, and protecting it from overuse or damage is just as important as maintaining your greenhouse or tractor.

Another option, especially for smaller-scale operations, is graywater recycling. Graywater is lightly used water—think from handwashing, rinsing herbs, or cleaning equipment. With the right setup, this water can be filtered and reused for non-edible irrigation, like watering trees, flowers, or compost piles. It's an ecofriendly solution that can reduce water waste and lower your monthly costs. But just as with septic, graywater systems may require permits depending on your state and how you plan to use the water.

For those going off-grid or building out incrementally, composting toilets can be a game changer. They're especially useful in outbuildings, processing areas, or guest spaces where installing full plumbing would be cost-prohibitive or unnecessary. A high-quality composting toilet reduces water use, limits contamination risks, and can help you meet sanitation needs while staying compliant. If you're hosting farm stays or public events, be sure to check local sanitation codes to make sure your system meets public health standards. Permitting requirements for composting toilets on farms can be tricky because they vary widely depending on state, county, and local health codes, so do your research.

Whether you're rinsing vegetables or cleaning canning supplies, wastewater has to be accounted for. It's part of your infrastructure plan—and in some states, it's part of your license or inspection process if you're creating value-added products. Think through your current needs, but also ask yourself: What might you be doing three years from now? Bottling more? Hosting larger groups? Washing bulk harvests? Your wastewater system should be ready to support the next phase of your farm.

Electricity and Internet

When it comes to utilities, electricity and internet access are two of the most critical—and often overlooked—components of your farm infrastructure. These may seem like givens if you're used to living in an area where you simply call the utility company and flip a switch. But when you're building a farm from raw land, especially in rural areas, these are major projects that require planning, patience, and investment.

Electricity

Let's start with electricity. Before Green Heffa Farms was a working farm, it was just land—no poles, no wires, no lights. My only prior experience with electricity was calling the city to start service at an apartment or a house. I had no idea what it took to actually bring power to an undeveloped property. Spoiler alert: It's a lot more than making a phone call. First, you'll likely need to pull permits and work with a licensed electrician to install new power lines and connect them to a service panel. Not every area has the same requirements, so check with your local jurisdiction before you make moves. You'll also need to think carefully about your energy needs. What buildings will be powered? What equipment will you be using—dehydrators, refrigerators, mixers, heaters? If you're planning to install a well, know that most pumps are electrically powered, too.

Another important consideration is whether or not you plan to host events, workshops, or farm stays—now or in the future. Many boutique farms evolve into gathering spaces, offering everything from tastings and classes to healing retreats and educational tours. But creating space for people is a different kind of buildout that comes with its own set of requirements. First and foremost, lighting becomes essential—both for ambience and for safety.

That means not just overhead lighting inside structures, but outdoor lighting along pathways, driveways, and gathering areas. Solar lighting can be a sustainable and low-maintenance solution, especially in places where hardwiring would be difficult or expensive. But if your events go into the evening, you'll want to make sure the lighting is strong enough for guests to safely move around. If you're already trenching to run electricity to a space, it makes sense to include wiring for exterior lighting at the same time—saving you from having to do it all over again later.

You may also need access to electricity for specialized event equipment. If you're setting up a workshop space or lodging units like tiny homes or domes, you may need dedicated electrical circuits, exterior outlets, and potentially even a separate panel depending on how far your structures are from the main service and how much power they require. I knew that I wanted to host events where a food truck would be included, so I made sure to install the appropriate exterior outlet on the herb cabin. That way, food trucks have a reliable and safe plug-in point, and I don't have to worry about overloading the system or running extension cords across the farm. It's a small detail, but it makes the whole experience more professional and welcoming for both vendors and guests. Planning for these possibilities doesn't mean you have to build everything now. But running conduit, adding a few extra outlets, or making sure your router setup can grow with your vision? Those are small steps that can save you major money and time down the road.

I began with a 200-amp service, which was fine initially. Three of our buildings are now wired, but as we've grown, so have our energy demands. We're now operating close to our electrical capacity, which means that with further expansion, we'll need to add another electrical panel. That might mean upgrading the service altogether or adding a subpanel to support a new processing shed or additional equipment. This is the kind of foresight I wish I'd had earlier. It's far easier—and cheaper—to plan for expansion from the start than it is to retrofit down the road. Alternative energy is worth exploring, too. Solar panels are a great option for supplementing your electrical needs and reducing long-term utility costs. Some farmers also use generators for backup during outages. On a farm, a sudden loss of power can mean spoiled products, halted processing, or loss of irrigation. Having a contingency plan in place protects your time, your products, and your peace of mind.

Internet Access

Let's talk internet. Coming from a suburban area where high-speed Wi-Fi was standard, I quickly learned that rural connectivity is a whole different game. Since the land was raw, there were no existing lines or service. The first step was figuring out which companies, if any, provided service in the area. And just because a provider *can* reach your farm doesn't mean they *will* anytime soon. After identifying a provider, I had to wait several months before they actually came out to install the lines. It was a slow process, and it taught me something critical: To get internet, you need more than just a provider—you need a functioning building with power in it. That means internet isn't the first thing you'll install. It has to come after your electricity and at least one building are in place. For those in areas where traditional broadband isn't available, there are other options worth considering. Satellite internet has come a long way and may be your best bet if you're in a more remote location. Some farmers also rely on mobile hot spots or fixed wireless solutions as a bridge until more permanent service is available. Starlink, though still pricey, is becoming increasingly popular in underserved rural communities. Just know that whatever you choose, reliable internet access is no longer a luxury—it's essential for running a modern farm. From managing sales to monitoring equipment to simply sending emails, your connection to the digital world directly impacts your ability to succeed.

When it comes to internet access, hosting events or offering agritourism experiences raises the bar on what your connectivity needs to look like. A stable, reliable connection becomes more than a convenience—it becomes part of your customer experience and your business operations. Whether you're processing on-site transactions, streaming a virtual class, or simply offering Wi-Fi to your guests, your signal needs to reach the places where people gather. That might mean investing in range extenders, setting up a mesh network, or even running ethernet cables to outdoor buildings or event spaces. And as with everything tech-related on a farm, none of that happens without power in place first—so again, plan your electrical layout with future expansion in mind. If you plan to install wired service, it's smart to designate a small, secure structure—like an office shed, studio, or even a converted shipping container—as your modem and router hub. This gives you a centralized location for your network setup and helps ensure your signal is protected from weather and wildlife. Reliable internet access may not be the first thing you think about when dreaming up your farm, but if you plan to host, teach, sell, or stay connected with your community, it's something you'll need to get right.

For Backyard Boutique Farms

For those of you starting from your home—which is how many boutique farms begin—there are still important utility considerations, even if you're not dealing with raw land. While you may already have electricity and internet, the question becomes: Do you have enough? Running a home and a farm on the same electrical service can strain your system, especially if you start adding equipment like dehydrators, refrigerators, heat sealers, or grow lights. You might find yourself constantly tripping breakers or noticing lights flickering when you run multiple appliances. In these cases, it's worth having a licensed electrician assess whether your panel can handle the extra load. Sometimes, something as simple as adding a dedicated circuit for your farm operation can make a big difference. Other times, you may need to upgrade your entire service.

If you're processing products from your kitchen, remember: Many states have cottage food laws that allow you to make and sell certain items from a home kitchen, but the requirements vary. Some jurisdictions may require specific upgrades like ventilation, sinks, or dedicated prep areas. That means your utility needs could shift based on compliance, especially if you're working toward certification or retail-readiness.

As for internet, working from home likely means you already have a connection—but ask yourself if it's reliable and fast enough to support your business. Can you host a live sale without buffering? Upload product photos quickly? Maintain a secure e-commerce website? If your signal struggles once you step outside or into your shed, consider installing range extenders, mesh systems, or even hardwired ethernet to ensure stable connectivity across your working spaces.

Starting from home doesn't mean you skip over infrastructure planning—it just means you adapt what you have to meet your business goals. Many successful farms began at kitchen tables and in converted closets. The key is making sure your utilities can grow along with your vision.

Structures

Once you begin building out your farm infrastructure, structures become the bones that support everything else. But let me be real with you—don't get caught up in the shiny farm builds you see scrolling through Instagram. Buildings are expensive. Material costs fluctuate, now more than ever. Labor is another major expense, especially if you have to hire outside help. And a lot of those folks with picture-perfect setups also have picture-perfect debt. If you're building in a rural area, just getting someone to show up and do the work can be a challenge in itself.

The very first formal structure on Green Heffa Farms was a high tunnel, which we converted into a greenhouse by using a gravel floor instead of natural soil. That one decision allowed us to better manage humidity and reduce pest issues, giving us more control over the growing environment. From there, we added the herbal tea cabin, followed by a tractor shed, then a tiny house for guests, another high tunnel, a second tiny house, and a third high tunnel. Next up was a storage shed for field tools and small equipment, a geodesic dome to house those who come here to learn, and a residence for me. Eventually, I plan to build a barn-style structure that will house our on-farm boutique apothecary and serve as a space for workshops, small events, and weddings.

I'm walking you through all of my plans not to overwhelm you, but to be transparent. These builds didn't happen overnight. They happened over years—based on budget, need, and strategy. That's why it's so important to begin with a clear understanding of function. Ask yourself: What do I need this structure to *do*? Are you drying herbs? Storing inventory? Housing animals? Teaching classes? Maybe you need a multipurpose space that can flex with the season or your evolving goals.

Each structure on this farm was built because there was a practical reason for it. Not because it looked cute in a photo but because it solved a real need. The truth is, you can do a whole lot with a converted carport, a repurposed shipping container, or even a reclaimed shed—especially if your budget is tight. A half-finished dream barn that drains your resources isn't a flex. A functional space that keeps your farm moving? That's the real win. You may want to start with a processing facility, a shed for tools, seeds, and supplies, a high tunnel or greenhouse to extend your growing season, and a shaded area for comfort, rest, and breaks.

Don't forget to consider your land's topography and your local climate. Do your structures need to withstand high winds, intense humidity, or heavy rainfall or snow? Do you need screens for airflow, or insulation for colder months? Think about how the sun hits your property and how water drains after a storm. Consider where your electricity and water lines will run. Good placement and smart design can save you so much trouble later.

It's also helpful to think ahead toward what your processing and storage needs *will* be—because chances are, your farm will eventually need space for both. That transition starts here, with how you design and prioritize your early structures. You don't have to build it all at once. Start with what you can afford, build what you actually need, and allow your farm to grow into itself over time. Taking the time to develop an infrastructure snapshot will help you decide what's manageable now versus what should be phased in later. It also gives you a realistic lens through which to assess whether farming part-time will allow you to meet your goals, or whether a full-time commitment—or support from others—will be necessary to bring your boutique farm to life.

Before you start laying a foundation or ordering lumber, it's important to think through several key considerations that go beyond just what you want to build. These are the less glamorous, often frustrating, but absolutely necessary parts of the process. And if you skip over them, they can cost you time, money, and peace of mind down the line.

First up: climate appropriateness. Your structures need to work *with* your environment, not against it. If you're farming in the South like me, you're dealing

Green Heffa Farms' herb blending kitchen, before the fire.

with humidity, heat, and seasonal storms. That means you need materials and designs that promote ventilation, resist mold, and can handle high winds. You might need hurricane strapping, roof vents, shade cloths, or reinforced doors. In colder climates, you may need insulation, snow-load-rated roofs, and frost-proof water lines. Think about how your climate affects not just your crops—but your buildings, your tools, and your ability to work year-round.

Next, check for any homeowners' association (HOA) restrictions. If you're farming in a suburban or peri-urban area, you may be dealing with an HOA. HOAs often have rules about what types of structures you can build, how they look, and where they're located. Some don't allow high tunnels or visible storage sheds at all. It might seem like your land is yours to do with as you please, but unfortunately, that's not always the case. Know the rules before you build.

Permitting is another critical step. In most jurisdictions, anything beyond a small shed will require a building permit. Even if you're out in the country, don't assume you can bypass your local planning department. Permits often require site plans, inspections, and code compliance for things like electrical and plumbing. It can feel like red tape, but trust me—it's better to deal with it on the front end than to be hit with fines or a stop-work order later.

It's also worth noting that many counties and municipalities have special allowances or exemptions for agricultural structures—but only if your land is recognized as agricultural. That's one of the many reasons I strongly encourage you to get a farm number from your local USDA Farm Service Agency. Remember, it's free. Having that designation can help you avoid certain building code restrictions, qualify for agricultural tax exemptions, or access cost-share programs for structures like high tunnels, processing sheds, or water systems. In some areas, ag buildings don't require the same permits as residential or commercial structures—but that only applies if you're recognized as a working farm. So don't skip that step. Getting a farm number doesn't just give you access to USDA programs—it helps you build with legitimacy and protection.

Speaking of electrical and plumbing, location matters. The farther your structure is from your main electrical panel or your well, the more expensive and complicated it becomes to run power and water. Trenches have to be dug, conduit has to be laid, and everything has to meet code. I learned the hard way that placing a structure "where it looked good" sometimes meant triple the cost to get utilities to it. If your structure needs electricity—whether for lights, fans, or equipment—consider how far it is from your breaker box. If it needs plumbing, know the location of your well, pressure tank, and water lines. This is not just about convenience—it's about cost and feasibility.

And let's not forget wastewater. In some areas, you can't build within a certain number of feet from a well or a body of water due to runoff and contamination concerns. If your land has a high water table or is prone to flooding, wastewater disposal becomes even more complicated. This is especially important for those of you who want to host events or build value-added product spaces on-farm.

A structure is more than four walls and a roof. It's a long-term investment, and it should be treated like one. The more you think through the details ahead of time—climate, location, compliance, and cost—the more resilient and functional your farm will be. You want your structures to support your growth, not slow you down.

Aesthetics: More than Colors and Filters

Your aesthetics are going to be informed by your brand's visuals and voice and also be a key deciding factor when it comes to making infrastructure decisions. Aesthetics don't just shape how your farm is seen—they shape how it is built. When you know the aesthetic you are going for, it becomes a compass that guides decisions around materials, layout, signage, color palettes, and even the types of structures you choose to erect. Now, do not go into debt to achieve an aesthetic. When it comes to infrastructure decisions, the impact on the environment and available resources should be prioritized. But think about how you want your farm to feel to someone pulling up for the first time. What stories do you want your space to tell? What do you want visitors to remember? How do you want to feel when you work there every day? Answer these questions early, so that you're building a cohesive experience instead of patchworking a farm together and hoping it feels right later. When people hear "aesthetics," they often think of pretty colors, flowers in bloom, or a perfectly styled Instagram post. But on a boutique farm, aesthetics serve a much deeper purpose. They help define your identity, tell your story without saying a word, and create a sensory experience that people remember. Aesthetics aren't just about what looks good—they're about what *feels* good. In this section, we'll explore how design choices, visual storytelling, and creative expression can turn your farm into a place of beauty, meaning, and profitability.

Ultimately, treating aesthetics as infrastructure means that your beauty is not accidental, it's intentional, foundational, and functional. Incorporating aesthetics into your infrastructure thinking isn't about vanity—it's about vision. It ensures that every choice you make contributes to a space that reflects your essence, delights your community, and becomes a place where both work and wonder can thrive. Aesthetics help turn a farm into a sanctuary, a workshop into a vibe, a shed into a scene. This is also an opportunity to

This lemon balm sign adds a personal touch to a practical piece of farm infrastructure.

Highlighting Local Artists

We commissioned a vibrant mural by artist Georgia O'Tardy, which was funded through an arts grant. It's not just paint on a building—it's a bold declaration of who we are: rooted in Black womanhood, land, culture, and healing. It draws visitors in, sparks conversation, and offers a powerful visual centerpiece that reflects our values. This is the kind of public art that doesn't just decorate—it educates, activates, and celebrates. Added bonus: Georgia also designed this book cover, providing us another opportunity to merge art and agriculture.

Georgia O'Tardy's mural on the herb cabin (Heffa's House of Happiness).

think about circularity: Aesthetics give you permission to repurpose, recycle, and reimagine—actions that are often kinder to both budget and planet. Start a Pinterest board. Visit antiques stores, flea markets, and local festivals.

Your aesthetic is a powerful branding tool because it communicates who you are without needing words. When done well, it creates cohesion across your products, your packaging, your online presence, and your physical farm environment. It draws people in, gives them something to remember, and can elevate a small operation into a signature destination.

At Green Heffa Farms, our aesthetic is rooted in a blend of Southern Black heritage, herbal elegance, and eco-conscious charm. We intentionally weave together tradition and creativity—honoring our roots while embracing a modern Black rural beauty. You'll find vibrant signage, antique furniture used as planter bases, upcycled bottles as propagation jars, and our signature color themes throughout. That didn't happen by accident. It was a series of intentional choices, guided by our values and our vision.

I will admit that for a brief moment, I felt overwhelmed with the idea of being responsible for building out 15 acres. When I first started, I convinced myself that I had to do everything at once. It felt like if I didn't have it all mapped out, built up, and branded immediately, I would fall behind. That mindset left little room for joy or creativity. Only when I stepped back and gave myself permission to grow at a pace that allowed grace did things began to shift. I had to remind myself that I was growing slow—on purpose. And in that slowness, I found clarity. I gave myself space to explore what I wanted the farm to feel like, not just look like. I started creating mood boards on Pinterest—not with pressure but with curiosity. At first I had just one board for overall farm design. As time went on, I began making boards for specific spaces and projects: the herb cabin, the field expansion, the outdoor classroom. Each board helped me translate vision into structure and aesthetics into action. The early building phases provided some of the best authentic content. It allowed me to build a genuine community with supporters who turned into customers. And I made it a point to enjoy the process. So, if you feel overwhelmed, know that's normal. Take your time. Let your vision evolve. Just make sure you're making space to see it.

Crimson clover cover crop at Green Heffa Farms.

For boutique farmers, aesthetics are part of placemaking—the act of turning land into an intentional, welcoming, and distinct space. It's the difference between a field and a farm experience. Do you want your field rows to feel wild and whimsical, or organized and modern? At Green Heffa Farms, we have both. Because rows are more efficient in harvesting larger grows, we utilize those—but I also have an educational space and many pollinator pockets that allow for less structured energy. No matter the size of your operation, it is important to identify your farm's core zones. These are the primary functional areas you plan to develop, which might include:

- Growing/production areas (fields, beds, greenhouses, hoop houses)
- Processing/prep areas (packing shed, cold storage, wash/clean zones)
- Storage (tools, feed, supplies, harvest containers)
- Animal housing or rotational grazing areas (if applicable)

A Cabin Called Happiness: The Story of Heffa's House

Let me tell y'all about a little building with a big story—Heffa's House of Happiness. When I first started thinking about where I'd process herbs and make products on the farm, I had visions of something small but sacred. I wanted a space that felt warm and grounded. What I found . . . was a cabin on Facebook Marketplace. Now let me pause right there and say: I do not recommend buying buildings off Facebook Marketplace. Learn *from* me, not *like* me.

The listing said it was an old sharecropper cabin. But when I stepped inside, it didn't feel haunted by that history. This building had never known Black pain. It felt different—like it had waited all this time for me. I knew absolutely nothing about relocating a building. Nothing. I didn't know I'd need permits. I didn't know how complicated moving it would be. I definitely didn't know how expensive it would be. Sis—by the time the cabin made it to the farm, I had already spent more than I planned. And that was just the beginning.

The structure needed a brand-new foundation. The roof had to be redone. Plumbing had to be installed. Electrical wiring, insulation, windows . . . it was a full-blown renovation. What I thought was a shortcut turned into a whole journey.

There were moments I second-guessed myself hard. There were even times I regretted the decision altogether. But today? I can't imagine Green Heffa Farms without this cabin. It's more than a building—it's a placemaker. We call it Heffa's House of Happiness, and that's exactly what it brings. It's where we make our teas, infusions, and body oils. It's where I feel most connected to the medicine of the land. The walls are made from old forest pine—dense, golden, fragrant wood that you can't even find in modern buildings anymore. We added a mural by a local Black woman artist, and now it's a whole vibe. The heart of the farm. So, yes, building or bringing in a processing structure can be a beast. Whether you're converting a shed, retrofitting a garage, or hauling in a century-old cabin, it will test you. But it will also ground your farm in a powerful way.

- Customer- or community-facing areas (farm stand, market setup, U-pick, events)
- Personal or staff space (shade/rest area, workspace, office)

Thoughtful aesthetics can deepen connection, increase engagement, and, yes, bring in revenue. People are drawn to places that feel good to be in. Don't underestimate the power of whimsy, like a repurposed bathtub in a

Heffa's House of Happiness before the renovations.

An early, in-progress photo of the herb cabin.

What I Wish I Knew Before Moving a Cabin

Moving a Building Is Not Cheap

Transport alone can cost several thousand dollars depending on distance, road conditions, and permits required. It's not a pickup-truck situation—it's a pilot car, escort vehicles, block-off-the-road type of thing.

Permits Are Essential—and Not Always Easy to Get

You'll likely need permits for transport, foundation work, and utility hookups. Call your local planning/zoning office early. Trust me on this.

Foundations Are Not Optional

Once the cabin arrives, it needs a proper foundation—pier and beam, slab, crawl space—whatever fits your land and structure. Factor in labor and materials.

Hidden Costs Lurk Everywhere

Even if the bones are good, you may need a new roof, plumbing, electrical wiring, HVAC, windows, insulation, or structural reinforcements. If it's an older building, get a full inspection before moving it.

Time Is Money, so Ask for Help and Hire Pros

What you think will take weeks may take months. And if you're DIY-ing parts of it, multiply that time by two. This is not a journey you want to take alone. Bring in experts where needed—especially electricians and structural engineers.

flower patch or a colorful chair in the middle of a field. Aesthetics give you permission to play—to think outside the rows and let your creativity shape your landscape. Whether it's a serene herb walk, a photo-worthy backdrop, or a product display that feels like art, your farm's visual language has real economic value.

Access and Security

As Black women, many of us move through the world with an ever-present awareness of safety. That same mindset applies when establishing your boutique farm. Access and security aren't just about gates and locks—they're about boundaries, peace of mind, and protection, both physical and digital. You're not just safeguarding your equipment and your products—you're protecting yourself, your investment, your time, and your energy.

A final but critical consideration for your farm infrastructure is accessibility—and this goes far beyond how something looks on a sunny day. Ask yourself: Can I access this structure easily, regardless of the season or weather?

Will delivery trucks, emergency vehicles, or even your own car be able to reach it after heavy rain? Will you need to install a gravel path, reinforce your driveway, or eventually pave certain entry points? These details might seem minor at first, but they become major when conditions change. And they will.

When we talk about access, we're also talking about the flow of movement throughout your farm. Where are the entry and exit points on your property? Are they clearly marked and logically placed? If you're working on multiple acres or plan to receive freight deliveries, you'll want to think through how large vehicles will navigate the space—turnaround space, clearance, and unobstructed paths matter. Poor access not only slows down operations but can become a safety issue in emergencies.

Security begins at the entry. On larger properties, fencing can help control access, but even a simple locked gate on a driveway or access road sends a clear message that your space is protected. Access points should be properly secured, and locks maintained. If you're just starting out and can't fence the entire property, focus on clearly defined boundaries and make sure your key structures are gated, locked, or otherwise reinforced.

Fencing is one of the most practical tools for both access control and security—and it doesn't have to be expensive at the start. Your first fence might be made from pallets, T-posts with wire, or reclaimed materials—something simple to mark your boundaries and keep out what needs keeping out. Over time, as your resources grow, you can upgrade to more permanent and durable solutions like welded wire, woven fencing, privacy fencing, or decorative wooden fencing that doubles as branding.

What you're fencing *for* matters, too. If your goal is to protect crops from deer or rabbits, you'll need taller, possibly reinforced fencing. If you're keeping in livestock, electric fencing may be a better fit—especially portable options that allow you to move animals for rotational grazing. Privacy fencing adds a layer of seclusion and can create a sense of sanctuary, which may be particularly important for those of us hosting events or offering wellness spaces.

Lighting plays a central role in both security and safety. Motion-sensor lights are ideal for outbuildings or perimeter zones where constant lighting isn't necessary. Outdoor lighting also improves the quality of security camera footage and deters unwanted activity. Motion-sensor lights around key entry points, structures, and walkways not only help you move safely after dark but also deter trespassers. Solar-powered motion cameras are great for farms, especially those in areas where running electrical lines isn't practical. They're easy to install, they're ecofriendly, and many offer app-based monitoring so you can check your property remotely. You can also consider an integrated security system, especially if you have structures storing high-value equipment or inventory. Make sure every building on your property is secured with reliable locks—sheds, greenhouses, processing rooms, guest lodging, even water spigots if theft or tampering is a concern. It doesn't have to be high-tech, but it does need to be consistent and intentional.

Surveillance is another key component of security and safety. There are many ways to approach surveillance. Game cameras are often a cost-effective option in rural or wooded areas, especially early on. They're great not only for detecting intruders but also for identifying which curious creatures are helping themselves to your crops at night. And yes, the boutique lifestyle does include critters. Mine apparently includes a groundhog who has decided that our natural space is just as sacred to him as it is to us. A few years ago, my son Asher and my son-in-law Josh (who's been part of Green Heffa since the beginning) were out in the fields when they encountered a groundhog. At first, he was just "the groundhog." But that day, when he popped up unexpectedly and the two men started arguing—shovel in hand—about who was going to "handle" him, he became Richard. Now he visits almost every evening at dusk, nibbling here and there but never causing real damage. He even samples my watermelons, but hey, it's his land, too. Richard might actually be Richardetta. We'll never know. Either way, they're part of the Green Heffa story now. As your farm becomes more established, or if you live in a residential area rather than rural, consider investing in a professional-grade security system. If you already have one installed in your home, ensure that your farm structures and growing areas are included in its range.

Signage is one of the simplest yet most effective tools in your access and security tool kit. Clear, intentional signs communicate expectations, reinforce boundaries, and reduce confusion for visitors, delivery drivers, and even neighbors. A basic PRIVATE PROPERTY or NO TRESPASSING sign can deter uninvited guests, while directional signage—like THIS WAY or WORKSHOP PARKING—can help guide those who are welcome without them wandering around. If you're running a business open to the public at certain times, be sure to include your hours, appointment policies, or check-in location. And signage doesn't have to be sterile or caustic—it can still reflect your brand voice while doing its job. Just remember: People can't respect your boundaries if they don't know where they are.

Physical protection is just one piece of the puzzle. In today's world, your digital presence affects your physical safety. If you're building a brand that stands out—which you likely are as a boutique farmer—you will attract attention. Most of it will be supportive. Some of it won't. Unfortunately, being visible—especially as a Black woman in agriculture—can invite unwanted energy. So, it's wise to develop boundaries for what you share online. Don't post your exact address. Delay real-time posting, especially if you're alone.

Why Green Heffa Farms Operates by Appointment Only

At Green Heffa Farms, we choose to welcome visitors by appointment only—not as a barrier but as an intentional boundary. Farming is sacred and consuming work. Every plant we grow, every product we craft, and every decision we make reflects care, labor, and vision. Operating by appointment allows us to protect that process, honoring both the land and our time. It also ensures that every visitor, every customer, is received with full attention and intention—not as a drop-in interruption but as a welcomed guest. We also offer scheduled on-farm pickup for online orders. This allows customers to choose a convenient time for collection, while giving us the ability to prepare their orders with care. It reduces waste, eliminates confusion, and reinforces the relationship we value most: the one between us and our community.

Appointments aren't about exclusivity. They're about alignment, respect, and practicing what we preach—intentionality, sustainability, and wellness for all, including the farmers.

Don't let folks know you are away from the farm in real time. Be selective about what areas of your farm you show publicly. It's not about moving in fear—it's about moving with foresight.

Your business address is another often overlooked layer of security. Using your home address publicly can put your personal safety at risk. That's why I recommend setting up a PO box early on. It protects your privacy while still giving you a professional mailing address. Many USPS locations now allow you to use a street-address format with your box, which can also accept packages from carriers like UPS and FedEx. Look into that option—it may give you more flexibility without compromising security.

Now let's talk about personal safety. I know pew-pews—aka firearms—are a sensitive subject. Here's my take: Do what aligns with your values and what brings you peace of mind. For those of us who choose to carry, "we keep our peace and we keep our piece." If you decide to go that route, please invest in safety training, understand the laws in your area, and follow proper storage protocols. Your safety is not up for negotiation.

As you grow your farm, you are also growing your visibility. And with that comes the responsibility of protecting what you're building—physically, emotionally, digitally, and spiritually. Safety isn't just about locks and lights. It's about building a farm that honors your well-being while allowing you to thrive. You don't need to operate from a place of fear, but you *do* need to operate from a place of wisdom. Access, safety, and security aren't just about reacting—they're about being proactive and setting clear boundaries that allow you to thrive in peace and sovereignty.

Tech Infrastructure

You don't need a high-tech palace to run a successful boutique farm—but you *do* need a few reliable tools to help you stay organized, professional, and connected. Your farm is not just a growing space; it's a business. And just like any other business, you need systems in place to manage your operations, communicate with customers, fulfill orders, and protect your data.

Start with a dependable laptop or desktop computer—something that can handle spreadsheets, design programs (like Canva or Adobe), video calls, and basic inventory management. An all-in-one printer/scanner can be surprisingly essential. You'll use it to print shipping labels, scan signed contracts, and make quick copies of documents for recordkeeping or licensing requirements. If you're shipping products frequently, you might also invest in a thermal label printer, which saves time and ink and gives your packaging a polished, professional look.

Your smartphone may become one of your most powerful farm tools. Beyond calls and texts, it's your mobile camera, content creator, inventory checker, payment processor, and customer service portal all rolled into one. If you plan to be active on social media or sell directly through your phone, make sure your device has a strong camera, decent storage, and a protective case for those inevitable outdoor drops. Don't overlook data security. Whether you're managing a small customer list or running multiple sales platforms, it's important to back up your data regularly. A simple external hard drive works well, but I also recommend setting up a cloud-based system—like Google Drive, Dropbox, or iCloud—to ensure you can access your files from anywhere and recover them if something goes wrong.

As your business grows, you may also want to explore farm-specific software tools for inventory management, email marketing, or accounting. But don't overwhelm yourself in the beginning. Start with the tech you truly need to function day-to-day and grow from there. The goal isn't to become a tech expert—it's to make technology work *for* your farm, not the other way around. This equipment helps you move professionally—whether you're sending an invoice, designing a flyer, or managing your ecommerce store.

Technology doesn't have to be overwhelming. When used with purpose, it becomes a powerful tool to support your creative flow, professional polish, and business growth—while leaving you more time to do what you love on the land. And when necessary, be willing to invest in professional help when it comes to technology. Just because you can DIY doesn't mean you should. When your resources allow, consider hiring a virtual assistant to help manage email, scheduling, or customer service as you grow. If you're ready to take your ecommerce or brand site to the next level, I recommend working with a professional web designer. If nothing else, booking a consultation with a tech-savvy friend to get your systems streamlined early can save you a lot of headaches down the line.

Think of it like fencing a pasture—it's a pain up front, but it protects what you're building long-term. As you continue on this path, remember that building a successful boutique farm requires ongoing education and adaptability. Engage with your local agricultural extension office or join farming associations to access resources, training, and support. By embracing your farm as a business and following these essential steps, you'll be better equipped to cultivate not just crops but a sustainable and prosperous future for yourself and your community. Embracing technology on your boutique farm is a journey. It can feel daunting, but with the right tools, you can make running your farm smoother, more efficient, and less stressful.

Create Your Digital Filing System Early

Digital clutter is real. You're going to accumulate a lot of files: permits, licenses, invoices, tax documents, vendor agreements, batch records, product labels, and more. Don't wait until your desktop is a graveyard of unnamed PDFs. Build a digital filing system now—before things spiral. Use a cloud-based platform like Google Drive, Dropbox, or iCloud so your files are accessible from anywhere and automatically backed up. Create folders by year, then organize within each year by category—admin, marketing, production, legal, events, and so on. This simple habit will save you hours down the road when you're pulling together grant applications, prepping for audits, or onboarding new help.

Recommended Digital Folders

- Business Formation Docs
- Financials and Taxes
- Permits and Licenses
- Product Labels and Packaging
- Marketing and Branding
- Contracts and Legal
- Inventory and Ordering

Don't wait until tax or grant reporting season to start organizing. Your future self will thank you—especially when you need to resend that EIN form or find a shipping invoice from two years ago.

Tech in Your Pocket

One of the most useful tools for beginner and seasoned farmers alike? Plant and animal identification apps. They turn your smartphone into a pocket field guide, helping you better understand your land, its biodiversity, and what's growing (or crawling) on it. One of my most-used apps is SEEK. A favorite among naturalists and farmers, it uses image recognition to help you identify plants, insects, birds, and fungi in real time. It's beginner-friendly and doesn't require an account. I've also included a list of other nature-ID apps in "Resources" at the end of this book.

With these apps you can quickly identify unknown weeds, volunteer herbs, or insects you've never seen before. Recognizing beneficial pollinators or invasive species helps you take more thoughtful actions and be a better land steward. Not only will you deepen your own knowledge, you'll be able to pass it along to team members, interns, or visiting youth. Some apps allow you to keep a running log of what you've observed over time—useful for both ecological insight and grant narratives.

Remember: No app is 100 percent accurate. Use multiple sources. Cross-reference identifications before acting on them—especially when foraging or removing anything. Keep data privacy in mind. Some apps track location and usage data. Read their privacy terms if that's a concern for you. And of course, apps are tools, not gospel. When in doubt, consult local extension agents, herbalists, or naturalists in your community. Take a walk with an app like SEEK once a season. You'll be amazed by what you've never noticed growing around you—and how your farm's ecosystem evolves. Be sure to catalog all of the new species you observe.

Farm Equipment with Tech Components

Today's farming equipment isn't just about muscle—it often includes tech that makes farming more precise and efficient. From GPS-guided tractors to automated irrigation systems, modern farm equipment helps manage labor and reduce strain. But for boutique farmers like us, the equipment doesn't have to be big and complex to make a significant difference. Even smaller tools like soil moisture sensors, weather monitors, and drone mapping can provide valuable insights to improve your growing practices and increase yields.

I'll share a personal example from Green Heffa Farms that shows just how powerful even small tech upgrades can be. Early on, we faced challenges with managing water use efficiently, which, on a small farm, can make or break your yield. Sometimes we'd forget to turn off the water at the right time, or we'd have to wait around to make sure different sections were adequately irrigated. The cost of water—in terms of both dollars and sustainability—was an issue we needed to solve.

So, we added timers to the water spigots and hydrants around the farm. It might sound simple, but those timers transformed our irrigation system. Now I could set a precise schedule for each zone, and the water would shut off automatically at the optimal time. Not only did this help us conserve water, but it also improved our crop health, since each section was getting just the right amount of hydration. We saw healthier, stronger plants with fewer water-related issues like root rot or stress.

This was a perfect example of how technology doesn't have to be intimidating or expensive to make a difference on a boutique farm. Those water timers saved us countless hours of labor and allowed me to focus on other tasks. More important, it was a reminder that technology—used thoughtfully—can solve real problems and help a farm thrive sustainably. So, when thinking about tech upgrades, focus on tools that address specific needs, no matter how small they may seem, because those small changes often lead to the biggest improvements.

Infrastructure Budgeting

Starting and maintaining a boutique farm requires a clear financial plan. From land costs to infrastructure investments, every dollar should be strategically allocated to ensure sustainability and profitability. So, when it comes to building your infrastructure, I encourage you to get the best that your resources have the capacity to provide, also taking into account your plans to grow. If you know that at some point, you are going to need a kitchen, a dishwasher, and three toilets, then plan for it when having your septic system installed if you are working on raw, rural land. Try to think ahead but also, optimize what you have. If there is a way to leverage resources, do so. Also, while there isn't money out there to "start a farm," there is funding to help expand operations, as we discussed in chapter 9.

Here's what you need to understand: You are going to build in phases. Unless you win the lottery or come into an unexpected windfall, your dream farm won't appear overnight. It will come together piece by piece, season by season. And that's not a setback—it's a gift. Because with each new milestone—whether it's growth in your yields, a bump in profitability, or customers who truly *see* and *respect* your vision—you'll find renewed energy to keep going. More doors will open. The right opportunities will start to align. You'll gain not just momentum but confidence.

I know, because I'm still building, too. At Green Heffa Farms, we have dreams that are still unfolding. I envision a small venue space where my oldest daughter can host boutique weddings and community events. I want to expand our herbal education programs and eventually add more production fields. At some point, we'll need another well. I also want to broaden our product line—which means investing in new facilities to match that growth. But even with those future plans in motion, I'm deeply fulfilled by where we are right now. My quality of life allows me to take vacations, rest, and be intentional. That's success to me. And here's something else I want to share: I have no desire to serve tens of thousands of customers with our physical products. That sounds stressful. I'd much rather have a few thousand loyal, thoughtful customers—folks who prioritize their well-being and resonate with what we do here.

Thanks to the personal brand I've built alongside the farm, I also get to be selective about the opportunities I say yes to. Growth, for me, is not about acquiring more land or scaling up just for the sake of it. I'm not trying to develop every acre. I'm about boutique living—a lifestyle rooted in intention, creativity, sustainability, and joy.

So, take your time. Build what you need. Expand only when it makes sense. And trust that your version of success doesn't have to look like anyone else's. It just has to feel right for you. A well-planned budget ensures your farm remains financially sustainable.

I encourage you to track your actual costs monthly—and adjust accordingly. Your farm isn't just built with seeds, soil, and sweat. It's a business, and it needs to be treated like one. Most aspiring farmers budget for the big things—land, tools, maybe some livestock. But often, it's the hidden costs that sneak up and throw your numbers off. These less obvious, yet essential, expenses can determine whether your boutique farm thrives or just survives. Here are the costs you are likely to encounter.

LEGAL AND COMPLIANCE COSTS

Licensing Fees: Some farmers markets require vendor licenses—and the fees can add up across multiple markets.

Attorney Fees: Whether it's leases, employee contracts, or vendor agreements, it pays to have a lawyer look things over. One bad contract can cost more than a good lawyer.

Tax Prep: Farms face unique tax challenges—income tax, sales tax, property tax, and ag exemptions. A tax professional who understands farming can save you thousands down the line.

Table 13.1. Sample Annual Budget for a Small Organic Farm (1–5 Acres)

Expense Category	Estimated Cost Range
Land lease/purchase	$500–50,000
Soil testing and amendments	$500–3,000
Organic certification	$750–3,000
Irrigation system	$500–5,000
Greenhouse/high tunnel	$2,000–10,000
Farm structures (storage, shed, etc.)	$5,000–30,000
Fencing and security	$1,000–10,000
Equipment and tools	$1,000–5,000
Website and branding	$500–3,000
Packaging and labeling	$1,000–5,000
Miscellaneous costs	$500–5,000
Total startup cost	**$13, 250–120,000**

RISK AND INSURANCE

Weather and Disaster Losses: Droughts, floods, and pests don't just hurt your crops—they hurt your cash flow. Plan for these risks.

Specialized Insurance: That truck, trailer, or ATV may need more than personal auto coverage. Look into commercial or ag-specific policies.

OPERATIONAL COSTS

Equipment Maintenance and Repairs: Tractors break. Irrigation systems clog. Mowers stop mowing. Build a repair-and-replace fund and stay on top of preventive maintenance.

Labor and Payroll: Even if you're solo now, there will come a time when you need seasonal or part-time help. Factor in fair wages, payroll taxes, and potential benefits.

MARKETING AND MARKET ACCESS

Branding and Promotion: This includes packaging, signage, website hosting, business cards, social media ads, and professional photography. If you want to be seen, it'll cost something.

Certifications and Memberships: Organic certification, GAP audits, or becoming a B Corp come with fees—but they also boost your brand's credibility and market value.

Infrastructure Beyond the Field

For those of us producing physical goods, the real backend work begins *after* the harvest. This is the unglamorous, behind-the-scenes infrastructure that often goes unseen—but it's absolutely essential if you want to turn crops into consistent income. We're talking about packaging, barcoding, batch tracking, inventory management, and fulfillment systems. These are the tools that help you stay compliant, fulfill orders efficiently, and present your brand professionally to buyers. A streamlined backend isn't just about looking good—it's what allows your business to scale and succeed over time. I'm always looking

Don't Forget the Pickup Truck

There's one piece of infrastructure that's easy to overlook—but once you have it, you'll wonder how you ever managed without it: the pickup truck. Whether you're hauling compost, delivering bulk orders, moving building materials, or transporting livestock feed, a reliable truck can quickly become one of the most used tools on your farm. It's more than just transportation—it's a mobile workspace, a field hauler, and sometimes even a makeshift delivery vehicle when orders pile up.

When choosing a truck, think about size and power. A half-ton (1500 series) is great for smaller loads and lighter farmwork, but if you're regularly hauling heavy equipment, livestock, or large quantities of soil or hay, a three-quarter-ton (2500 series) or even a one-ton (3500 series) with a strong engine can save you time and wear and tear. Four-wheel drive is worth the investment if your farm has rough terrain, muddy fields, or snowy winters.

There are also special considerations that can make your truck more farm-friendly. Many states offer farm vehicle tags or plates, which can reduce registration fees and sometimes allow for heavier load limits. In addition, if your truck is used exclusively for farm operations, you may be able to claim tax deductions for depreciation, fuel, maintenance, and repairs. Always check with your accountant or local DMV to understand eligibility and proper documentation.

You don't need a brand-new model or a showroom shine. In fact, a well-maintained used truck with a strong bed and decent tires can be a smart, budget-friendly investment. Both of my pickups were purchased used—though perhaps a brand will read this and be interested in working with me to put me in a brand-new model. Just know that as your farm grows, so will your hauling needs—and a good truck will save you time, labor, and a whole lot of frustration.

for ways to improve our backend systems—those internal operations that support everything from order fulfillment to inventory tracking. But I've also learned to extend myself grace. I'm not Amazon. I'm an herbal farmer and boutique herb farm owner learning as I go and giving my best along the way. Fortunately, we attract customers who understand and respect that, too.

When most people hear *infrastructure*, they picture barns, tractors, or maybe a greenhouse. But boutique farm brands need to think bigger. Infrastructure is also digital, operational, and strategic. It's the solar panels powering your drying shed. The walk-in cooler preserving your harvest. The website that accepts orders while you sleep. The point-of-sale system that

GROUNDWORK

Mapping Your Infrastructure for Impact

This exercise will help you define, prioritize, and plan the physical, digital, and operational infrastructure needed to support your boutique farm brand—on your terms.

Step 1: Audit What You Already Have

Divide a page into three columns labeled PHYSICAL INFRASTRUCTURE (sheds, fencing, water systems, storage), DIGITAL TOOLS (website, Wi-Fi, point of sale, farm management software), and OPERATIONAL SYSTEMS (labeling/packaging, recordkeeping, SKUs/UPCs). In each column, list what's working well, what needs improvement, and what's missing or holding you back.

Step 2: Identify What You Actually Need Next

For each column, ask: What would reduce stress or save me time? What's preventing me from earning more or scaling? What will help me meet compliance or customer expectations? Circle one or two priorities in each area. Don't overcommit—focus on what will have the biggest impact with the least resistance.

Step 3: Check the Alignment

For each priority, ask yourself: Can I afford this now—or do I need to budget, barter, or seek funding? Will this support my sustainability—physically, financially, emotionally? If an item doesn't align, table it for now. Infrastructure should support your well-being, not sabotage it.

Step 4: Plan Your Next Ninety Days

Choose one or two infrastructure goals to act on in the next three months. Outline what steps you'll take, who can support you, and what success will look or feel like.

tracks your income, your inventory, and your growth. It's the SKUs and UPCs that help you move products, and the Customer Relationship Management system that helps you nurture customers. It's your team. Your tech. Your time.

Whether you're bottling herbal teas, running retreats, or selling fresh-cut flowers, the systems you build now will shape how your business runs, how it grows, and—just as important—how sustainable it feels to *you*. Don't let pressure or perfectionism push you into premature decisions. Take your time. Trust your instincts. And only build what truly serves your mission. Infrastructure isn't just your foundation—it's your freedom. When you invest in systems that work for *you*, you're not just building a farm. You're building a life that reflects your values, supports your vision, and protects your peace.

And that, sis, is the real harvest.

LAST WORD

The Harvest Is Yours

When I first set foot on my farm, the land was quiet. It had been harshly farmed for many years and now lay fallow. Void of earthworms yet full of potential. I didn't have a blueprint. I didn't have a full staff or a trust fund or a team of consultants. What I had was vision. A stubborn kind of hope. A belief that I could grow something beautiful and bold in a space where no one had handed me permission to do so.

And now here you are—still reading, still curious, maybe still afraid, but also still here.

Photo courtesy of Maddy Gray.

Let me remind you: Choosing to build a boutique farm as a Black woman is a revolutionary act. Whether you grow herbs in containers on your porch or cultivate 10 acres with a crew and a customer list, you are doing something powerful. You are claiming space. You are honoring your ancestors. You are planting seeds not just in soil but in spirit—yours and those of everyone who will be nourished by your work.

Throughout this guide, we've talked infrastructure, finances, regulations, products, and practices. We have dug into the gritty, unglamorous pieces of the process. Because this life isn't curated for social media. It's real. It's dirt under your nails, late nights with spreadsheets, and mornings spent walking your land and asking it what it needs from you.

I didn't write this book to give you all the answers. I wrote it to offer what I wish I had when I started: honest stories, real numbers, cautionary tales, and reminders that you can absolutely do this—and do it your way. No matter what you grow or raise, your boutique farm has a unique fingerprint. The visuals and voice of your brand are how people get to know you, believe in you, and support you.

So, sis, don't play small. Show up. Be seen. Let your story be told and the beauty of your farm reflect the power of your purpose. If there's one truth I want you to hold onto, it's this: You do not need to ask for permission to farm beautifully, abundantly, and on your own terms. This path won't be easy. But it is yours.

To the Black women reading this, as you grow—your crops, your business, yourself—I hope you remember that you are part of a rich agricultural lineage of Black women who have always known the power of the land. Whether we were forced to work it, pushed off it, or determined to reclaim it, we have always had a connection to growing, healing, and creating life from soil. You are not alone. You are not late. You are not behind. You are exactly where you need to be—seed in hand, sun on your face, ready to grow something that matters.

May your farm be abundant.
May your boundaries be firm.
May your funding be fair.
May your freedom feel full.
And may your harvest be joyful.
With soil-covered hands and an open heart,
—Farmer Cee

Resources

Finding a Graphic Designer

Upwork (www.upwork.com): A freelance platform that allows you to post jobs or browse designer profiles. You can filter by industry, experience level, and budget.

Fiverr (www.fiverr.com): A great option for quick, one-off design needs like logos, social media graphics, or product labels. Fiverr lets you search by style, price, turnaround time, and designer reviews. Tip: Look for designers with "Pro" status or strong portfolios in wellness, herbal, or sustainable branding for best results.

Black Women Photographers (https://blackwomenphotographers.com): A beautifully curated global community, directory, and support hub that, according to their website, includes over 2,100 Black and African creatives across more than sixty countries and thirty-five US states. This is an excellent place to find Black photographers, videographers, and cinematographers who understand the cultural, community-centered nuances of your brand.

Instagram (via Hashtags and Creative Collectives): Instagram doubles as a live portfolio. Use hashtags like #BlackGraphicDesigner, #LatinaDesigner, #BrandingForWellness, or #CreativeFarmBrand to discover aligned creatives. Many designers post their work regularly and welcome DMs or email inquiries. You can also follow design collectives and directories like @blackgirlgraphics or @thebrandidealist to tap into a broader network of talent.

Local Universities and Design Schools: Don't overlook the up-and-coming talent right in your community. Reach out to graphic design departments at nearby HBCUs, community colleges, or art institutes. Many students are looking for real-world portfolio projects and are open to collaborating at lower cost—or even for course credit or barter (especially if your farm offers something unique in return). Bonus: You may also find interns who grow with your brand long-term.

Crowdfunding Platforms to Explore

IFundWomen: Especially supportive of women-led, mission-driven businesses

Kickstarter: Great for specific product launches or creative campaigns

Indiegogo: Offers more flexible funding options

Seed at the Table: Focused on Black founders and culturally aligned enterprises

Kiva: Offers 0 percent interest micro-loans with a crowdfunding model

AI Name Generators

Shopify Business Name Generator: This tool is designed specifically for business names, making it a great choice if you're naming your entire brand or a product line. It has the added benefit of showing you which domain names are available, so you can start planning your online presence at the same time.

Oberlo Business Name Generator: Like Shopify's tool, Oberlo's name generator is great for e-commerce and product branding.

Namelix: Namelix allows you to set filters based on name length, word combinations, and even the type of names (for instance, invented words or real words). It's especially useful if you're looking for something a bit more out-of-the-box.

Wordoid: Wordoid creates catchy, made-up words that sound natural and are easy to pronounce. This tool is perfect if you're open to using a more whimsical or abstract name that's still brandable. You can specify language preferences, length, and quality of the wordoid.

Business Name Generator: Enter your main keywords, choose your industry, and refine your preferences for length and style. It's a no-frills option that still delivers plenty of inspiration for product and business names.

Fantasy Name Generators: If you want something with a unique twist, like a line of teas inspired by herbal folklore or a name for a special limited-edition product, this is a great choice. It offers everything from plant name generators to mystical word combinations, perfect for boutique farming brands looking for a name that's rich in character.

Nature Identification Apps

SEEK by iNaturalist: A favorite among naturalists and farmers, and one of my most-used apps, SEEK is a gamified app that provides immediate identification and allows users to win badges and complete challenges. It is a great free resource to help you identify plants, insects, birds, and fungi in real time. For those of us who aren't tech-savvy, it is beginner-friendly and doesn't require an account.

PictureThis: Great for identifying plants and flowers with high accuracy. It includes care tips and information on medicinal uses, but be cautious—it can sometimes recommend chemical solutions not aligned with organic practices.

PlantNet: A crowdsourced database driven by contributions from scientists and users alike. Very useful for wild plant identification and regional info.

iNaturalist: A bit more advanced, iNaturalist is a community-driven platform that provides more research-quality data. It is perfect for building your own observations log and contributing to citizen science. It does require an account, and it also shares observations and location data publicly. Great for tracking wildlife, beneficial insects, and more.

Merlin Bird ID: Ideal if you're tracking birds on your farm. It uses sound and photo recognition.

Financial Education Resources

Two of my go-to financial literacy resources are: (included) CPG and Rodale Institute's Farmer Training (RIFT). But there's a third one I want to lift up: RAFI's Farmers of Color Network. Together, these three give you different lenses on how to manage money, leverage community, and grow your farm and brand. One of RAFI FOCN's standout tools is their Farmer Financial Crisis Hotline, which you can call when you're in a bind and need immediate guidance. I received a small grant from them after my farm's fire, which came at a critical time. RAFI FOCN understands that financial literacy for farmers of color isn't just spreadsheets. It's about navigating inequities, getting plugged into networks, and having backup when the unexpected (weather, market volatility, et cetera) happens.

Bibliography

Caruth, Nicole. "Farmers of Color Offer Community Wellness at 'Healing Farms.'" *Civil Eats*, September 3, 2025. https://civileats.com/2025/09/03/farmers-of-color-offer-community-wellness-at-healing-farms/

Green 2.0. *Transparency Report Card: Philanthropy and Environmental Nonprofits 2023* (2023). https://diversegreen.org/reports/2023-transparency-report-card/

Lucidpress. *The 2020 State of Brand Consistency* (2020). https://www.marq.com/blog/state-of-brand-consistency

Markets and Markets, "Knowledge Management Market by Component, Deployment Mode, Organization Size, Industry, and Region—Global Forecast to 2026." https://www.marketsandmarkets.com/PressReleases/knowledge-management.asp.

Smith, Tyler. "US Sales of Herbal Supplements Increase 4.4% in 2023." *Journal of the American Botanical Council* 141 (Summer 2024).

US Department of Agriculture. 2022 Census of Agriculture (Washington, DC: United States Department of Agriculture, National Agricultural Statistics Service, 2022). https://www.nass.usda.gov/AgCensus/

"What Is a UPC (Universal Product Code)?" GS1 US. https://www.gs1us.org/upcs-barcodes-prefixes/guide-to-upcs

"What Percentage of Businesses Fail? Averages by Time, Industry, and Locale." Vena Solutions. September 26, 2024. https://www.venasolutions.com/blog/what-percentage-of-businesses-fail

Index

Note: *Italic* page numbers indicate images.

A

abundance mindset, 32–33
access, for infrastructure, 220–224
ACCOUNTABILITEA, 23, 100
accounts, business, 78
acronyms, 69
Acumen, 124
ad revenue, 160
adjusted gross income (AGI), 11
administrative support employee, 118
advertising, 89–91
aesthetics, for infrastructure, 214–220
affiliate marketing, 160, 162
agency, reclaiming, xiv–xv
agricultural agencies, 107–111
agricultural extension service, 109–110
agricultural/nursery license, 78
agriculture, harms in, xiii. *See also* boutique farming; farming
agritourism, 9–10, 55–56, 157–159
AI name generators, 236
Alston, Cheryl (Mama Cheryl), 27
Amber Grant for Women, 134
Angelou, Maya, 16
Animal Welfare Approved (AWA), 170
animal welfare certification, 173
animals
  considerations for, 52–53
  drain fields and, 207
  Grass-Fed and Ethical Livestock Farm, 56
  infrastructure and, 203
  livestock insurance for, 85–86
  photo of, *56*
  specialty crops for, 53
anxiety, 3–4, 17
Appropriate Technology Transfer for Rural Areas (ATTRA), 132
artificial intelligence (AI), 103–105, 236
Asana, 131
aspirations, 42
attorney fees, 228
authenticity, 98
auto insurance, 84
awards, 179–182

B

B Corp (Certified B Corporation), 170–171, 174, 175
B Lab US & Canada, 170, 175
Babcock, Lori, 58–59
Babcock, Ruth, 58–59
Backstage Capital, 124
balance, 44
Barfield, Christa, 55
basil tomato sauce, 150
Bed Head Plant Nursery (East Point, Georgia), 192–194

Bee and Pollinator Conservation Farm, 59
beekeeping, 203
Benefit Corporation, 170–171
besties' trip, 37
bias, 108
Big Hemping course, 20, 143
Black Farmer Fund, 133
Black women
  access of, 124
  advice for, 24–25, 45, 93, 193–194
  assumptions regarding, 119
  statistics regarding, 183
  underrepresentation of, 22
Black Women Photographers, 235
Bloom Ranch (Los Angeles County), 56–57
Bonfire, 147
boundaries, setting, 42
boutique farming. *See also* farming
  advice for, 24–25, 45, 93, 193–194
  benefits of, 3, 5–6
  choosing, 3–8
  claiming space for, 14–15
  community in, 19
  connection in, 62
  cool factor of, 7–8
  credit score for, 36–37
  customer experience at, 7–8
  as customized joy, 3, 27
  decision weight in, 46
  defined, 1
  demands of, 22
  diversity in, 44–45
  downsizing for, 19
  education for, 19–20
  finding your footing in, 17–23
  focus of, 7
  intention in, 46, 51
  invisible labor of, 18
  legacy in, 50
  luxury in, 3
  mentorship in, 19
  milestones in, 21
  models for, 54–59
  niche in, 51
  power of, 1
  prosperity potential of, 6–8
  relationships in, 62
  research in, 19, 51, 60
  revenue streams in, 54–59
  sharing knowledge in, 21
  silver lining in, 21–23
  softness in, 2
  thriving, 7
  values in, 1
brand book, 71
brand/branding
  assets of, 61, 72
  basics of, 71–72
  benefits of, 62
  budget for, 229
  color palette for, 101
  connection in, 62–63
  consistency in, 102
  defined, 90
  dual, 64
  importance of, 61
  loyalty to, 159
  name in, 65–71
  overview of, 89–91
  partnerships, 159–162
  personal, 63–65
  profitability and, 159–162
  as revenue engine, 61–62
  roots for, 62–63
  trust in, 181
  visibility, 154
branded merchandise, 146
Brenda's Balm, 146–147
budgeting, 130, 227–229
bugs, 22
bulk orders, defined, 153
Burke, Tarana, 198

business
  accounts for, 78
  failures of, 2
  insurance for, 79–87
  lessons regarding, 93
  making it official, 77–88
  permits for, 78–79
  real talk regarding, 76, 88
  registering, 77
  spending statistics of, 20–21
  structures of, 74–76
  websites for, 78
business address, 223
business interruption rider, 86–87
Business Name Generator, 236
business owner, embracing role of, 32–33
butterfly pea flowers, *18*

C

calendula, 53
Camelback Ventures, 124
cannabis, 20
Canva Brand Kit, 71, 72
Carolina Farm Stewardship Association (CFSA), 116
case packs, defined, 153
cash on delivery (COD), 153
certifications, 167–176, 229
Certified B Corporation (B Corp), 170–171, 174, 175
Certified Humane, 170
challenges, innovation in, 23
cities, farming in, 12
Clark, Patrice, 93–94
clients, customers *versus*, 162–166
climate, structures and, 212–213
collaborative product lines, 160
color palette, 101
commercial farm vehicle policy, 84
community, 19, 100
composting toilets, 207
conferences, 176–177
connection, 98–99, 113, 163
Conservation Stewardship Program (CSP), 139
consignment, defined, 153
consistency, 98
consistent revenue, defined, 153
consulting services, 165
consumers, 7
cooperative farm model, 191
core pillars, 106
corporations, 76
cost of goods sold (COGS), 148–152
cost-share programs, 137–138
cottage food laws, 210–211
county planning and zoning departments, 111
CPG, 237
credibility, building, 144
credit, 34–39
crop failures, 10
crop insurance, 84–85, 87
crowdfunding, 122, 139–141, 236
Cruz, Victoria Santa, 89
Culinary and Agritourism Farm, 56–57
cultural inspiration, 69
Current Good Manufacturing Practices (cGMP), 170
customer service, 163, 164
customers, 106, 162–166

D

DAFgiving360, 142
data security, 224
Davines Group, 180
debt, 120
debt/income ratio, 36
delivered pricing, defined, 153
de-stemming, 81
Detroit Black Farmer Land Fund (DBFLF), *110*

digital filing system, 225
digital identity, 106
digital land, 78
digital presence, 91–101
digital products, 143–144
digital protection, 222–223
discrimination, *29*, 108, 137
diversity, equity, inclusion (DEI), 155, 157
Dixon, Bea, 61
documentation, 93, 130
Doing Business As (DBA), 77
domain name (URL), 78
donor-advised funds (DAFs), 141, 142
Dovetail Workwear, 64, 160, *161*
downsizing, 19, 39
drain fields, 207
dreams, connecting to, 28
drip irrigation, 205
drop shipping, defined, 153
Dropbox, 225

E

Earth People Farms, 24–25
Earthseed Farm (Sonoma County, California), 55–56
Economic Prosperity pillar, 6, 41
Economic Research Service (ERS), 135
education
    course buying guidance for, 178–179
    financial, 32, 237
    investing in, 176–179
    profitability in, 157–159
    real talk regarding, 178
    on social media, 99
    taking and leaving in, 19–20
    workshops and classes for, 165
Education pillar, 43
electricity, 208–209, 210–211, 214
emails/email list, 91, 92, 94, 95, 105
Emerald Roots Farm Collective (Phoenix, Arizona), 93–94, *145*
Employer Identification Number (EIN), 77
empowerment, social media, 100
engagement, social media, 100
entry, security at, 221
Environment pillar, 41
Environmental Quality Incentives Program (EQIP), 138–139
EP Farmacy, 55
EQUIP, 122–123
Equity pillar, 41
ethical certification, 172–173
European Regenerative Organic Center, *122*, 180
events, profitability in, 157–159
expectations, business, 118–119
expenses, core, 199
experience-based revenue, 159

F

Facebook, 100
Fair for Life, 170
fair trade certification, 172–173
Fair Trade USA, 170
fair-trade, 169
family foundations, grants from, 128
Fantasy Name Generators, 236
farm equipment with tech components, 226–227
farm incubators, 190–191
farm mood board, 68
farm operations support employee, 117
farm plan, infrastructure and, 199–200
farm property insurance, 83
Farm Service Agency (FSA), 10, 11, 108, 214
farm tract number (farm number), 10–11, 14
farm use endorsement, 84
farm vehicle insurance, 83–84
Farmer Cee
    awards of, *179*, 180

branding of, 38, 64–65
as inspiration, 193
name meaning of, 65
photo of, *41, 110, 112, 114, 129, 144, 161, 175, 179, 189, 204, 233*
social media of, 94

FarmerJawn (Elkins Park, Pennsylvania), 55
farmers, 8–12, 26
Farmers of Color Network, 237
farmer-specific tax exemptions, 122, 141–142
farming. *See also* boutique farming
balance in, 44–45
beliefs of, 29
business of, 29
business planning stage of, 33
eligibility for, 9
establishment phase of, 33
financial foundation for, 31
groundedness in, 45
income intent in, 9–10
income supplementation for, 17
lessons regarding, 93, 193
luxury in, 3
partnering in, 13
perceptions of, 1
as physical, 27
proof of work in, 9–10
as reclamation, 54
rooted resilience in, 120
statistics of, 17
stretching in, 22
in suburbs or cities, 12
as teacher, 194
"why" for, 44, 46, 93, 192–193

Fearless Fund, 124
Featured Farmer (Hemp History Week) award, 180
Federal Housing Administration (FHA), 36
fencing, 221, 225
fiber and craft products, 146
Fidelity Charitable, 142
50/50, defined, 153
finance support employee, 118
financial education resources, 237
financial literacy, 35
financial management
abundance mindset in, 32
business accounts for, 78
credit and, 34–39
education for, 32
foundation for, 31
intimacy with numbers in, 32
revenue stream diversification in, 32
vision and, 30–31

financial mindset, 31
firearms, 223
5 V's (Values, Vision, Visuals, Voice, and Validity), 89, 144
Fiverr, 235
Floral and Apothecary Farm, 57
floral products, 145
Floyd, George, 155
followers, ideal, 106
Food Animal Concerns Trust (FACT), 159
food handling permits, 79
food trucks, 209
Ford Foundation, 128
Foundation Directory Online (FDO), 133
4 E's (Economic Prosperity, Environment, Equity, and Education), 6, 41–43. *See also specific pillars*
Foxx Winship, Samantha, 59
free products *versus* value exchange, 161–162
Freight on Board (FOB), defined, 153
French Kiss Life, 93
FreshBooks, 78
FruitGuys Community Fund, 134

funders, listing of, 123
Fyfe, Andy, 175

G

Gaia Herbs, North Carolina, *41*
game cameras, 222
garden and home goods, 146
general liability insurance, 82, 87
GoDaddy, 78
GoFundMe, 141
Good Agricultural Practices (GAP), 170
Good Farmer Award, 180
Good Ground Initiative, 190
Gooding, Phoebe, 54
Google Domains, 78
Google Drive, 225
grants
- considerations regarding, 127–128
- corporate, 128, 135–136
- data for applications for, 135
- discrimination in, 137
- foundation, 128, 135–136
- government, 127, 134–135
- introduction to, 125–127
- overview of, 121–122
- quantitative language in, 135
- real talk regarding, 136
- research regarding, 131–134
- resources for, 133–134
- subgrants, 136–137
- success in, 128–131
- technology, 127
- tips regarding, 130–131
- types of, 132–133

Grants.gov, 133
graphic designers, 235
Grass-Fed and Ethical Livestock Farm, 56
graywater recycling, 207
Green Heffa Farms
- aesthetic of, 216–217
- appointment only policy of, 223
- awards of, 122
- brand insights of, 72
- brand of, 63–64
- certification of, 168
- as Certified B Corporation (B Corp), 175
- color palette of, 101
- as corporation, 73, 76
- customers of, 163
- digital products of, *143*
- educational content of, 99
- electricity and, 208
- email list of, 94
- farm loan for, 36
- farming approach in, 168
- fire at, 79–81
- grant application of, 134–136
- Heffaisms of, 147
- Heffa's House of Happiness, 218–220
- holiday card of, *8*
- Juneteenth event at, *130, 158*
- land acquisition of, 187–189
- logo of, 66, 71
- marketing material of, *91*
- name meaning of, 65, 70–71
- niche for, 51
- origin of, xiv–xv, 5, 13
- photo of, *10, 62, 96, 123, 168, 183, 201, 213, 216, 217*
- products of, *99, 104, 156*
- signage at, *215*
- social media of, 94, 97–101
- structures of, 211–212
- technology at, 226–227
- vision for, 16
- water access and, 203–204

greenhouse farming, 197
groundedness, 45
groundhogs, 222
groundwork
- Accessing Your Own Wisdom, 28

- Claiming Your Growing Space, 14–15
- Clarifying Guiding Principles, 42–43
- Crafting Your Mission Statement, 49
- Creating Your Vision Statement, 47
- Credit Check, Reality Check, 38
- Cultivating Your Customer Culture, 164
- Cultivating Your Digital Voice, 106
- Cultivating Your Email List, 95
- Cultivating Your Relationship Ecosystem, 113
- Customizing Your Boutique Farm's Model, 60
- Mapping Your Infrastructure for Impact, 231
- Nailing Your Name, 68–70
- Root Your Brand in Trust, 181

grow slow so you don't owe approach
- adaptability in, 199
- cost-share programs and, 137–138
- crowdfunding and, 139–141
- Environmental Quality Incentives Program (EQIP) and, 138–139
- grants and, 125–137
- introduction to, 33, 120–123
- miscellaneous external funding and, 141–142
- venture capital (VC) and, 123–125

Growing Urban Farmers, 13
GS1, 155
guiding principles, clarifying, 42–43

H

Hamer, Fannie Lou, 29
Hamilton, Arlan, 124
hashtags, 100–101, 235
Hawk's Nest Healing Gardens (Durham, North Carolina), 54
Healing-Centered Farm, 54–55
Heffa's House of Happiness, 218–220
heirloom tomato analogy, 63
hemp flower (*Cannabis sativa*), 17, *149*
herbal and botanical products, 145
herbal market, boom in, 51
herbal medicine, benefits of, 20
herbal tea industry, growth in, 51
herbs
- benefits of, 51
- characteristics of, 51
- de-stemming, 81
- grown *versus* purchased, 148–150
- specialty crop pricing for, 51

Herrick, Rachel, 44–45, 56
Hersey, Tricia, 2
hiring, picking the right team in, 114–119
holistic health, benefits of, 17
holy basil, 20
home occupation permits, 79
home ownership, 36
homeowners' association (HOA), 12, 14, 213
honesty, 118
honey production, 203
horticulture, healing power of, 3–6

I

IBISWorld, 135
iCloud, 225
IFundWomen, 140, 236
images, access to, 161. *See also* photography
Impact X Capital, 124
imposter syndrome, 21
iNaturalist, 237
income. *See* profitability
Indiegogo, 236
indoor growing, 196–197
infrastructure
- access and, 220–224
- aesthetics and, 214–220
- animals and, 203
- audit of, 231

infrastructure (*continued*)
- for backyard boutique farms, 210–211
- beyond the field, 230–232
- budgeting for, 227–229
- electricity and, 208–209, 210–211, 214
- farm equipment, 226–227
- internet access and, 209–210, 211
- introduction to, 198–202
- Mapping Your Infrastructure for Impact, 231
- model and, 200
- plumbing and, 214
- processing and, 202–203
- production setting and, 202
- research and, 200
- sanitation and, 206–208
- security and, 220–224
- storage for, 202–203
- structures and, 211–214
- technology, 224–226
- wastewater and, 206–208, 214
- water access and, 203–206

inspiration, on social media, 100
Instagram, 100, 235
insurance
- crop, 84–85, 87
- farm property, 83
- farm vehicle, 83–84
- general liability, 82, 87
- getting coverage for, 87–88
- livestock, 85–86
- overview of, 79–82, 229
- product liability, 82–83
- riders, 86–87
- tractors and, 85

intention, 2, 46, 51, 155
Internal Revenue Service (IRS), 77
internet access, 209–210, 211
inventory, maintaining, 147

J

J. M. Kaplan Fund, 128
Jennings-O'Byrne, Gayle, 124
joy, customizing, xii–xiv, 3
Juneteenth event, 130, *158*
JustFund, 133

K

Kickstarter, 236
Kiva, 236
knowledge, leveraging, 20–21

L

lack mindset, 33
Lacrete, Patty, 192–194
land
- buying *versus* leasing, 184–189
- cleared *versus* wooded, 188
- cooperative models of, 191
- farm incubators and, 190–191
- indoor growing and, 196–197
- introduction to, 183–184
- land trust assistance, 189–190
- small space growing and, 196–197
- soil quality and, 195–196
- statistics regarding, 183

land host model, 13
land leasing, 13
land trust assistance, 189–190
lavender, 22
lead time, defined, 153
learning, embracing journey of, 28
leasing, land, 184–189
liability, 74
licensing fees, 228
lighting, for infrastructure, 221–222
limited liability company (LLC), 75
line sheet, 154
LinkedIn, 100
literature, inspiration from, 69
livestock. *See* animals

Livestock Gross Margin (LGM), 86
livestock insurance, 85–86
livestock rider, 87
Livestock Risk Protection (LRP), 86
loans, 121
local certification, 174
local health departments, 111
Local Initiatives Support Corporation (LISC), 133–134
local inspiration, 69
logo, 71
Lopez, Hector, 54
Lucy Daniels Center, 5
luxury, 3
Luxury U-Pick Experience, 55–56

M

market access, budget for, 229
market reach, defined, 154
market research, 51
marketing, 66, 89–91, 117–118, 229
meat processing, 203
media relationships, 111
memberships, 229
mentorship, 19, 194
Merlin Bird ID, 237
Micro Farm insurance, 84–85
Micro-Dairy and Artisanal Cheese Farm, 58–59
mind map, 42, 68–69
Minimum Order Quantity (MOQ), defined, 153
mint, 53
Mintel, 135
mission statement, 48–50
misunderstandings, 118
Mitchell, Amirah, 58
money. *See also* financial management; revenue
    contention regarding, 35
    credit and, 34–39
    foundation for, 31
    healthy relationship with, 199
    intimacy with, 32
    minding, 30
    mindset regarding, 33
    strategy regarding, 33
Mother's Finest Urban Farm (Charlotte, North Carolina), 59
motion-sensor lights, 221–222

N

name generators, 69–70, 105, 236
Namecheap, 78
Namelix, 236
naming, business, 65–71
Nappily Naturals & Apothecary (Los Angeles), 57
National Agricultural Statistics Service (NASS), 135
natural disasters, 9–10
Natural Resources Conservation Service (NRCS), 108–109, 195
natural skincare and body products, 145
nature, inspiration from, 69
nature identification apps, 226, 236–237
negotiation, 155
net 30/net 60, defined, 153, 155
nettles, 53
network, mapping, 113
New Communities (Albany, Georgia), 57–58
New Voices Fund, 134
niche, finding, 51
nine (number), significance of, 120
Non-GMO Product Verified, 170
Norman, Jamila, 167, 194
North Carolina Botanical Garden, 5
North Carolina State College of Design, 116
North Star, 46
Notion, 131
nursery farming, 197

O

Oberlo Business Name Generator, 236
online presence, importance of, 66–67
operational costs, 229
operational efficiency, 154
order fulfillment employee, 117
organic, defined, 168
organic certification, 171–172
O'Tardy, Georgia, *216*
ownership, land, 184–189

P

paid content, 162
pain points, identifying, 144
parasocial relationships, 96
partnership
  brand, 159–162
  challenges in, 155
  cooperative models of, 191
  dissolution of, 201
  overview of, 75–76
  profitability and, 159–162
Patagonia Environmental Grants, 134
payment, 45, 153
pecan orchards, 58
percolation test, 206–207
performative partnerships, 155
permits, business, 78–79, 213, 220
personal finance, 31
personal safety, 223
photography, 101–105
pickup truck, 230
PictureThis, 237
Pigford era, 29
Pinterest, 100
placemaking, 217
PlantNet, 237
plants, 4–5, 52
plumbing, 214
Potlikker Capital, 124
prepaid, defined, 153
primrose, *5*
Printful, 147
Printify, 147
private foundations, grants from, 128
processing, for infrastructure, 202–203
produce and pantry products, 145
product liability insurance, 82–83
production setting, for infrastructure, 202
profitability
  brand partnerships and, 159–162
  cost of goods sold (COGS), 148–152
  customer *versus* client, 162–166
  digital products for, 143–144
  diversification of, 32
  events and, 157–159
  line sheet for, 154
  physical products for, 144–148
  real talk regarding, 162
  retail and, 152–157
  social media and, 159–162
  sustainable, 61
  value and, 6
  wholesale and, 152–157
program-related investments (PRIs), 141, 142
Project Diane, 124
project management, 131
public foundations, grants from, 128
Public Service Loan Forgiveness Program, 35

Q

QuickBooks, 78

R

racism, 119
Rare and Indigenous Crop Farm, 58
rebranding, 67
recognition, 179–182
reflection, 42

Regenerative, Carbon-Sequestering Farm, 57–58
regenerative certification, 172
regenerative farming, 52, 168–169
registering, business, 77
regulations, 200
relationships. *See* sustainable relationships
reputation, 42
resilience, 28
RESILIENCEE, 81–82, 100
Resourceful Communities Program, 134
resources, 33, 123, 235–237
rest, 2, 45
retail, 152–157
revenue. *See* profitability
riders, insurance, 86–87
risk, 229
Risk Management Agency (RMA), 85, 86, 87
Rodale Institute, 122, 180
Rodale Institute's Farmer Training (RIFT), 237
Rural Energy for America Program (REAP), 139

S

Saffron, Sierra, 57
salary, paying yourself, 150–152
sales and marketing employee, 117–118
sales channels, 152–153
sales tax license, 78
sanitation, 206–208
satellite internet, 209–210
saving, 37–38
scarcity mindset, 30, 33
security, for infrastructure, 220–224
Seed at the Table, 236
seed keeping, 58
SEEK, 226, 236
self-care, 25, 94, 96–97, 194
self-doubt, 21
seller's permit, 78
selling, relationships in, 152
septic system, 206–207
service-based revenue, 164–166
sexism, 119
Shenzhen Nongke orchid, 12
Sherrod, Shirley, 58
shipping, terms for, 153
Shopify Business Name Generator, 236
shopping, boundaries for, 38
Shumaker Family Foundation, 128
signage, 222
Simone, Arian, 124
singleness, 23–26
Sistah Seeds (Philadelphia), 58
Skin Soothing Balm (EP Farmacy), 55
Sky High Farm Grants, 134
Slow Farm, Cameron, North Carolina, 44–45
slugs, 22
Small Business Administration (SBA), 111
Small Business Development Centers (SBDCs), 111, 133
small businesses, failures of, 2
small space growing, 196–197
small-scale questions, 200
smartphones, 102–103, 224, 226
social equity, as value, 49–50
social impact funding, 121–122
social media
  artificial intelligence (AI) and, 105
  creative expression in, 94–97
  function of, 92
  of Green Heffa Farms, 94, 97–101
  handles for, 78
  principles for, 98–101
  profitability and, 159–162
softness, 2
software, 224
soil, 4, 195–196, 206–207

Soil and Climate Health Initiative Verification, 168
soil and water conservation districts (SWCDs), 109
solar lighting, 208
sole proprietorship, 75
solopreneurs, 117
soul questions, 49
sounds, for naming, 69
South Carolina Black Farmers Association, *114*
Sow Green Society, 5, 57
speaking engagements, 165
Specialty Crop Block Grant Program (SCBGP), 53–54
specialty crop certification, 173–174
specialty crops, 51, 53–54
Specialty Fruit and Vegetable Farm, 55
sponsored content, 160
Starlink, 210
starting point, 28
state certification, 174
Stock Keeping Unit (SKU), 156–157
storage, 202–203
storytelling
- for grant applications, 130
- photography and, 103
- in products, 146–148
- on social media, 99
- trust and, 181

structures, for infrastructure, 211–214
subscription options, 160
suburbs, farming in, 12
Sundance, Cheyenne, 194
Sundays, 45
surface water, 205
surveillance, 222
sustainability, as value, 49
sustainable, defined, 169
Sustainable Agriculture Research and Education (SARE), 133
sustainable certification, 172
Sustainable Mushroom and Exotic Crop Farm, 57
sustainable relationships
- agricultural agencies for, 107–111
- challenges of, 112
- connection messages in, 113
- county planning and zoning departments, 111
- Cultivating Your Relationship Ecosystem, 113
- farmer and maker communities, 112
- with funders, 128–129
- introduction to, 107, 110–111
- local health departments, 111
- media, 111
- picking the right team for, 114–119
- priorities in, 113
- in selling, 152
- service providers, 112
- Small Business Administration (SBA), 111
- Small Business Development Centers (SBDCs), 111

Swanson Family Farm (Georgia), 56
symbolism, for naming, 69

T

tagging, 100–101
taglines, 105
taxation, 74, 122, 141–142, 187, 228
team, building, 114–119
technology infrastructure, 224–226
thank-you notes, 7
Thomas, Najmah, 24–25
thresholds, 22
Tieton Farm & Creamery (Tieton, Washington), 58–59
TikTok, 100
timers, water, 227
tractors, 85

trade shows, 176, 177–178
trees, 188
Trello, 131
Triangle Land Conservancy (TLC), 190
trust, 181
turning point, 28

U

Universal Product Code (UPC), 156–157
Upwork, 235
URL (domain name), 78
US Department of Agriculture (USDA)
  Agricultural Census, 135
  building relationship with, 14–15
  discrimination in, 29
  Economic Research Service (ERS), 135
  Grants and Loans, 133
  National Agricultural Statistics Service (NASS), 135
  organic, 170
  overview of, 8
  in person *versus* online, 11

V

value exchange *versus* free products, 161–162
Value-Added Producer Grants, 54
value-added product, 150–152
values
  actionable, 42–43
  defining, 42
  as framework, 50
  importance of, 40
  of intangible riches, 45
  practices for, 49–50
  refining, 43
  reflection on, 42
  revisiting, 43
  trust and, 181
  understanding, 166
  vision an, 40
  visual representation of, 43
  as "why," 40
  of your farm, 40–43
vanity metrics, 97
venture capital (VC), 121, 123–125
Vera, Yvonne, 73, 107
verifications, 167–176
vision
  defined, 43, 46
  financial management and, 30–31
  guiding principles and, 42–43
  statement for, 43, 46–48
  values and, 40–43
vision board, 47
visuals and voice
  artificial intelligence (AI) and, 103–105
  branding, marketing, or advertising in, 89–91
  connection in, 96
  Cultivating Your Digital Voice for, 106
  digital presence in, 91–101
  introduction to, 89
  photography and, 101–105
  social media and, 94–97

W

W-2 employees, 116
W-9 contractors, 116
Walker, Madam C. J., 120
Washington, Karen, 1, 183
wastewater, 206–208, 214
water access, 203–206, 227
Wave, 78
Weaver, Fawn, 40
websites
  Amber Grant for Women, 134
  Black Farmer Fund, 133
  Black Women Photographers, 235
  as digital homestead, 91
  Fiverr, 235

websites (*continued*)
  Foundation Directory Online (FDO), 133
  FruitGuys Community Fund, 134
  Grants.gov, 133
  Growing Urban Farmers, 13
  GS1, 156
  JustFund, 133
  Local Initiatives Support Corporation (LISC), 133–134
  New Voices Fund, 134
  Patagonia Environmental Grants, 134
  Resourceful Communities Program, 134
  Risk Management Agency (RMA), 86
  securing business, 78
  Sky High Farm Grants, 134
  Sustainable Agriculture Research and Education (SARE), 133
  Upwork, 235
wellness industry, 6, 7
wells, 203–205
Whole-Farm Revenue Protection program, 84–85
wholesale, 152–157
wisdom, accessing, 28
Wocstar Fund, 124
word association, 68–69
word combinations, 69
wordmark, 71
word-of-mouth marketing, 66. *See also* marketing
Wordoid, 236
workshops, 165
World Wide Opportunities on Organic Farms (WWOOF), 159

X

X (formerly Twitter), 100

Y

YouTube, 100

About the Author

Tunisa Rice

Clarenda Stanley is a visionary entrepreneur, farmer, herbalist, and advocate for ethical business and sustainable living. Known affectionately as Farmer Cee, she founded Green Heffa Farms in Liberty, North Carolina, in 2018. Raised on her maternal grandparents' farm, with an awarded professional background in marketing and environmental fundraising and a deep and profound respect for the Earth, Farmer Cee dedicates her life to promoting holistic health and wellness practices that honor the interconnectedness of all living things. Green Heffa Farms is also the first Black-owned farm to achieve Certified B Corp status. Beyond her work as an executive, farmer, and herbalist, Farmer Cee is also a passionate educator and community leader. Through workshops, classes, and speaking engagements, she empowers others to support their health by incorporating herbs into their well-being program.

the politics and practice of sustainable living

CHELSEA GREEN PUBLISHING

Chelsea Green Publishing sees books as tools for effecting cultural change and seeks to empower citizens to participate in reclaiming our global commons and become its impassioned stewards. If you enjoyed reading *The Black Girl's Guide to Building a Boutique Farm*, please consider these other great books related to farming and herbal wellness.

AFRICULTURE
How the Principles, Practices, Plants, and
People of African Descent Have Shaped
American Agriculture
MICHAEL CARTER JR.
9781645023012
Hardcover

FARMING WHILE BLACK
Soul Fire Farm's Practical Guide
to Liberation on the Land
LEAH PENNIMAN
9781603587617
Paperback

THE ACCIDENTAL SEED HEROES
Growing a Delicious
Food Future for All of Us
ADAM ALEXANDER
9781915294432
Hardcover

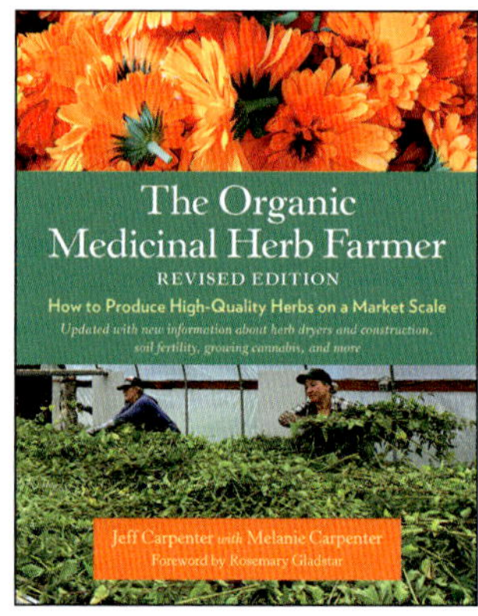

THE ORGANIC MEDICINAL HERB FARMER
REVISED EDITION
How to Produce High-Quality Herbs on a Market Scale
JEFF CARPENTER with MELANIE CARPENTER
9781645021124
Paperback

For more information,
visit **www.chelseagreen.com.**